# DOUGLAS HAIG

*By the same author*
British Generalship in the Twentieth Century
Eisenhower as Military Commander

# E.K.G. SIXSMITH

# DOUGLAS HAIG

Weidenfeld and Nicolson
London

Copyright © E.K.G. Sixsmith 1976
Published by George Weidenfeld and Nicolson Limited,
11 St John's Hill, London sw11.

ISBN 0 297 77149 3
Printed in Great Britain by
Butler & Tanner Ltd,
Frome and London

# CONTENTS

List of Illustrations     vii
List of Maps     viii
Introduction and Acknowledgements     ix
1 The Victorian Years     1
2 Haig and his Contemporaries at the Staff College     11
3 First Experience of Active Service:     16
The River War
4 The War in South Africa     30
5 'The Educated Soldier'     51
6 Subordinate Commander     67
7 The First Army Offensives:     85
Neuve Chapelle to Loos
8 Commander-in-Chief:     107
Strategic Considerations and Allied Dialogue I
9 Strategy II:     132
Mud, Blood and Disaster, but by Faith to Victory
10 A Tactical Study     164
11 Morale, Leadership and Character     172
12 Haig and his Critics     185
Appendix 1     194
Roll of Officers who were students at the
Staff College with Haig 1896–7
Appendix 2     197
Haig's Special Order of the Day, 11 April 1918
Notes     198
Bibliography     203
Index     207

# ILLUSTRATIONS

1 Rachael Haig
2 The Haigs' wedding day, 11 July 1905
3 17th Lancers polo team which won the Inter-Regimental Cup in 1903
4 Generals Sir Douglas Haig and Sir Charles Monro, Brigadier-General J. Gough, Colonel Perceval, Western Front, 1914
5 The Somme, 1916: Allied troops advancing through the wire
6 Aerial view of the Somme offensive in the French sector
7 Lloyd George, Haig, Joffre and Thomas at the 14th Army Corps HQ, Meaulte, 12 September 1916
8 King George V with General Joffre, President Poincaré, General Foch and General Sir Douglas Haig at Château Val Vion, Beauquesne, 12 August 1916
9 Haig on his charger 'Poperinghe'
10 Brigadier-General J. Charteris, head of 'Intelligence' GHQ, is presented to Queen Mary at Blendecques, 5 July 1917
11 Passchendaele, 6 October 1917
12 Field-Marshal Sir Douglas Haig with General Sir Arthur Currie and staff looking towards the German lines from Bouvigny Hill, 28 February 1918
13 A *Punch* cartoon depicting Haig's success at Cambrai, November 1917
14 Field-Marshal Sir Douglas Haig with the Army commanders, Cambrai, 11 November 1918
15 Haig in his GHQ train 1918

The author and publisher are grateful to the following for their kind permission to reproduce the illustrations: Lord Haig and the Huntly House Museum, Edinburgh, for 1, 2 and 3; Roger Viollet for 6; *Punch* for 12; and the Imperial War Museum, London, for 4, 5, 7, 8, 9, 10, 11, 13, 14 and 15.

# MAPS

1 The Sudan                                                    18
2 South Africa                                                 32
3 France and Belgium: the British Theatre of Operations        68
4 The Somme                                                    114
5 Nivelle's Plan for 1917                                      122
6 The Flanders Campaign 1917                                   136
7 German Gains in 1918 Offensives                              151

# INTRODUCTION
# AND ACKNOWLEDGEMENTS

It may be asked why another book on Field-Marshal Haig is necessary. Two biographies published soon after his death have the advantage of close personal acquaintance by the author, and the military and political experience of Brigadier-General Charteris and Duff Cooper (Lord Norwich) respectively. Then there are two expert military studies: *Douglas Haig, the Educated Soldier* by John Terraine, and *Haig as Military Commander* by General Sir James Marshall-Cornwall. Regrettably, all of these are now out of print. I gladly acknowledge my debt to all four, but it cannot be said that the last word on Haig has been written. The life and the place in history of a man who held such a position at such a time will be the subject of debate and controversy for many years to come, as are those of Marlborough, Wellington, Napoleon, Grant and Lee.

Mention must also be made of Lord Blake's *The Private Papers of Douglas Haig 1914–1919*, in which Haig is able to speak for himself and in which the story is woven together by the remarkable Introduction and Notes of the editor. I have gone to the original papers, but must confess to the advantage of having had at hand at all times this most valuable collection.

Since the publication of the last biography, other private papers have become available in the Liddell Hart Centre for Military Archives at King's College, London, and at States House, Medmenham. There, the Liddell Hart, Kiggell, Edmonds, Howell and Robertson papers have been of inestimable value to me. I acknowledge with gratitude my debt to the Trustees and to Lady Liddell Hart for the privilege of reading and using them. I wish also to thank Miss Julia Sheppard, the Archivist, for her most valuable help and Mr Brian Bond, Lecturer in Military History, King's College, London, for his help and advice and Mr Angus, the Librarian. At this stage, I also pay special tribute to the late Sir Basil Liddell Hart whose books and whose help in my previous work have meant so much to me.

In the preparation of my book I have had every assistance from the present Earl Haig, and I am most grateful to him for the trouble he has taken in answering my questions and allowing me to quote from his father's papers. My thanks go also to the Field-Marshal's daughter Lady Victoria Scott for her help. I am much indebted to Mr J. S. Ritchie, Keeper of the Manuscripts, National Library of Scotland.

I wish to thank Mr R. W. A. Suddaby, Head of the Department of Documents, Imperial War Museum, and Major Cyril Wilson for permission to quote from the Wilson papers. Also, the Chief Librarian and staff of the Ministry of Defence Library, particularly Mr C. H. Potts, Lieutenant-Colonel G. A. Shepperd, Librarian at the Royal Military Academy, Sandhurst, Lieutenant-Colonel W. W. Leary, Curator at the Intelligence Corps Library, and Mrs Meg Weaver, Librarian of South West District Library, who has been most helpful to me in finding and obtaining books.

In my enquiries I acknowledge the help I received from General Sir James Marshall-Cornwall, John Terraine, the Marquess of Anglesey, Major-General H. Essame and Major-General Ralph Younger, Brigadier C. N. Barclay, Colonel Roderick Macleod, Mrs Duncan and Mr Charles Sisson.

In writing my book I owe a great debt to my brother, Mr Guy Sixsmith, and to Brigadier L. F. Heard, both of whom read every chapter, to my wife and Lieutenant-Colonel Stuart Cameron, who helped in reading the proofs and to my son Angus, who helped with the research. My brother spared no pains in trying to keep me within the bounds of lucidity and good English, and Brigadier Heard has given me the benefit of his wide reading and military knowledge. I am indebted to Commander John Smallwood (RN Retd.) for helping with the maps and to those who have given permission to reproduce their photographs. I should also like to thank Miss Greta Williams for her care in typing the manuscript.

Finally, I owe thanks to Lord Chalfont for introducing me to the publishers, Messrs Weidenfeld and Nicolson, and also to Miss Ruth Baldwin of their staff for her help.

Quotations from the Haig Papers can be identified by the dates, all other quotations are acknowledged in the notes and full details of authors and publishers, to whom I am grateful, are given in the Bibliography. Acknowledgement is also made in the list of illustrations.

## NOTES

1 Names of army officers are given without ranks except where it is significant and not obvious from the text. The final rank reached by officers is given in the index.
2 Abbreviations are kept to a minimum and only those which are most familiar have been used.

E.K.G.Sixsmith
Langport, Somerset
January 1976

# 1

# THE VICTORIAN YEARS

Douglas Haig was born on 19 June 1861 at 24 Charlotte Square, Edinburgh. He was destined to be Commander-in-Chief of the largest army ever put into the field by Britain and to command it in circumstances more difficult than those that have ever existed before or since. The Great War of 1914–18 came in an industrial age, but one in which manpower was still predominant. With difficulty the nations of Western Europe could make the weapons and munitions of war, maintain the minimum necessary home organization, grow and transport the food and still have sufficient men for armed forces to face each other in a continuous line of battle from Switzerland to the North Sea. In addition, they could provide forces for the war at sea and, to a limited extent, in the air, and could fight each other in distant theatres. In earlier times no nation had the capacity to raise, feed and transport such enormous forces so that, for example, Marlborough, fighting over the same territory as Haig, always had room to manœuvre. More recently, the increased mechanization of life and the resulting material standards have so absorbed the labour force that highly-developed nations can only maintain much smaller forces in the field. Moreover, enormous air forces have taken up much of the manpower available for the other armed forces. As a measure of the difference, Haig had more than sixty divisions in the field, Montgomery never more than fifteen.

Haig came to his supreme task experienced and prepared. His life had been given up to the study of the art of soldiering; he served his apprenticeship in the Sudan and South Africa and he moved on through the normal stages of major commands to his eventual position as Commander-in-Chief. The early history of the Haigs is that of an ancient Scottish border family established at Bemersyde since the twelfth century and taking part, usually on the Scottish side, in the affrays and wars that were part of the Border life. Although he was bred with this strong blood in his veins, Douglas was born in easier circumstances, the fifth and youngest son of John Haig, a well-to-do whisky distiller, head of a firm still renowned the world over. In such home surroundings the Haigs may be judged to have spent a comfortable youth but, with the rough and tumble of a large Victorian family, five boys and four girls, there was little chance of leading a sheltered life. Moreover, the Covenanting stock from which the Haigs came were not used to the easy life and Haig's mother, Rachael, a strict Presbyterian, brought up her children to acknowledge the way of the Lord. It does not always follow that a strict upbringing has the result that is intended, but few will deny the life-long influence of a mother's teaching and the part she might play in the kindling of a strong faith. Haig's mother died before he was twenty and he felt the loss deeply. There is no doubt that it is to her that he owed the strong faith, the religious conviction and the strict sense of duty that were so essential a part of him throughout his life.

Haig's education followed the normal course of his day. He went first to a day school, Orwell House, near Edinburgh, and then at the age of fourteen to Clifton College. His school reports show that he was certainly no scholar, but they do show that the habit of industry developed early. They also show that he was good at games and, perhaps surprisingly, that he was a boy of high spirits. Haig's father and mother died within a year of each other and at nineteen, a young man of independent means (some £500 a year), he entered Brasenose College, Oxford. Here he read English under Walter Pater and it is possible that it is to Pater that Haig owed his facility for expressing himself on paper and his ability to write lucid prose. Haig believed that it was, but Duff Cooper affirms there was little evidence, even in his third year, of his master's influence on his style. Like Wavell after him, Haig developed a facility to express himself in writing that he always lacked in speech. He had no small talk, nor had he the ability to throw off an easy extempore speech on some minor formal occasion. He could state clearly what he thought ought to be done and could explain his plans, but he could not engage in political exchanges in which ideas were sold by rhetoric and argument.

Haig seems to have partaken fully of and derived every advantage and enjoyment from the life at Oxford. Duff Cooper has recorded the impressions and reminiscences of Haig's contemporaries[1] who were alive when he wrote his biography of Haig. Dr Craddock, who had been Principal of Brasenose for twenty-seven years, gave two pieces of advice to undergraduates at their first interview. One was 'Ride sir, ride – I like to see the gentlemen of Brasenose in top boots.' The other was 'Drink plenty of port, sir, you want port in this damp climate.' We do not know whether or not Haig preferred the family whisky to port – he was not likely to have taken either to excess – but we do know he took the first counsel. It was at Oxford that he became a skilled horseman and there that he learned to excel at polo. The game was only just being introduced to Oxford; in fact, Haig and his friends were instrumental in getting permission for the first time to play in the Parks. Haig wrote the formal request to the Curators for this permission and supported the request with the plea that the game was of great antiquity, said to have been introduced to Europe by the great explorer Marco Polo. He thus preceded the Staff College candidate who, in one of his papers, referred to 'Marco Polo, the great cavalry leader'.

It was not only Haig's skill as a player that helped Oxford, but also his ability to keep good ponies. In his diary Haig describes the match against Cambridge (there were five in a team in those days):

> Portman's two ponies inferior. Cator had only one. Gosling two, but he himself as well as ponies was a moderate player – Charrington had two excellent ponies being himself such a duffer he might as well have been off the ground! I had one very good pony and another moderately good one. I got the only goal on our side, but we ought to have had several had our fellows backed me up. The Cam team only got one also, so the match was a draw.

Polo provided Haig's recreation in the summer. In the winter, he hunted regularly with the Bicester, but he also entered fully into the social life of the University. His diary shows that he had a wide circle of friends and he was elected a member of a number of clubs, including the Bullingdon. But despite his gay and carefree life, Haig did not neglect his work. Lord Askwith has said, 'No dinner and no club deterred Haig if he was not prepared for a particular lecture or essay. As to wine and cards he was more than abstemious. His object was to pass his schools, and to pass them quickly, and he cut or left a social gathering for his books with singular tenacity of purpose.'[2] This must not be taken to indicate that Haig was a solitary academic shunning the convivialities of his contemporaries. For one thing, he had no pretensions to being a scholar, he was only reading for a pass degree. For another, his diary, begun in his last year, shows how much pleasure he took in club politics, breakfast, luncheon and dinner parties, the taste in dress of his fellows, and the conversations – worldly and religious – that would be expected of an undergraduates' party. One such entry has a modern ring in 1976: 'We discussed the merits of the Channel Tunnel. Most people thought that the only advantages to be got from it would be that fresh spring vegetables and flowers would be brought to the London market quicker.'

Haig had no difficulty in passing his final examinations but, owing to illness, he had missed one term of the obligatory period of residence – so he could not formally take his degree without making good the lost term. Early in his Oxford career, Haig had expressed his intention of going into the army and he was not prepared to delay further his entry to his chosen career. In those days there was no direct University entry to the army with its antedate in seniority, but University graduates were allowed into Sandhurst up to the age of twenty-two without further examination. Accordingly, Haig entered the Royal Military College in February 1884. He did not continue his diary while at Sandhurst and there are few contemporary records, but it is here that the idea of Haig as an aloof and taciturn man first appears. It is not difficult to imagine the reason. Coming down from a life at Oxford among men of his own age and ready for a more mature life, he found himself instead among boys of seventeen and eighteen who had hardly shaken off the outlook of their schooldays. It is little wonder that a man of Haig's reserved nature and industrious habits kept very much to himself. The exceptions were polo and hunting which, in addition to being his chosen recreations, were an important element in the training of the cavalry officer. Edmonds, later official historian of the campaigns in France and Flanders 1914–18, records that Congreve, Haig's contemporary at Sandhurst, and later, one of his corps commanders in France, said that each day Haig used to write up the notes of the instruction he had received. Edmonds adds that he is probably the only cadet before or since who has ever done so.[3]

Haig's industry was rewarded: at the end of his time he passed out first and received the Anson Memorial Sword. This is not, as is sometimes supposed, the same as the Sword of Honour. This last award, which goes to the cadet adjudged to be the most outstanding and is not tied to position in passing out, was not introduced until 1890. It is of some interest that the winner of the Anson Memorial Sword in the year before Haig had been Maude, Commander of the army which won the first major victory in the Great War, the capture of Baghdad in 1917. Maude was also a student at the Staff College with Haig, but in the year senior to him.

Haig was commissioned into the 7th Hussars on 7 February 1885. Haig's diaries at this time contain only the trivialities of a subaltern's regimental life and there is nothing to match the colour of his Oxford days. Nor are there any records to show what his contemporaries thought of him, but his late entry to Sandhurst had put him out of step in age in relation to seniority and it was not until his arrival at the Staff College eleven years later that he was really on equal terms with officers of his own age. The regimental history of the 7th Hussars contains few references to Haig except to record him as a member of the polo team on many victorious occasions. The 7th Hussars won the Inter-Regimental trophy in each of the last four years before they went to India in 1886. Haig's skill at the game was recognized outside the Regiment also and he went to America in that year as a member of the English team which easily defeated the United States.

Haig went to India with the Regiment and was first stationed at Secunderabad, one of the most peaceful of military stations in the heart of what was sometimes known as the 'Sloth Belt'. But there was no sloth about Haig, and the conscientious and assiduous care with which he went about his duties is shown by the fact that, after only three and a half years' service, he became Adjutant. John Terraine has suggested that Haig had no very deep affection for the Regiment.[4] It is true that later loyalties were perhaps stronger, but it is unlikely that in a man of Haig's nature there did not remain a strong feeling of affection for his first Regiment. Major-General Ralph Younger tells of his own first Regimental Dinner with the 7th Hussars in 1927, which was attended by Haig, at which the Field-Marshal told him what a fine Regiment he had joined.[5] Whatever others in the Regiment may have thought of the young Haig, there is evidence that the Regimental Sergeant-Major thought the world of him. It is also significant that in the oft-quoted letter of April 1894 in which the Commanding Officer, Lieutenant-Colonel Hamish Reid, took leave of him he addressed him as 'Dear Douglas'.[6] That would be a matter of course now but in those days Christian names were not commonly used, especially between a commanding officer and a junior officer.

On 23 January 1891, during his tenure as Adjutant, Haig was promoted Captain and later that year he was selected to become Brigade-Major during cavalry training exercises near Delhi. During the next year, he gained further staff experience with the headquarters of the Bombay Army at their training camp at Poona. After these staff attachments he had command of a squadron, but it would have been surprising if so ambitious a soldier had not determined to try for the Staff College. In those days there was no Staff College in India and it was necessary for Haig to obtain home leave to sit for the examination for Camberley. This he did, but unhappily he failed to qualify on two counts. He failed to get the necessary minimum in mathematics, a compulsory subject, and he was adjudged by the medical board to be colour blind. Haig protested against the latter decision and, in the light of his later admission to the Staff College, it must be assumed that the medical opinion which he proffered was accepted. But there is no doubt that Haig *was* colour blind and this was a subject which his later associates did well to avoid.

Haig was bitterly disappointed, but this serious set-back did not abate his ambition and, before returning to India to rejoin his Regiment, he obtained leave to attend French cavalry manœuvres at Touraine. This attachment was to prove of great importance to him because the long report which he made on the manœuvres and on the French cavalry was forwarded by the Military Attaché in Paris to the War Office with the comment that Haig had been 'afforded unusually favourable opportunities of seeing and judging all that was done'. Haig's report came to the notice of Evelyn Wood who had just become Quartermaster-General, and he at once saw that the report had been made by an officer of ability and promise. At that time the Quartermaster-General was not, as at present, the master of the material side of the army but did much of the work now done by the General Staff. Evelyn Wood was an influential member of the so-called 'Wolseley Ring' and one of those forward-looking officers who was determined to make a truly professional body out of the corps of officers. It was natural, therefore, for Wood to look beyond the ordinary rules of seniority and procedure.

On his return to India, Haig found himself only second-in-command of his squadron, which had been taken over by a captain senior to himself. The tone of the commanding officer's farewell letter, to which reference has already been made, shows that Haig did not let this demotion affect his keenness or the quality of his work. But he remained only a few months more with the 7th Hussars before leaving them once more. Probably as the result of the favourable notice of Evelyn Wood, he was offered appointment as Aide-de-Camp to General Sir Keith Fraser, the Inspector-General of Cavalry at home. This appointment gave Haig the opportunity of another visit to the French Army and an even more important visit to the German Army. We are able to picture the course of events during the attachment from the illuminating letters which he wrote to his youngest sister Henrietta Jameson. Henrietta was ten years older than Douglas and at the age of eighteen she had married William Jameson. The Jamesons had no children and, after the death of their mother, Henrietta had taken her place in Douglas's life, so that a deep bond of affection always remained between them. William Jameson, like Haig's father, was a whisky distiller and was a man of considerable wealth and influence. He was *persona grata* with the Prince of Wales, afterwards King Edward VII, and it was through him that Haig was later introduced to court circles.

In his first letter from Germany, Haig told how all the German officers did everything possible to help him. He went on:

The only officer who does not go out of his way to assist me is Colonel Swaine, our own Military Attaché. He has been here nine years, is a friend of the Emperor's and can do pretty well anything he likes. . . . I did not want his help except once: that was for yesterday. The Emperor inspected 4 Battalions on the Tempelhofer Feld. My Regiment (The 1st Guard Dragoons) had been ordered to parade also – to attack the infantry or some game of that sort. . . . The officers suggested that if I went with Swaine and the other attachés, I would see everything. I suggested this to Swaine. He said there would be nothing to see and that I would be much better to be at the side of the field where the crowd is allowed to stand; in fact where you could see nothing. However I did not mind this, but got my horse from the Regiment as usual. Luckily von Loë, the Governor of Berlin, on whom I had called with a letter from old Keith, met me on my way to the Tempelhofer Feld, introduced himself and took me on to the ground. I rode about without molestation until the firing and tactical inspection began,

when a mounted policeman of sorts rode up and said it was for-
bidden for me to be where I was. Old von Loë saw the man coming
and at once galloped up and rode beside me for the rest of the day
– asked senior officers what orders they had received etc., simply
for my information. I therefore saw everything and knew more
about what was going than if I had been with Swaine. . . .

In a later letter he tells of his attendance at the special parade
dinner given by the Emperor (the Kaiser William II who had succeeded
to the throne seven years before) in his pavilion:

I found myself not among the foreign officers but at the end of the
table opposite the Emperor. . . . On my right was a Colonel
Crosigk who commands the Fusilier Guards here – and a great
friend of the Emperor. After we had been a certain time at dinner
the Emperor drank his health, then signalled to him that he
wished to drink my health. So I stood up and emptied my glass to
the Kaiser in the usual style – *nae hieltaps*. He did the same. . . .
After dinner we went into the picture gallery and the Emperor
asked me about my Regiment, about Keith Fraser and what I was
anxious to do and the length of leave which I had. Altogether he
was most friendly.

Haig cut short his leave in Germany when he heard that there was
to be a Staff Ride in England conducted by Evelyn Wood. He was
able to take an active part in the exercises by acting as staff officer to
French, commanding the cavalry on one side, whom he thus served
for the first time. During the manœuvres Evelyn Wood, who had
previously dealt with him only on paper, sought him out and
questioned him about the German Army. Their conversations confirmed the good opinion that the Quartermaster-General had
formed of the young officer and Haig was able to write to Henrietta
saying, 'Sir E.W. is a capital fellow to have upon one's side as he
always gets his own way.' Later the same year, the fruit of Evelyn
Wood's interest was borne when Haig received a nomination for the
Staff College.

In the interval before going to the Staff College, Haig was made
responsible for completing the new edition of the *Cavalry Drill Book*
which had been begun by French, who had now taken over a new
appointment. This was the last of the Duke of Cambridge's thirty-
nine years as Commander-in-Chief. Wolseley, who was to succeed

him, and ought to have done so years before, was struggling to improve the training and readiness for war of the army in the face of the Duke's opposition to all change. The composite work of French and Haig which was issued in 1896 was, in the light of the military thought of those days, a practical manual; nevertheless, all the emphasis was on the supreme importance of the cavalry charge. Lip service was paid to the effect of the improved firearms, but it was thought that, even in the face of the heavy casualties that would result, the cavalry charge would be the victorious turning point in any battle.

Haig joined the Staff College at Camberley in February 1896 for the two-year course and it may be said that his apprenticeship was over. His earlier failure in the examination and his rejection on medical grounds had made him a later entrant than he had hoped. Even so, he was still below the maximum age for admission and he now found himself for the first time in his military life on equal terms with officers of the same age whose ability and interest in their profession was commensurate with his own. There was nothing unusual about his nomination. A number of entrants each year entered by nomination and Haig had shown by his regimental record and by his reports on the French and German armies that he was in every way suitable for the Staff College.

From this time forward, his career was marked by clear steps to the top. The development of his military character will, it is hoped, be shown as the story unfolds, but it is not always easy to see beneath the resolute soldier the man himself. Reference has already been made to his religious faith, a faith which grew with him and of which the conviction that he had an essential mission to play became a part. His wealth did not spoil him. He certainly partook of the good things that wealth could give and took naturally the social advantages that followed. But he never allowed worldly pleasure to captivate him, to turn him from his duty, or to affect his judgment of right and wrong.

General Sir James Marshall-Cornwall, one of the few officers still living who served personally under him, believes he did not have a sense of humour and that beneath manners of perfect courtesy his nature was cold.[7] Haig's daughters do not agree: they say he was always full of fun in the family circle and that, although he was reserved, it is quite wrong to consider him cold. Lady Victoria Scott wonders whether the myth that her father had no sense of humour stemmed from the fact that he never showed any taste for dirty stories. He enjoyed every other form of joke and in his home there was care and warmth, happiness and laughter. Lady Victoria continues, 'Everyone around him, everyone who had served with him, the servants, the dogs, and us children were absolutely devoted to him. No cold person would have been so loving and so universally loved.'[8] A gallant and still-living veteran of the South African War and both World Wars, Brigadier R.S.G.Stokes, who had social dealings with Haig between the wars, agrees with the daughters.[9] From his description it seems that any show of humour or high spirits was usually on the initiative of Lady Haig, so it is possible that Haig's perfect manners gave the mark of his acceptance.

Haig's very full diaries are, except for the Oxford days, too formal and too restrained to give us much help, but he is much more revealing in his other personal writings and these support his daughters' opinion. He was quick to see the promise in a brother officer, especially a junior officer, and to do what he could to help him. Nor did he forget those who served him. His personal letters to them show a warmth of feeling which is absent from his diaries and, more understandably, from his official correspondence. In particular, there is an understanding and a generous humanity in his letters to Kiggell,[10] afterwards his Chief-of-Staff in France, and to Philip Howell, who served him as a junior officer in India and was killed as a Brigadier-General on the Somme, and to Howell's widow.[11]

# 2

# HAIG AND HIS CONTEMPORARIES AT THE STAFF COLLEGE

Before going to the Staff College, Haig's zeal in mastering his profession had been that of the lone wolf assiduous and pre-eminent in his regimental duties and taking every advantage from visits to foreign armies in his periods of leave and from his brief introduction to staff work. Now that he was working with his peers, he could no longer take for granted the rightness of his views and he found that he was subject to frank criticism and free discussion from his fellow students and his instructors alike. At this time the army had many senior officers who could not see beyond the drill book, the regulations and the barrack square but, thanks to Wolseley and his disciples, like Evelyn Wood, and to Roberts in India, the seed was beginning to produce good fruit.

Some of it had, in fact, already reached the Staff College. Hildyard, the Commandant, had his limitations, but he was a sound and thoughtful soldier who was determined that instruction should lead to the absorption of ideas rather than the cramming of facts. Hildyard's subsequent performance as brigade and divisional commander in the South African War was not undistinguished, certainly in the light of the unpredictable mistakes of Buller and Warren, his immediate superiors. But the real genius of the Staff College teaching came from Haig's Chief Instructor, Henderson, author of the incomparable biography of Stonewall Jackson and of *The Science of War*. Henderson was at one with the Commandant in the object of the instruction and he set original and far-sighted tactical exercises based on recent campaigns, particularly the American Civil War

11

and Franco-Prussian War, exercises which evoked almost as much discussion in leisure time as in hours of work.

Haig's fellow-students were in every way worthy of this instruction. His own year included Allenby, Edmonds, Capper, a brilliant officer who was killed at the battle of Loos when commanding the 7th Division, Furse, Quartermaster-General at the end of the Great War, Haking, later one of the corps commanders in France, and Macdonogh, Head of Intelligence at the War Office and becoming Adjutant-General in 1918. There were only thirty students in each year's batch, so truly it was a vintage year.

In the two batches which overlapped there were also some most talented students.[1] In the senior year were Maude and Lawrence, who became Haig's Chief of Staff in 1918, and in the junior year were Robertson and Murray, both of whom rose to become Chief of the Imperial General Staff. There was also Barrow, who was to command the Yeomanry Division under Allenby in the capture of Jerusalem. Barrow has written some illuminating comments on Haig at the Staff College and an interesting comparison of Haig and Allenby:

> Haig did not stand out among his fellows at the College because of any intellectual superiority. It was not brains that brought him forward; there were several who had bigger and better-stored brains than he. Neither was it tact, of which he had little; nor imagination of which he had none. It was not hard work, for others worked as hard, some harder. It was his personality and his power of concentration. . . . His was the dominant personality that made itself felt in every company, in every place, in the office, on the polo ground, in the mess, in the field.[2]

Barrow thought that the chief difference between Haig and Allenby was in breadth of outlook. Haig thought of little outside the army, except for moments given to polo, while Allenby, besides matching Haig's skill with horses, had wide interests in nature, in literature and in music. He was a fellow of the Zoological Society and kept his own aviary. Barrow wrote, 'It was a pleasure to go for a walk with him, when he would point out and name and discuss the tendencies and peculiarities of all the birds, trees and flowers we passed on our way.'[3]

As will be gathered from Barrow's account, Haig and Allenby, both cavalrymen, were the two outstanding men of their year, although in knowledge and detailed work they were always eclipsed by Edmonds, and possibly in personality, wit and imagination by Capper. Edmonds had passed first into the Staff College by a record number of marks, and some well-read wit attached to him this description by Goldsmith[4] of a country parson:

> The more we gazed the more the wonder grew
> That his small head contained the half it knew.

In comparing Haig with Capper, Barrow said the difference was that, if opposed by Capper, you would never know what he was going to do and would always be afraid of being surprised, whereas you would know exactly what Haig would do.

Wavell, too, has made a comparison of Haig and Allenby, although this is at a later stage than the Staff College. He says:

In spirit and body they were fellows – strong, enduring and upright, but in mind there was a wide difference between them. Allenby had the greater perception and the greater knowledge. His intelligence had . . . a wide range and many interests outside soldiering; he took every opportunity to visit new places and to acquire fresh learning. He was earnest and thorough in his profession, but it was by no means his only, probably not even his first, interest. Haig, on the other hand, had a single-track mind, intensely and narrowly concentrated, like a telescope, on the one object. Except for his profession of soldiering, and later his family, he had no real interests of any kind, and little knowledge; nor had he any desire for knowledge, unless it bore on his own special subject. Very quick of temper in his youth, he had so disciplined his mind and body to serve his fixed purpose that he seldom showed anger or impatience. Allenby, by nature of a more tolerant humour, indulged as the years went on in frequent outbursts of violent temper. Haig, secure in his own self-confidence, seldom listened to the opinion of others; Allenby, equally strong-willed, would always pay heed to those who had knowledge. . . . Haig had a deeply religious strain, and was a regular church-goer; Allenby, though a constant student of the Bible, made little observance of the outward forms of religion.[5]

Haig says little in his diaries of his Staff College days but, in addition to Barrow's reminiscences, Edmonds wrote a good deal for a book which was never published. He summarized the records of the thirty-one officers of his batch, which bears out the belief that it was a vintage year. Four (of whom two were generals) were killed in action, one was wounded and died of enteric in Ladysmith, two were wounded and invalided out of the service and one died. Of the remainder, two became field-marshals, and fifteen became generals. One, the youngest, got no further than colonel; three others retired before 1914, one resigned when he came into a fortune and one, 'the bravest of the brave', shot himself, his mother-in-law and her lawyer in one terrible *drame passionelle*.

According to Edmonds, the subjects taught at the Staff College were Military History and Geography, Fortifications, Artillery, Staff Duties, Topography, Military Law and one obligatory language. Curiously he makes no mention of strategy and tactics, but presumably these were included in Military History and Geography in which Henderson was the professor. That the subjects were studied in a realistic manner is shown by Edmonds's own papers on the subjects which are preserved in the *Edmonds Papers* and by his comments on the outdoor exercises.

Edmonds's judgment of Allenby at this time was less flattering than that of others. He described him as a very popular member of the batch who had not much to say for himself and was 'very much out of his depth at Camberley'. Henderson liked to set Haig to work with Edmonds because he said Edmonds was a man of detail and Haig was inclined to take too general a view. Henderson hoped they might cure each other. Edmonds recounts how Haig outraged his fellow students within a few days of arrival at Camberley by writing his name in the leave book with a request for 'three days' leave to shoot and to meet the Prince of Wales'. Edmonds commented that Haig's manners then were very abrupt and unsympathetic, but 'so very different later'. However, Haig and Edmonds got on very well, although Edmonds, perhaps with intellectual pride, found him 'slow in the uptake' and remarked upon the great disadvantage of his being colour blind. This probably arose from Edmonds's lavish use of coloured chalks in his topographical sketches. They must have been a good pair; Edmonds tells the story of how, when intending to work together, they went to Brighton to study the invasion of the south coast, and Edmonds went off to study the beaches and landing areas while Haig looked for a covering position on the hills inland. Things did not always go so smoothly. In one of the passing-out exercises in the field, set by Plumer, who was an outside examiner, Haig asked if he and his friend Blair, an officer of the King's Own Scottish Borderers, could ride with Edmonds. They did so on the first two days, but, on the third, Edmonds went off alone because he had found them so slow that they were holding up his work. Haig reproved Edmonds for leaving them and was very cool towards him for some time.

Many of Haig's Staff College papers have been preserved. They show his interest in military history, particularly the campaigns of the nineteenth century in which Henderson was so expert. He also made a special study of the organization and mobilization of an expeditionary force. The remarks of Henderson and the other instructors show their appreciation of Haig's practical outlook and amazing industry. Henderson's understanding went deeper. In the mess ante-room, he remarked one night to a group of students, 'There is a fellow in your batch who is going to be Commander-in-Chief one of these days. No, not any of you! Captain Haig.'

Edmonds, one of the listeners, noted this. He did not wait until the prophecy was fulfilled, but recalled it to Haig when he wrote to congratulate him on getting the Aldershot Command in 1911. In his letter of thanks to Edmonds, Haig said, 'I think dear old Henderson must have been talking very much through his hat when he said he thought I would ever be Commander-in-Chief of the British Army. I only wish to be of some use somewhere.'[6]

Enough has been said to show to what extent Haig's fellow-students rated him, but there is one additional indication. The appointment of Master of the Drag Hounds at Camberley has always been a highly-coveted honour for which selection was at that time by vote towards the end of the first year. Given the skill in horsemanship and the inclination to hunting, the selection usually went to the most highly thought-of officer of the batch soon to pass from the junior to the senior division. In 1896 there were only two possibilities – Haig and Allenby. Allenby was elected by a comfortable majority. The two men had never been friends; indeed, both quick-tempered men, they rather grated on each other. It was sometimes said that Haig was jealous of Allenby because of his election as Master, but this is to ascribe a pettiness and small-mindedness which was not in Haig's nature. Barrow, who talked of the matter with Allenby in his last interview before his death, says that Allenby did not believe that it was so.[7]

15

# 3

# FIRST EXPERIENCE OF ACTIVE SERVICE:
## The River War

As Haig passed out of the Staff College, all military eyes were turned towards Egypt, for there lay the hope of active service and of glory. A decade earlier, in 1882 after Wolseley's victory at Tel el Kebir, the British had occupied Egypt, disbanded the Egyptian Army and raised a new one with Evelyn Wood as the first British Sirdar or Commander-in-Chief. Most of the officers now came by secondment from the British Army. Despite the occupation of Egypt, the Gladstone Government refused to accept any responsibility for the Sudan, which had been under Egyptian rule for sixty years. The Sudan was in the throes of a revolt against Egypt led by Mohamed Ahmed, son of a boat-builder who, in 1881, had proclaimed himself Mahdi, or Messiah. The Mahdi, whose claim to supernatural powers was supported by a remarkable personal magnetism, soon had a large army of Dervishes with which he imposed a despotic control over almost the whole of the country. The British Government disclaimed responsibility, but the Egyptian Government was bound to take steps to protect or withdraw the Egyptian civil population and garrisons scattered about the country. The Egyptian authorities obtained the services of a retired Indian Army officer, Colonel Hicks, and sent him to command a force of 7,000 infantry and 1,000 cavalry against the Mahdi. In November 1883, Hicks and his entire army were annihilated at El Obeid, some 200 miles south-west of Khartoum.

Gladstone was now stirred to intervention. The Foreign Office instructed the Egyptian Government to withdraw all troops and civilians from the Sudan and despatched a one-man relief force to

Khartoum, in the shape of General Gordon, a former Governor-General of the Sudan. Gordon, who in a Victorian manner matched the Mahdi in personality and religious fervour, was instructed to report on the military situation, the safety of Europeans in Khartoum and the possibility of withdrawal. The Mahdi's answer was the close investment of Khartoum. After hesitations and delay, the British Government suggested to Gordon that he should withdraw and sent an expedition under Wolseley to rescue him should it be necessary. The uncertainties and vacillation of the Government were not redeemed by any skill in the handling of the relief force. On 22 January 1885, Khartoum fell to the Mahdi while the leading column was still two days' march away and Gordon and the whole garrison were massacred. Gladstone still had no intention of occupying the Sudan and the relieving force was withdrawn to Egypt. This was a bitter blow to Britain's pride; nevertheless for twelve years the Mahdi, and his successor, the Khalifa, were left in undisputed control of the Sudan.

In 1896, Kitchener, who had become Sirdar four years before, with a combined force in which the Egyptian Army was supplemented by units of the British garrison in Egypt, had conquered the province of Dongala. The next year he organized the construction of a railway across the loop of the Nile from Wadi Halfa to Abu Hamid, an act of foresight and an engineering feat which considerably simplified the administrative problem. There had been several changes of Prime Minister since Gladstone had suffered the opprobrium of Gordon's murder, but all governments, Liberal and Conservative alike, were determined that the reconquest of the Sudan should be primarily a matter for Egypt and that it should be paid for by Egypt.

By 1898, Kitchener was ready to mount a force which would be predominantly Egyptian. His only requirement outside the garrison of Egypt was for British officers for secondment to the Egyptian Army. There was a rush of British officers to apply and Haig was one who did so. Only a small proportion of the applicants was chosen, but Haig quickly got a telegram from Evelyn Wood saying that he would be accepted. By one of those games of musical chairs in high places which so distress the aspirants below, Sir Evelyn had now become Adjutant-General. Moreover, when Kitchener cabled the Adjutant-General asking him for three first-class officers who had just passed out of the Staff College, Evelyn Wood nominated Haig,

17

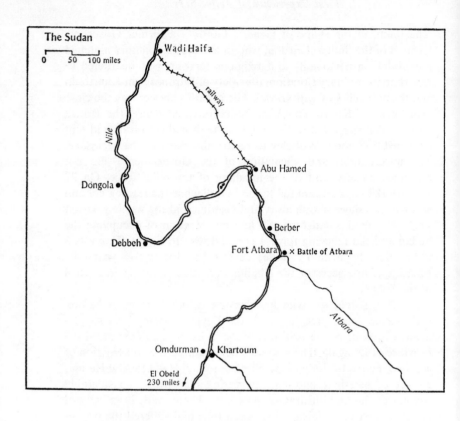

The Sudan

0    50    100 miles

Wadi Halfa

railway

Nile

Abu Hamed

Dóngola

Berber

Debbeh

Fort Atbara ✕ Battle of Atbara

Atbara

Omdurman ● Khartoum

El Obeid
230 miles

his friend Blair and Capper. Haig was instructed to report to the War Office four days later; there he was interviewed by the Adjutant-General himself and told to start for Cairo in the next week. Sir Evelyn, always ready to cut official channels, told Haig to send by private letters his personal account and comments on the handling of operations.

Haig had spent the three weeks since he left the Staff College at the Jamesons' hunting lodge in Warwickshire and he now returned for a few more days' hunting. Whilst there, he was commanded to spend his last week-end before embarking with the Prince of Wales at Sandringham. Haig's efficiency for once deserted him and he lost the train by going to Liverpool Street instead of to St Pancras so that he did not arrive until after dinner on Saturday. Among the party were the Duke and Duchess of York (King George V and Queen Mary), Evelyn Wood and the Bishop of Ripon. The happy combination of Sunday observance and personal leisure is shown by an entry in Haig's diary: 'The Princess and some go to church about 11.30. The Prince . . . and self go in at 12. Excellent sermon by the Bishop on Gordon – Hebrews Ch. XI, verse 8.' The afternoon was given to gardens and stables, but after dinner the conversation turned to serious military matters. Haig was surprised at the difficulty in finding in the Royal household a good map of Central Asia. When the discussion turned to the Sudan, the Prince asked Haig to write regularly to him from Egypt.

Haig arrived in Cairo on 3 February and, after a few days, proceeded down the Nile. He was now an officer in the Egyptian Army, wearing the drill uniform he had had in India with the addition of the tarboosh, of which he had bought three in Cairo. This most unsuitable military headdress was worn by all ranks of the Egyptian Army with, on field service, the addition of a khaki cloth cover to protect the back of the neck and shade the eyes. In his five days in Cairo, Haig had met several old friends and had spent part of his time in trying and buying two horses. From the gossip of his friends, he learned how others had fared in their applications to serve in Egypt and wrote: 'The longer I stay here the more lucky I seem to be in having got to this Egyptian Army. The crowd of fellows that have asked to be taken and been refused is very great . . . Kitchener will only take the best now and picks and chooses from hundreds who are anxious to come.'

After the journey by train and river to Wadi Halfa, Haig was introduced to the Sirdar and received a more forthcoming and friendly welcome than the austere Kitchener was wont to give. On a second meeting he commented to his sister Henrietta: 'I saw the Sirdar again at the station here before he left. He was very affable and pleasant. He is very anxious for me to take in hand a squadron which is at Debbeh and which has been up to date commanded by a native officer and is not very first class.'

Kitchener's orders were soon altered and Haig went instead to command a squadron in Broadwood's Egyptian cavalry brigade. Broadwood had been at the Staff College seven years before, although he was only a few years older than Haig, and had spent all the time since with the Egyptian Army. They were to serve together again in the South African War when Broadwood commanded a brigade in French's cavalry division.

Broadwood quickly perceived Haig's qualities and took him as his brigade-major, but not before Haig had seen active service with a squadron. He found that in training his squadron he was given a free hand and he was able to compare his experience very favourably with that of Blair and Capper who had gone to infantry battalions and whose commanding officers allowed them no responsibility or initiative. In his first report to Evelyn Wood, Haig gave his early impressions of the Egyptian Army and brought out the general failure of commanders to delegate responsibility and to ensure that their subordinates, British and Egyptian alike, learned their true function as commanders. He also included a detailed account of his first action, although this was little more than a skirmish between outposts and reconnaissance patrols. The long report showed Haig's interest in tactical detail and his ability to see where training methods needed adapting to meet the lessons of behaviour in action. In his general comments, he regretted the scarcity of machine guns. His interest in this weapon, which had been introduced into the British Army eight years before, is significant. He had shown his understanding of its importance by giving up two days of his embarkation leave to visit the Enfield small arms factory to study its working.

It is customary now to decry the exploits of the British Army and the native armies which they trained against uncivilized enemies, but the power which Kitchener set out to destroy was certainly not one to be despised. The Dervish army which had destroyed Hicks's force and harassed the withdrawal of Wolseley's relieving columns had shown its skill in the surprise attack and its fanatical courage.

Winston Churchill, who was for part of the campaign also in the Sirdar's army but serving in a British Regiment, the 21st Lancers, wrote the story of the several Nile campaigns in his first book, *The River War*. He has described in his own inimitable style how the Dervish hordes could appear from nowhere in an apparently empty desert and could disappear as quickly.

At the end of February, when Haig joined Broadwood's brigade, the Khalifa had mustered some 40,000 men north of Khartoum and was preparing to move north to join a force of 20,000, under his chief lieutenant, Mahmud, which was gathered almost 200 miles away near the confluence of the Atbara with the Nile. Kitchener had a force of 14,000 of all arms, including thirty guns and six maxims at Berber. It was his intention to destroy Mahmud's force before it could be joined by the Khalifa. Mahmud was strong in cavalry, but chose to take up an entrenched position well protected by hedges of prickly pear and with its back to the north bank of the Atbara. He was curiously inactive. It was Kitchener's plan to advance behind a screen of cavalry and then to launch his attack with Hunter's division of three Egyptian brigades, reinforced by one British brigade. The cavalry were to be used not only to cover the advance, but also to allow a thorough reconnaissance of Mahmud's position by all the commanders concerned.

It was in the action to cover the final reconnaissance that Haig had his first real taste of battle. He appears to have been used by Broadwood as a roving staff officer, a rôle which allowed him to show considerable initiative and powers of decision. Haig sent a very full account of the action to his sister and it is to be hoped she was able to comprehend all the military detail that was included:

On Tuesday, April 5th, the Cavalry Brigade with a Horse Artillery Battery and 2 Maxim Batteries and Company Camel Corps started as soon as it was light (5 am) to reconnoitre the Dervish camp again. . . . General Hunter, who commands all the Egyptian forces, was here and is a first-rate fellow, I think. There were a few other hangers-on as well, who came on one pretence or other. But the management of the whole force rested with Broadwood, Commanding Cavalry. We got opposite the Dervish *dem* or camp . . . and General Hunter was able to see all he wanted of the right of the enemy position. He then said he would like us to move so as to let him see the left. We therefore proceeded to retire towards the enemy left. We had scarcely begun to do so when the horsemen whom we had already repulsed advanced up a sort of dip in the ground and came round our flank from upstream. The Dervish infantry left their trenches and came at top speed towards us. And the cavalry which had gone downstream came directly across our line of retreat. The situation was a difficult one, and to add to it a strongish north wind prevented our seeing clearly the moment a squadron moved.

I had just been to Baring to get him into position on the right of the guns to cover them during our withdrawal when I noticed our left rear (Le Gallais) attacked. Broadwood was on the left of guns retiring at a trot. I galloped to him and told him the left rear was strongly attacked. He could not see this from where he was because of the dust. Broadwood attacked with the squadrons (Le Gallais) and fortunately the enemy (infantry and cavalry mingled) gave way before us. As we advanced B. gave me orders to see to the safety of the guns which meanwhile were trotting gaily on to the rear. Mahon was halted waiting for guns to pass, so as to get into formation ordered for retirement.

He could not see anything for dust. I told him that 2 squadrons (Le Gallais) were attacking, and asked him what he was going to do, so that I might get remainder of Brigade to conform. Mahon is a sound fellow and said, 'I can't see what has happened, what do you suggest?' I at once said, 'Place one squadron on flank (i.e. west) of guns and support Le Gallais with your other two on *his* left. I will then bring Baring and remaining three squadrons on your left rear as third line.' Mahon advanced. I gave Baring his orders, putting all three squadrons under him. I then galloped on to find Broadwood (who I knew must be with Le Gallais' squadrons) in order to know his wishes as to the action of the guns.

On my way I found the 2 squadrons coming back at full gallop. We were able to stop them (the horses were pretty well beat) and they advanced a little way. I thought there was no time to ask for orders, so I went direct to the maxims and told them they must come into action against the most threatening of the enemy (which I indicated) as soon as the cavalry cleared their line of fire. I then went off to Broadwood (who was still in front) to get him to lead the cavalry to a flank. I met him coming back with Mahon's squadrons, which were now pretty unsteady, as well they might be, for the infantry was round their flank and only 500 yards off and firing like blazes. Broadwood at once led off the cavalry to the flank and the maxims were able to open fire. This saved us for the moment, and the squadrons again being steadied, we were able to fight our way out of the reach of infantry fire. Had the Dervish horsemen been all the papers say of them we would never have got away. Fortunately they ran away the moment we showed a bold front, and only came on when we turned our backs.

Our casualties were pretty severe, 30 and 10 killed. We had over 20 horses shot and many wounded. The cavalry did very well, I think, and the Sirdar came out and met the squadrons as they returned, and complimented some of them. . . . Broadwood was much obliged to me for my assistance, and told the Sirdar so. He, Broadwood, was wrong to charge as he did with the first line, for the whole Brigade then passed from his control. But he is a very sound fellow and excellent at running this show.

Even if we make allowances for Haig's desire to make a good story for his loving sister, there is no doubt that he came extremely well out of the battle. He showed himself a most capable staff officer, knowing when to act and when to refer to his commander. He even disclosed a considerable degree of that tact which Barrow thought he did not possess. He certainly sensed the feel of the battle and showed a knowledge of minor tactics. It is, moreover, significant that he realized there are occasions when machine-gun fire is more effective than a cavalry charge. Broadwood recognized the ability that had been shown and, on his recommendation, the Sirdar put up Haig's name for a Brevet Majority.

Churchill's account of this action does not mention Haig, although he names Broadwood and all the squadron commanders concerned. Contrary to Haig's opinion, he commends Broadwood for his charge. He says Broadwood ordered the two squadrons 'to right about wheel and charge. Thus headed by Broadwood himself, and with their British officers several horse-lengths in front, the Egyptians broke into a gallop and encountered the Baggara line, which numbered not fewer than 400 men, but was in loose order, with firmness. They struck them obliquely and perhaps a third of the way down their line, and breaking through, routed them utterly.' But despite this praise, Churchill does admit that 'the shock and confusion broke both squadrons and, although successful, they came through the Dervishes and back on to the river flank in some disorder'. He also suggests that it was the maxim fire and the use of carbines by the other squadrons which checked the enemy without the remainder of the brigade being 'involved in the disorder of the squadrons which had just charged'.[1]

After this reconnaissance in force, Kitchener had sufficiently fixed the enemy to deliver his main assault. In the resulting Battle of the Atbara, on Good Friday 8 April, Mahmud was utterly routed and himself captured and subjected to considerable indignity. The cavalry did not take any notable part in the battle, but Haig was able to note what happened and to make a critical report to Evelyn Wood. First he criticized the exaggerated accounts of the victory which appeared in the British press. The headlines in the *Daily Telegraph* seemed to him to suggest that the victory surpassed that of Waterloo. He tells how the cavalry did all that the Sirdar would allow them to do by driving the enemy cavalry across the river and that this gave him a good view of all that was going on. He thought the day's movements would provide a good basis for a tactical discussion and that the first question to be answered was why the attack was frontal. He continued:

It seemed to me from the very first day that we reconnoitred the place, that an attack on the enemy's right offered great advantage. The enemy would have been forced to retreat across the open desert to the Nile without being allowed time to fill waterskins etc for the march. What actually happened was that we drove the enemy from the right bank. He easily crossed the sandy bed of the river and retired up the left bank. There is a belt of scrub and palm about 2 miles wide on left bank opposite the *dem*. While on right bank it averages about ½ mile only. Now it seems to me there would have been little or no risk (had we attacked enemy's right) in sending a brigade across the river bed with all the cavalry and some guns. I am aware that to reach the enemy's right we should have had to make a flank march in front of an enemy 'in position'. But it would have been to our advantage had he left his trenches and attacked us during the movement.

Next, what about the use made of the artillery? Distant fire was not required; in fact, the first and only range was some 700 yards. Our side says the guns did tremendous damage. Mahmud and 300 (enemy) questioned by Fitton (who is a sort of Intelligence officer here) say, 'We did not mind the guns: they only hurt camels and donkeys. The infantry fire was what destroyed us.' As far as I can

make out the artillery fire frightened a good many of the spears-
men and they bolted. The deep nature of the trenches prevented
shrapnel searching it. It was interesting to see an old camel during
the artillery bombardment, hopping about in and out of the weak
places of the zariba. This was nothing of an obstacle, and there
were many roads through it.

Another point is the formation of the force for the attack. Each
brigade attacked on a front of about 300 to 400 yards. (For a
straight line of 1000 yards would more than reach from the
enemy's right to his left). So looking on, it struck me that our
formation was extraordinarily deep. This may have accounted for
our severe losses. Egyptians had 483 casualties; British 120–603.
I see in the whole Tirah operations the losses are 1,050. (My
Egyptian figures are correct, for the hospital is next door here and
the 2 doctors live in our mess). Briefly, my plan of attack would
have been to establish as many infantry as the front admitted, in
a fire position as quickly as possible. The *dem* being at the foot
of the slope (400 yards from crest on average) the ground lent
itself to this. Moreover, it was possible from more than one place
to enfilade the front trench with machine guns. Two brigades would
have more than sufficed for this. A third brigade, guns and cavalry
to have destroyed the fugitives *in* the river bed (600 yards wide
or more), in the scrub beyond and in the desert. The 4th brigade as
a reserve. The weak point in my plan is that I calculated as if I
had troops that can shoot and manoeuvre. It would be unwise to
rely upon the Blacks doing either *well*. So all the more credit is
due to the Sirdar for limiting himself to a moderate victory
instead of going for annihilating Mahmud's army.

This long extract is worth study, for it shows Haig's understanding
of the nature of battle and his interest in minor tactics. He was able
to sum up the battle as a tactical exercise and yet not to forget the
human element. Significant was his realization of the importance of
small arms fire, of the use of ground, especially of the interplay of
the various arms and of the value of enfilade machine-gun fire.
Despite his somewhat patronizing apologia for Kitchener, he showed
himself far in advance of his commander in these matters; but that
Great Man never showed any interest in tactics. Evelyn Wood, on
the other hand, was fascinated by the report. He had served both in
the cavalry and the infantry,[2] and there was no more experienced

fighter at that time in the army. In acknowledging the report, he told Haig that he could safely write freely and that his letters would be shown to no one. In expressing his interest, he said, 'You gave me an excellent description of the reconnaissance and your little rough diagrams made it all so clear I could almost fancy I was there. . . . What you write about the effects of the artillery fire is borne out by all the officers I have seen. . . . Your observations on the tactical teaching are I think worthy of all consideration. It is rather sad to me to think I am getting too old to think how I might better your tactics of Good Friday.'

The battle of the Atbara ended the fighting for the season and the next four months were taken up with preparations for the final defeat of the Khalifa. By the end of August, Kitchener had a considerably augmented force, some 8,200 British and 17,600 Egyptians and Sudanese, but he was greatly outnumbered by the Khalifa's army of more than 50,000, many of them well armed and all of them fanatical in their cause. The Dervish army was drawn up on the west bank of the Nile at Omdurman, just north of Khartoum. Kitchener advanced to contact on 1 September, but next day it was the Dervishes who attacked. Haig was in command of the leading squadron of Broadwood's cavalry drawn up on the extreme right of the line, furthest from the river. The Khalifa's main attack was launched against the infantry, which lay with their backs to the river within a zariba of thorn bushes. There was also a subsidiary move by the left wing, under the Khalifa's son, to outflank Broadwood's cavalry, which was outside the zariba. Kitchener sent Rawlinson, one of his staff officers, to order Broadwood inside the zariba, but Broadwood saw that this would allow the position to be outflanked and, on his own initiative, he retired to a line of hills to the north. Haig commanded the rearguard in this move, which drew off much of the Khalifa's army and probably saved the day. Rawlinson saw Haig's squadron in action and commented:

> At length we could see our contact squadrons under Douglas Haig gradually withdrawing as the Dervishes advanced. . . . I rode out to him over ground which an hour later was heaped with dead and wounded Dervishes. When I reached him he was within about 600 yards of the enemy's long line, and I noticed that his confident bearing seemed to have inspired his fellaheen, who were watching the Dervish advance quite calmly.[3]

Broadwood held the threat to the flank and, in the meantime, the main advance came under heavy fire from Kitchener's artillery and, as it progressed, was further mown down by machine-gun and rifle fire. None of the Dervishes got within 300 yards of their enemy line and the field was strewn with their dead and wounded. But the battle was not yet over because the Khalifa still had his reserve of 20,000 men in possession of a rocky hill, the Jebel Surkab, which dominated the route to Omdurman. Kitchener came forward to direct the battle for this eminence and, as was his habit, issued his orders direct to all and sundry, by-passing the chain of command, and getting everything into confusion. However, superior fire power won the day and the Dervishes were driven off the hill. In the last action of the battle, Kitchener tried to cut off their retreat by ordering a charge by the 21st Lancers along the line of the river. This was the Regiment in which Winston Churchill had with some difficulty found a place. Earlier, Kitchener had offered him to Haig, saying he was much bothered by people of influence trying to get him to place officers. But Haig had said he did not want him in his squadron.[4] Whether this refusal was from personal acquaintance or from a dislike of politicians is not apparent. His rejection of Churchill, however, did not prevent Haig from entrusting him with letters to Evelyn Wood and to Henrietta when Churchill went back to Cairo by the Nile steamer after the battle.

These letters contain criticism of Kitchener for his failure to capture the Khalifa and for the hardship imposed on the cavalry in the pursuit. There was also harsh criticism of the handling of the battle as a whole. To the Adjutant-General he wrote:

The officer in chief command (be he the Sirdar or Hunter) insisted on doing every detail himself, in place of trusting a staff officer to allot the camping area to units. I had occasion to see this, for on 24th August I covered the advance of the Egyptian Army with my squadron, two maxims and one company Camel Corps. . . . The plan of having two bodies of cavalry (the 21st Lancers and ourselves) under independent commanders, but employed in advance of the army with one objective, cannot be too strongly condemned. It led to much waste of horseflesh, to say the least; and had the enemy possessed even 500 horses, might have resulted in disaster. . . .

You will hear a lot of the charge made by the 21st Lancers. It

27

took place at 9 am south of Signal Hill, into an arm of the Khor Shambat. The Sirdar was then meditating an advance on Omdurman and the 21st were to precede the infantry. The Regiment seems to have advanced without any patrols in front. Seeing a few men in front, the Colonel thought it a good moment to charge. He seems to have marched parallel to the enemy in column of troops, then wheeled into line to the right and charged. While in column of troops they were under a hot fire, so his suspicions might have been aroused, especially as Slatin before had told him of the nullah. Away the Regiment went, four squadrons in line, and came down in this nullah filled with rifle and spearmen. The result was scarcely as bad as might have been anticipated, for the two flank squadrons suffered little. Two troops of the centre squadron were, however, practically wiped out. A rally with their backs to the river followed, the enemy meantime going on to join the attack on MacDonald (commanding one of the Egyptian brigades). The loss inflicted on the enemy (judging by the corpses) was trifling, 14 or 15 at most. . . . We onlookers in the Egyptian cavalry have feared this all along, for the Regiment was keen to do something and meant to charge something before the show was over. They got their charge, but at what a cost? I trust for the sake of the British cavalry that more tactical knowledge exists in the higher ranks of the *average* regiment, than we have seen displayed in this one. Yet this commanding officer has had his command extended. . . . I cannot think that the Promotion Board fully appreciate the responsibility which rests with them when they put duffers in command of regiments. I am writing to you just what I think, and now one word on the battle as a whole.

I had ample time to appreciate the situation on the 1st and 2nd morning. The enemy halting as he did on the upper pools on the Khor Shambat on night 1–2 Sept abandoned the key of the position – Signal Hill – to the Sirdars. The latter hill has long sloping shoulders and, to my mind, should have been occupied on evening of 1st. Why should the enemy not have taken it? And what losses would we not have suffered in turning him out? Lastly, occupied and used as a pivot, and keeping our army concealed to the east of it with gunboats and heavy guns on position protecting the flanks, we could anticipate any move of the enemy. Then on morning of 2nd when the enemy had divided his forces, the Sirdar's left should have been thrown forward to this hill, and gradually drawing in his right and extending his left south-westwards, he might have cut the enemy off from Omdurman and really *annihilated* the thousands and thousands of Dervishes. In place of this, altho' in possession of full information, and able to see with his own eyes the whole field, he spreads out his force, thereby risking the destruction of a brigade. He seemed to have had no plan, or tactical idea, for beating the enemy beyond allowing the latter to attack the camp. This the Dervishes would not do in force, having a wholesome fear of gunboat fire. Having 6 brigades, is it tactics to fight a very superior enemy with one of them and to keep the others beyond supporting distance? To me it seems truly fortunate that the *flower* of the Dervish Army exhausted itself first in attack and pursuit of the cavalry. Indeed the prisoners say, 'You would never have defeated us had you not deceived us.'

It is difficult to surmise what Kitchener would have said had he known that his tactical deficiencies had been the subject for an essay by a junior officer for the Adjutant-General, but there is no doubt that the letter must have delighted Evelyn Wood.

In common with most of the officers specially seconded to the Egyptian Army, Haig left the Sudan after Omdurman. He returned to the 7th Hussars in Norwich as a squadron commander. On 16 November, a few days after his arrival, the Brevet Majority which he had been awarded by Kitchener appeared in the *London Gazette*.

# 4

# THE WAR IN SOUTH AFRICA

On 8 May 1899, Haig left the 7th Hussars for the last time; he was appointed Brigade-Major to the 1st Cavalry Brigade at Aldershot. There, he worked again with French, who was the brigade commander. Some idea of their trust in each other and of Haig's generosity may be gained from the fact that French borrowed £2,000 from Haig. He had been investing in the South African gold market and had got into financial difficulties. There is no evidence that this loan was ever repaid; certainly in December 1903, writing to his trustees, Haig said that he would prefer to lose the money rather than that French should be pressed for it. Although after long and faithful service to him, Haig did eventually lose faith in French, this was on military grounds, and there was never any indication that this debt had anything to do with the lost friendship.

At the time Haig joined the brigade, it already seemed likely that the British would be forced into some military action against the Boer republic of the Transvaal. A month later, in June, a decision was taken that, if armed action became necessary, a corps of three divisions and a cavalry brigade, under Sir Redvers Buller, then commanding at Aldershot, would be sent to South Africa. The military authorities were faced with a time and space problem not unlike that of Britain and France in the Suez Canal crisis in 1957. The mobilization, despatch and concentration overseas would take at least three months and, in the meantime, the British colony of Natal was extremely vulnerable to invasion from both the Transvaal and the Orange Free State. The garrison of Natal was then two regiments of cavalry, five hundred sabres in all, three battalions of infantry, two thousand-odd bayonets, two field batteries, in all twelve guns, and one mountain battery of six guns. There was no possibility of reinforcement from Cape Colony on anything but a small and temporary basis, because in that colony were only three and a half battalions of infantry, one field battery and some coast defence guns. Against these small forces, the Boers could be expected to bring some 50,000 well-armed and well-mounted burghers, with an efficient, regular cadre of artillery. In July, it was decided to send some 10,000 men to reinforce the Natal garrison. This was irrespective of Buller's force, which had still not been mobilized. The reinforcements were to come principally from India and Malta and would bring the garrison of Natal to roughly a division, plus a cavalry brigade.

In those days there was no field or expeditionary force ready for despatch overseas. Wolseley had for years been calling for the establishment of such a force, but the Government view was that the army at home existed for home defence and the upkeep of overseas garrisons. Any overseas expedition that became necessary had to be extemporized from the forces thus maintained. There was not even any policy for sending out existing formations, such as the 1st Cavalry Brigade. Instead, units were mobilized and grouped as required and commanders appointed from a mobilization list. In accordance with this haphazard procedure, Sir George White, the Quartermaster-General, was sent out to command in Natal and French was sent to command the cavalry brigade with Haig as his principal staff officer.

Haig embarked on 23 September in the Union Castle liner *Norman*. He shared a two-berth cabin with his commander, on the top deck where he had access to the captain's bath. These were the days when there was no means of getting news at sea and they arrived at Cape Town on 10 October thirsting to know what had happened in the meantime. It was, in fact, the day that the ultimatum made by Kruger expired. Haig, with his customary belittlement of politicians, thought that 'even Lord Salisbury' could not submit to the insolent demands of the Transvaal President. He was right and next day the war began. Haig and French still had five more days at sea before reaching Durban on 19th October. They went up at once by the night train to Ladysmith and arrived next morning.

On 11 October, the Transvaal and Orange Free State removed all

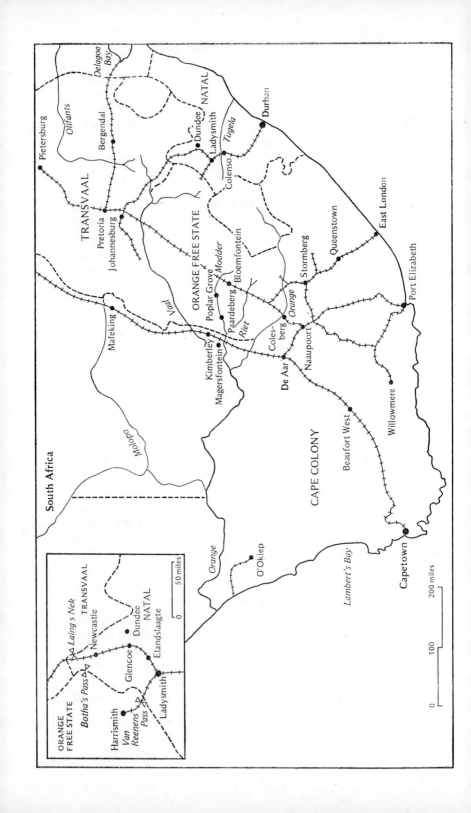

South Africa

Pietersburg

*Delagoa Bay*

*Olifants*

Bergendal

Dundee NATAL
Ladysmith
*Tugela*
Durban

TRANSVAAL

Colenso

Pretoria

Johannesburg

ORANGE FREE STATE

East London

*Modder*
Poplar Grove
Paardeberg Bloemfontein

*Vaal*

Queenstown

Stormberg

*Orange*

Coles-
berg

Mafeking

Kimberley
Magersfontein

*Riet*

Naauwpoort

De Aar

Port Elizabeth

*Molopo*

CAPE COLONY

Beaufort West

Willowmere

*Orange*

O'Okiep

*Lambert's Bay*

Capetown

200 miles

0        100

ORANGE
FREE STATE

△ *Laing's Nek*

TRANSVAAL

Newcastle

Dundee

Glencoe

Elandslaagte

△ *Botha's Pass* ▽

Harrismith

*Van Reenens Pass* ▽

Ladysmith

50 miles

0

doubts about the war by moving to the invasion of Natal. Other attacks were made against Mafeking and Kimberley but, despite the encouragement of Boer sympathizers on both sides of the border, President Steyn of the Orange Free State assured the Premier of the Cape that he would not invade Cape Colony. Buller's corps had not been mobilized until 7 October, but the last of the reinforcements for Natal arrived on the day hostilities began. White had arrived in Natal on 7 October and was immediately involved in a difference of opinion with the officer then in command, Major-General Penn Symons, who was supported by the Governor. The question was whether to defend the rich coalfield area of Dundee and Glencoe or, as White wished, to concentrate at Ladysmith. The Governor considered a withdrawal from Glencoe would be disastrous, since it would cause the Dutch in Natal and perhaps the Cape, to throw in their lot with the Boers and might also lead to the disaffection of the Zulus. White's reasoning was that Ladysmith was the furthest point north where the British could meet the converging threats from the Transvaalers through Laing's Nek and the Orange Free Staters through Van Reenen's Pass.

Against his better judgment, White allowed Symons to remain at Glencoe. That gallant warrior thought that a British brigade could dispose of any number of Boer burghers. Accordingly, when the situation offered, he launched an ill-devised attack against a superior force at Talana Hill and, courageously in the lead himself, was mortally wounded. The Boers, under Joubert, showed a surprising lack of initiative and Talana was at first seen as a British victory, despite the heavy casualties they incurred. There was, however, one bold move by the Transvaalers which gave Haig his first opportunity of action against a civilized enemy. A raiding force under Kock was sent to cut off the Glencoe brigade from Ladysmith by destroying the railway at Elandslaagte. French and Haig, with a small mounted force, went out to reconnoitre the area, but were recalled as soon as they made contact with the Boer piquets, because of a threat from another column from the north-west. They dined with White to receive their orders, but the threat did not materialize and instead they were ordered to move at four am next day to clear the enemy from Elandslaagte and cover the repair of the railway and telegraph. French's force consisted of part of two British cavalry regiments (the 5th Dragoon Guards and the 5th Lancers), two batteries of artillery and five squadrons of the Imperial Light

Horse, volunteer units raised in South Africa, mostly from Uit-landers in Johannesburg. He was supported by an infantry brigade commanded by Ian Hamilton. French had at this time no battle experience and doubtless leaned heavily on Haig's thoughtful study of the problems of the attack, albeit against a less sophisticated enemy.

Haig had no restful dinner, but immediately set about preparing the orders for the move and making the march table. The attack next morning surprised the Boers, but, with those tactics that were to become so familiar, they did not stand and instead rode off to the adjoining hills. From there, they brought disconcertingly accurate artillery fire to bear on the cavalry. The infantry brigade was then only in the process of arriving, and the position taken up by the Boers in the horseshoe of hills overlooking the railway seemed strong, particularly as the Boer artillery outranged the British. French therefore telephoned White for orders. This does not seem much like the dashing cavalry leader, but Haig in a note made at the time explains it thus: 'It appeared that the decision of fighting the enemy in a chosen position was one upon which the Commander-in-Chief alone could give an opinion. A defeat or victory must have important results on the campaign. It was for the Commander-in-Chief to decide whether either the political decision in South Africa or the military situation in Natal (which an officer commanding a detachment for a day could not thoroughly know) demanded that a battle should be risked.'

White said that the enemy must be attacked without delay and driven out. Haig immediately prepared the orders and the attack was launched that afternoon. It was in its nature a classic battle. The Boers occupied one arm of the horseshoe and three *kopjes* at its north-east end. Hamilton's infantry formed up along the other arm. The Devons advanced frontally along the mouth of the horseshoe, while the Manchesters and the Gordons worked along the ridge to roll up the enemy from the southern flank. The cavalry watched both flanks and were ready when the moment came for the pursuit.

The infantry attack succeeded but not without a hard struggle. At the end, a counter-attack of fifty Boers emerged from cover, led by old General Kock himself in his top-hat and frock-coat. Kock was mortally wounded. The end of the battle is best described in Haig's own words to his sister:

All the leaders were either shot down or taken prisoner; none escaped. The Boers say they never thought the British could have taken their position. They abandoned their tents, waggons, everything in fact, and took to flight. Some 1815 brandy was found in one of the waggons. [Some will be shocked that a member of a famous distiller's family should thus perpetuate the romantic myth of Napoleon brandy.] They were wild with the way the fugitives were killed with the lance! They say it is butchery, not war. But as they use express rifle bullets, I don't quite see where the difference comes in.

White had come forward to see the battle, but had not interfered with its conduct. He returned to Ladysmith the same evening and was informed that Boer columns were approaching Ladysmith from the north-west; he was also given a message that had come in his absence from Brigadier-General Yule, who had taken over from Symons. Yule asked for reinforcements and described his difficult situation. White decided he must revert to his original plan of concentrating for the defence of Ladysmith and he recalled French. The cavalry arrived back in Ladysmith on 22 October and two days later were sent out on an offensive operation to cover Yule's withdrawal. This accomplished, and Yule's depleted and exhausted brigade having been given a few days' rest, White decided to attack the Boer column which had now arrived within striking distance of Ladysmith. White's plan involved a complicated move to strike the enemy in flank while a force under Carleton moved by night to cut off the enemy retreat.

The resultant battle of Lombard's Kop on 30 October was one of those in which everything went wrong. Carleton's column was itself surrounded and captured, while the main infantry attack hit the air and was itself outflanked. White felt bound to confess himself defeated and ordered the withdrawal to positions for the close defence of Ladysmith. The cavalry did no better than the infantry in this battle. French's brigade was supposed to cover the flank of the infantry, but dawn had found them much too far back to do so. Nor is there any indication that the brigade was used effectively to cover the withdrawal to Ladysmith. White denied in his evidence to the Elgin Commission that the withdrawal was a rout and he talked of artillery fire having halted the enemy follow-up. But, according to *The Times History of the War*, 'For reasons which it is difficult to understand, the cavalry were allowed to save themselves by their speed alone. No attempt was made at a judicious withdrawal by regiments. Troop officers were not even given the time to form their troops. A seething mass of clubbed and broken cavalry charged down the narrow nek on the west of Lombard's Kop.'

How this can have happened is unexplained; it was certainly against all Haig's teaching. That Haig's opinions were, even at this early stage in his career, of some account is shown by the fact that White took him on his ride round the area to select the defences and asked him his views on the position. Haig gave advice which was well in advance of his time. He was against thinly spreading the troops around a long perimeter, but preferred holding strongly the important features, which he indicated, and keeping a strong reserve with cavalry and artillery for counter-attacks. But Haig was not to remain to see the defensive battle of Ladysmith fought out. When he returned from a successful raid on a Boer laager at midday on 2 November, he found that White had received a signal from Buller, who had arrived at the Cape on 31 October, asking that 'French should take command of Cavalry Division on its way from home and it is my wish that he and Haig should come here if you can spare them possibly.'

Accordingly, two hours later, the two officers left with a small personal staff in what proved to have been the last train to get through before the cordon of siege was closed. They were the sole passengers in a mixed train and had been warned to keep out of sight for two hours. The party, including the two future commanders-in-chief, can be imagined in a rather undignified posture along the seats and floor of a first-class coach. They were fired on several times and a three-inch shell did some damage to Haig's personal baggage.

Haig sailed from Durban and arrived at Cape Town on 8 November. There he stayed at the Mount Nelson Hotel, where he shared a bedroom with French. They had ten days to wait and Haig used this time to review the lessons he had learned from the fighting in Natal. He committed them to paper as his 'Tactical Notes'. What the more frivolously-minded French thought of his room mate's industry is not recorded. The significance of these notes lies in their indication of the situation that was going to develop in South Africa. They show the impotence of the infantry attack against an enemy that cannot be fixed, the strength of infantry in defence provided they remain concealed, the limitations of artillery shrapnel, and the value of cavalry armed with the rifle or carbine. Haig's views on mounted troops are particularly interesting. He wanted to abolish the lance; the sword is not mentioned, but there is ample evidence elsewhere that he regarded the ability to charge with the sword as essential. Apart from this unstated opinion, all he said about the tactics and equipment of the cavalry pointed to a mounted infantry – the horse for movement and movement to be followed by dismounted action.

Nevertheless, in a letter to Henrietta in which he stated the need for more cavalry, he said: 'The Mounted Infantry craze is now I trust exploded. So far they have proved useless, and are not likely to be of use *until they learn to ride*. You had better not give these views to Sir Evelyn, for both he and Lord Wolseley are the parents of the Mounted Infantry.' As has already been stated, Evelyn Wood served both in the infantry and the cavalry and he was the originator of the idea that each infantry battalion should train one mounted company. These companies were later grouped with specially-raised units to form mounted infantry brigades or columns and used extensively throughout the campaign. Haig was possibly moved by the understandable suspicion of the professional for the amateur, but what he should have seen was that mounted infantry were as effective as cavalry provided they were skilled in horsemanship and horse-mastership. The Boer commandos formed a skilled mounted infantry and, as often as not, were a match for British cavalry.

Buller had arrived in South Africa determined to advance astride the railway to Bloemfontein and on into the Transvaal. Events in Natal and the clamorous demands of Cecil Rhodes, besieged in Kimberley, to be relieved had altered the situation. To add to Buller's problems, Steyn had, on 1 November, withdrawn his undertaking not to invade Cape Colony. Buller decided to split his force. With the main body, he would go to the relief of White at Ladysmith and he would send Methuen's division to relieve Kimberley. For the defence of Cape Colony, he sent Gatacre with a brigade to Stormberg and ordered French's cavalry division to cover the border between Methuen and Gatacre, to harass the enemy where possible and eventually to form the screen behind which Buller would regroup his forces for the advance on Bloemfontein. Except for French's division, all this came to disaster in 'Black Week' – 10–15 December. Gatacre was defeated at Stormberg on Sunday, Methuen at Magersfontein on Wednesday and Buller failed at Colenso on Friday.

The cavalry division moved up on 19 November to the important rail junctions of De Aar and Naaupoort and was soon in action against the Boers who had crossed the border and occupied a commanding ring of *kopjes* about Colesberg. The regular British cavalry regiments, augmented by mounted infantry units, were at first no match for their very mobile opponents, but they learned from experience and French's command did much to prevent the disasters which might have followed Stormberg and Magersfontein. Much of the credit for this must go to Haig, who was so apt at learning and teaching. Laycock, father of Major-General Sir Robert Laycock, Chief of Combined Operations in the Second World War, one of French's Aides-de-Camp, recorded how adept Haig was in framing concise orders and instructions which made absolutely clear to units what they had to do. Another staff officer who worked with Haig at this time was Herbert Lawrence, who had joined the division as DAAG Intelligence. They had been together at Camberley and their paths were often to cross again.

The disasters of Black Week caused the Government to send out Roberts to take over chief command, although Buller was left to continue with the operations for the relief of Ladysmith. Roberts had Kitchener as his Chief of Staff and Henderson, Haig's teacher at the Staff College, as his chief Intelligence Officer. A fresh spirit was put into the conduct of operations and French's cavalry division had a most important part to play in the new plan. Haig remained on French's staff, as indeed he did right up to the end of 1900, but for a short time, however, he had to take second place. Colonel Lord Erroll, who had just arrived in South Africa, was appointed Assistant Adjutant-General to French, leaving Haig as a Major and DAAG. In vain, French telegraphed to Kitchener pointing out that Haig had been specially appointed to him as his Chief of Staff with the local rank of Lieutenant-Colonel, and saying that Haig's service in the recent operations had been invaluable. The answer came back that the Commander-in-Chief fully realized the excellence of Haig's service, but that the appointment was one for a more senior officer. Erroll only remained in the post for just over a month and Haig took over again with the rank of Lieutenant-Colonel. During that month, Haig had the opportunity of returning for a few days to Cape Town, where he was brought to discuss the situation with Henderson. The period of his supersession (18 January–21 February 1900) was, ironically enough, that in which the cavalry division carried out their most exciting and successful operations of the whole war. But Haig was present throughout these operations and there is no doubt that he remained the linchpin of the headquarters and signed the essential orders. As further proof of the position, after the successful operations were over, French sent one of his aides to Kitchener to tell him that Erroll had not proved satisfactory and to get him moved to another appointment.

The task given to the cavalry was the essential part in Roberts's plan to make a surprise move to capture Bloemfontein from the west and at the same time to relieve Kimberley. French's first task was to cross the river Modder and to screen the concentration of three divisions which were to deal with Cronje's force that was investing Kimberley, before advancing on Bloemfontein. French carried out this task and then, in a brilliantly executed dash, culminating in a fine cavalry charge, he relieved Kimberley and cut off Cronje from the Transvaal. Cronje sought to escape along the Modder and was pursued by Roberts's main body of infantry. The cavalry, dispersed in the pursuit and somewhat spent by their battle for Kimberley, then had the task of dashing south-east again to cut off Cronje at the Klip Drift on the Modder. This they succeeded admirably in doing, with the result that Kitchener, temporarily in command while Roberts was ill, was able to compel Cronje's surrender at Paardeburg.

After Klip Drift, French put Haig in command of a brigade, but that only lasted a day or so because, on 21 February, he again became French's chief staff officer. De Wet with his Free Staters was in the vicinity of Paardeburg, having tried fruitlessly to relieve Cronje. Roberts's next move was an attempt to round him up in the same way that he had dealt with Cronje. The ensuing battle of Poplar Grove was far from a complete success, the reason being bad staff work and lack of co-ordination for which Haig cannot be held blameless. Roberts had made an admirable plan and had given out orders orally on a *kopje* east of Paardeburg on the afternoon of 6 March. De Wet, with about 5,000 men, was twelve miles to the east along the Modder. Roberts planned to throw the cavalry by a wide detour to the south – about seventeen miles – thus cutting off De Wet from Bloemfontein, while the 6th Division and the Guards Brigade put in an attack from the south on a shorter axis and two more divisions attacked direct, one each side of the Modder.

No timings were given in the orders, but it was obvious that the cavalry would have to be well clear to allow the move of the 6th Division. The cavalry did not move off until three am, while 6th Division had moved at two am and had had to halt. Even with their late start, the cavalry halted for two hours for daylight and again at seven am to water their horses. The result was that, so far from being cut off, De Wet moved away before a direct attack and a half-hearted pursuit by the cavalry. This was all the more unfortunate as it was later ascertained that Kruger and Steyn had been with De Wet.

The historians of the war have tended to underestimate the importance of this action. Even the *Official History* in which Roberts's orders and the order for the cavalry divisions, signed by Haig, are given in full, makes little of the failure. Roberts himself was in no doubt at the time that he had lost a golden opportunity of ending the war. Ladysmith had been relieved a few days earlier and the Boers were very dispirited. Kitchener, as Chief of Staff, and French were chiefly to blame. There is evidence that French was in a temper because of some dispute with the staff about forage for his horses and he certainly left Roberts's conference before the end so that there was no opportunity for questions or tying up details. But it is certain that Haig, usually so punctilious in these matters, ought to have cleared the times with 6th Division before he issued the orders. Roberts, with that absence of bitterness and recrimination which characterized all his evidence, said to the Elgin Commission:

. . . but owing to the darkness of the night, the Cavalry Division was delayed and, when day broke, instead of being as I had hoped, well round the enemy's left flank, it had gone little more than a couple of miles, and for some time blocked the way of the 6th Division. . . . The Poplar Grove Day, however, was a most disappointing one for me, as I had quite calculated on cutting the enemy off from the Bloemfontein road, and forcing him to get entangled in the difficult drifts of the Modder; but, notwithstanding the comparative rest the horses had had after Cronje's surrender, they were in extremely poor condition, added to which the ground was very heavy owing to recent rain. Had the mounted troops been able to move more rapidly, they could undoubtedly have intercepted the enemy's line of retreat, for when I reached Poplar Grove late in the afternoon with the infantry and heavy artillery, their rearmost troops were still visible. Immediately on sighting them, I hurried off a staff officer to tell General French what a short way off the enemy were, and to urge him to follow them up. The reply I received was that his horses had come to a standstill. The failure to effect my object was the more mortifying when I learned that the Presidents of the Orange Free State and South African Republic had been present during the engagement. . . .[1]

Haig's own account of the day to Henrietta does not give any indication that the move of the cavalry division was not in accordance with Roberts's intentions. He said:

. . . we marched at 3 am and moved round the left or southern flank of the Boer position which they had been strengthening with entrenchments for some days. We got completely round the enemy and quite surprised them. The Boers left their trenches and some took up new positions to try and check our advance. We lost fairly heavily in turning some Boers out of a farm and off a ridge, but nothing of course to what infantry would have suffered had they tried to dislodge the Boers by an attack on the position. Old Kruger and Steyn were among those who ran away! We hear now that Kruger had fixed a meeting for 9 am that day. He of course had to go off before the meeting took place. I well remember seeing a light 4-wheeler waggon drawn by six horses making off and our guns shelled it. One shell fell very close and the driver (who lives in Bloemfontein) says he never drove so fast in his life before! We did not know of course that Kruger was in the waggon, otherwise his capture would have been very well worth a lot of horses' lives. I have never seen horses so beat as ours on that day. They had been having only 8 lb of oats a day and practically been starving since we left Modder River on 11 February. So many Colonial Skallywag Corps have been raised that the horses of the whole force could not have a full ration. The Colonial Corps raised in Cape Colony are quite useless, so are the recently raised Mounted Infantry. They can't ride and know nothing about their duties as mounted men. . . . You will see that the success of the Cavalry Division has been in spite of these ruffians, and notwithstanding short rations.

It must be admitted that there is a certain sinful pride about these observations and certainly a complete lack of understanding of the reason why Roberts's plan went awry. Due allowance must be made for the condition of the horses, but that points to the fact that a preliminary move should have been made the evening before. The ration of 8 lb oats to which Haig refers is 2 lb short of the normal 10 lb. The ration also included 12 lb hay. This would probably not have been issued in full because, at that time of year, there was ample grass, suitable in rest periods but no substitute at times of action. The Boer ponies lived off the *veldt* all the year, and it may be remarked that the despised colonial mounted infantry were, broadly speaking, the same material as the Boer enemy.

After the capture of Bloemfontein, Roberts halted for six weeks before advancing into the Transvaal. The pause was necessary for the reorganization of communications and the collection of a reserve of supplies, as well as to give time for the mounted troops – or rather their horses – to rest and recuperate. But Roberts used the time also to try to persuade the Orange Free Staters to bring in their arms and return to their peaceful occupations. De Wet saw to it that Roberts should not get his way in this; he was everywhere organizing raids and ambushes to the discomfiture of British units. In one of his most successful ventures at Sannah's Post, Broadwood, Haig's former commander and now commanding 2nd Brigade of the cavalry division, was completely outwitted and lost seven guns, much ammunition, and a number of prisoners and horses. Roberts tried to put an end to all this by rounding up De Wet between French's cavalry and the mounted infantry which had been organized as a mobile force under Ian Hamilton, now freed from the Ladysmith siege. But De Wet evaded them both and slipped over the Vaal.

When Roberts resumed his advance astride the railway to Pretoria, it was the same story. French was working on the left and Hamilton on the right and, at each successive river obstacle, the plan was for the mounted troops to hold the Boers while the infantry attacked. But when the cavalry reached the Boers, they slipped away and the cavalry were too exhausted to pursue. Before they were half-way to Johannesburg, the cavalry division, which had left Bloemfontein with 5,900 horses, were down to 3,470 and had to halt for six days to rest and bring up remounts. However, the Boers could only keep in the field by giving up their towns. By the first week in June, Johannesburg and Pretoria were captured and, to the exuberant joy of the British people, Mafeking relieved. On the Queen's official birthday, 24 May, Orange Free State had been annexed to the Crown as Orange River Colony.

After the fall of Pretoria, Roberts fought two battles, Diamond Hill and Bergendal, along the Delagoa Bay railway. In each of these, Roberts used his cavalry to turn the flank and force the enemy to face the infantry attack. In both battles, the cavalry division was on the left or northern flank in boulder-strewn country very difficult for mounted action. At Diamond Hill, the division was almost surrounded by De La Rey, one of the most formidable of the Boer leaders. It was forced to fight dismounted and was only saved by the action of Ian Hamilton's mounted infantry on the other flank. It can hardly be said that the operations since Bloemfontein confirmed Haig's strictures on the mounted infantry or conviction of the superiority of the cavalry. At Bergendal again, the cavalry was ineffective and the battle was won by infantry under Buller, at last arriving from Natal after about six months' inexcusable delay, punctuated by promises to Roberts and subsequent procrastination.

The battle of Bergendal on 27 August 1900 was the end of Boer resistance by a field army, but the leaders had already met to agree that they would continue resistance by guerilla warfare. Kruger had fled from the country, but Steyn stayed on to direct the campaign. The British thought the war was over, but in fact it was to drag on for more than eighteen months. To clear up what was thought to be the last flicker of resistance, the British divisional system was broken up and replaced by a system of mobile columns and, on 30 October, one month before Roberts handed over command to Kitchener, the cavalry division was broken up. This gave Haig his first opportunity of command. From now on he was to have a group of columns, varying from three to seven, working directly under him, in what were largely vain attempts to round up the principal Boer leaders. At first, Haig was still working under French, who was in command of operations against De La Rey near Pretoria. Haig got his chance of independent command when De Wet made his first attempt to invade Cape Colony in December. On 1 January 1901, Haig was moved down to Orange River Colony to join in the pursuit. De Wet got away, but he was foiled in his attempt to get into Cape Colony.

In the turmoil of the pursuit, however, two detachments from his force did get across to Orange River, one under Kritzinger, a Cape rebel, and the other under Hertzog, later to be Prime Minister of the Union of South Africa. Haig, in the temporary rank of Colonel, had four columns to deal with this incursion which had caused considerable alarm in loyal circles in Cape Colony. Haig operated between the Cape Town–Kimberley and the Port Elizabeth–Bloemfontein railways. Kritzinger was some 150 miles north-north-west of Port Elizabeth, and Haig got his columns to the south and east of him and sought to encircle him round the north. But Kritzinger, dividing his force by detaching Scheepers, another Cape rebel, got away to the west and was soon only sixty miles from the sea between Cape Town and Port Elizabeth. There was considerable consternation in the coastal towns and farms, which was only soothed by the arrival of HMS *Doris*, whose commander Captain Grant organized local defence and communication with Haig. The subsequent arrival of HMS *Widgeon* further eased the situation.

It was the difficulty of communication and of getting information that proved to be one of Haig's chief problems once he got away from the railways. His next effort to close in on the enemy was almost successful; Scheepers, surprised at his breakfast, was nearly captured. But although hemmed in by a watch on all the mountain passes to the north, both Boer leaders broke out in darkness and hurried north hotly pursued by two of Haig's columns under Byng and Grenfell, both later to become field-marshals. But on 17 February, the hunt was called off for operations against a more dangerous foe. De Wet had not been deterred by his narrow escape and had made another attempt to invade Cape Colony and join Hertzog. This time he had succeeded in crossing the Orange River and Kitchener had come down to take personal charge of all available columns to round him up. De Wet was hemmed in in the rectangle between the Orange River and the three railways to the south. Plumer was hot on his heels and, with the river swollen, seemed certain to catch him. But at the last possible crossing-place before the Colesberg railway (the fifteenth he had tried), De Wet found a ford dangerously high but just passable. He had failed in his purpose, but he escaped capture.

De Wet's failure and escape coincided with the end of a tremendous drive by French in which the whole of the East Transvaal had been laid waste so that it could no longer sustain the guerillas. Here also, Botha had escaped capture, but Kitchener's object was nearly enough achieved for Botha to accept an offer to discuss terms. Kitchener and Botha were very close to agreement and it is probable that peace would have ensued if it had not been for the intransigence of Milner, the High Commissioner, and Joseph Chamberlain, the Colonial Secretary, and unfortunate advice to continue the struggle from Kruger in the Netherlands. In April, Haig was ordered back to the Cape Midlands in command of all the columns there. At this time, Kitchener was beginning to embark on his immense policy of parcelling out the Boer lands by a system of blockhouses and wire fences supplemented by guards along the railways and rivers. He thus hoped to destroy the mobility of the enemy and to keep them out of the Cape, where fear of a rising in favour of the Boers haunted Milner and others. But Cape Colony itself became the field of what the official historian described as 'kaleidoscopic operations in an immense space of command'. He continued:

> On the one side were Kritzinger, Fouché, Scheepers and Malan, and many lesser leaders, sometimes adroit in various combinations, sometimes separate, now joined by some foe of minor standing whom they absorbed, now by officers more noted than themselves who for the time dominated the scene; on the other side were British columns varying from 15 to 20 in number, pressing now this, now that commando with such tireless industry and infinite complexity of movement that the symmetrical vagaries of the kaleidoscope present actually the truest image of their activities.[2]

It would be fruitless to try to follow the fortunes of Haig in the circumstances described above, but by 9 June 1901, when he again came under French's command, he had worn down some two-thirds of the Boer commandos, although he had still not captured even one notable leader. French came down to command operations over the whole of Cape Colony and Haig still had command of five columns. One of these columns was the 17th (Duke of Cambridge's Own) Lancers and, on 17th July, while retaining his colonelcy and his group, he became a substantive lieutenant-colonel in command of that Regiment. This promotion had one personal consequence; Herbert Lawrence had joined the Regiment three years before Haig had been commissioned and, as a most capable officer, might reasonably have expected to get the substantive promotion. There is no reason to believe that this led to any personal estrangement between them, but soon after the war Lawrence retired to enter the City. On recall to the service in 1914, he gave distinguished service and, in 1918, became Haig's Chief of Staff.

So little effect had the drive through Cape Colony that Scheepers who, with only 300 men, was hunted by almost 15,000 men, was able to tell De Wet in a letter where he would lie up so that he could sally forth to Cape Town when the rains came. He did not quite achieve his aim because the hunt drove him north where, for ten weeks, he marauded the districts on the Indian Ocean. There he was laid low with an attack of appendicitis, was captured and, as a rebel, was shot. But before this happened, a more dangerous enemy appeared in the Cape. In July, the Transvaalers had agreed to invade the Cape. A commando of about 300 men was to go first under Smuts and to be joined later by a larger force under De La Rey. Information of this reached Kitchener, and French was given the task of preventing Smuts crossing the Orange River. After six weeks of near capture, Smuts did cross the river on 3 September and Haig was sent in pursuit. When Smuts was near Queenstown, Haig was able to get the 17th Lancers around him to bar his progress. But Smuts got information from a farmer of the trap that was being laid for him and, watching for his opportunity, in misty weather he surprised a squadron which had unsaddled in a gorge for their midday meal. Smuts' commando helped themselves to rifles, ammunition, horses and stores and made off west. Haig told the story to Henrietta in a letter dated 22 September:

I trained the Regiment from Stormberg ... to head Smuts's Commando, which had broken south-west from near Dordrecht. The squadron in question under a most capable officer (Sandeman) was holding a position ... to prevent the enemy coming south. ... Next morning was very foggy. However the patrols reconnoitred the two passes at the exits of which Sandeman had his camp. All was reported clear, but about noon a message was sent to Sandeman that Boers were advancing to attack his camp. A troop moved out at once. The officer-in-charge saw some men in khaki whom he took to be some of Gorringe's column which was expected north of the post. These levelled their rifles at him when about 200 yards distant. He shouted at them, 'Don't fire. We are 17th Lancers.' (These irregular corps often fire at one another by mistake.) The Boers, as such they proved to be, opened fire at once and emptied several saddles. Before the troop got back to camp the enemy had worked up a *donga* to the rear of the camp. Again their khakee dress assisted them. ... Seeing khakee-dressed men in rear of camp they were allowed to approach quite close before fire was opened on them. Our men held the position to the last and not a man surrendered. Out of 130 men, 29 were killed and 41 wounded. The other men were still fighting when the next squadron came up. . . . All the officers were either killed or wounded. Such nice fellows too.

Although Smuts roamed the West Cape at large for the next six months, hunted assiduously by Haig's columns, and although the commando force increased to ten times its original number, the rising in the Cape on which the Boers had fixed their last hopes did not come about. Most of the Boer sympathizers and all the waverers were unwilling to show their hand until there was a more certain prospect of success than the evasion of the hunted and the occasional spectacular coup. Smuts was one of those far-sighted enough to see that isolated success gave no promise of eventual victory and so, in April 1902, Smuts was called by Kitchener to a conference with Botha and the other guerilla commanders. At the end of May, peace came at last.

Haig's lack of success in hunting Smuts and others may give colour to the remark of Colonel Wools-Sampson, a famous intelligence officer, when he heard that Haig had been given independent command. 'Haig will do nothing. He's quite all right, but he's too damned cautious; he will be so fixed on not giving the Boers a chance, he'll never give himself one.'[3] This harsh judgment will be tempered by the knowledge that the more dashing commanders like French, Ian Hamilton, Allenby and Byng did no better.

Haig was often critical of the generalship in the campaign, but he does not appear to have chafed, as did French, under the close control and detailed instruction exercised by Kitchener. Haig also criticized the peace terms, which he considered too lenient, but here he was able to blame his favourite scapegoat the politician, forgetting perhaps that it was the austere Kitchener who had been the advocate of moderation. Haig had apparently been warned by the Prince of Wales, through Henrietta, that he must be careful not to be too critical because he wrote to a friend to this effect, adding that he had received the same admonition after the Sudan campaign from Sir George Holford. He went on:

My criticism, says H.R.H., may be correct, but it does not do. Now, I never criticize people except privately, and what a stupid letter it would be if I did not express an opinion. Besides, I think we would have better generals in the higher ranks and the country would not have had to pass through such a period of anxiety had honest criticism, based on sound reasoning, been more general in reference to military affairs during the last twenty years.

Haig did not return immediately from South Africa but remained in command of the West Cape, an area including the railway from Cape Town to Kimberley and comprising almost 2,000 square miles. In June he went to see French off on his homeward journey and commented that the 'little man' got a great send-off and was almost in tears as he bid Haig good-bye. Haig asked Henrietta to ensure that there was no nonsense about his own greeting on return. He wanted no crowd of relatives, only Henrietta and a friend. Before he left South Africa, Haig wrote a personal letter which expressed much of his philosophy of life. He was advising his nephew who had himself served in South Africa, whose father Hugo, sixteen years older than Douglas, had recently died.

It would be absurd for a lad of your years and without any experience of the Empire and its inhabitants to settle down into a turnip-grower in Fife. Leave these pursuits until you get into the doddering age! Meantime do your best to become a worthy citizen of the Empire. . . . How would you now feel if you had not been out here, had you not starved with the 'Old Colonel' . . . in fact were not an officer in Her Majesty's 2nd Hussars? It has been your *good fortune* not only to become a soldier, but to have served and risked your life for the Empire – you must continue to do so and to consider that it is a privilege and not that by doing so you are losing time and money! . . . possibly a word or two of patriotism would not be wasted on some of your home loafers such as. . . . Let him use some of his wealth in buying land in the newly-acquired territory and send out settlers to ensure the unity of the country. There are a thousand other ways in which these rotters can become useful members of society, once they realize what rotters (from the point of view of British Citizenship) they are in their present mode of living. The gist of the whole thing is that I am anxious not only that you should realize your duty to your family, your country and to Scotland, but also to the whole Empire – 'Aim High [as the Book says], perchance ye may attain.' Aim at being worthy of the British Empire and possibly in the evening of your life you may be able to own to yourself that you are fit to settle down in Fife. At present you are not, so be active, and busy. Don't let the life of mediocrities about you deflect you from your determination to belong to the few who can command or guide or benefit our Great Empire. Believe me, the reservoir of such men is not boundless. As our great Empire grows, so there is a greater demand for them, and it behoves everyone to do his little and try and qualify for as high a position as possible. It is not ambition. This is *duty*.

In September, Haig returned home. He reverted to his substantive position as Commanding Officer of his own Regiment, the 17th Lancers, which he brought to Edinburgh. At the age of forty-one, he was now firmly established as one of the rising stars of the army. For his services in the war he was promoted Brevet Colonel and he became a Companion of the Bath and ADC to the King. The war, coinciding as it did with the obviously growing rivalry of the powerful German Empire, had awakened political and other civilian interest in military matters and a commission under Lord Elgin was set up in October 1902 'To enquire into the military preparations for the war in South Africa . . . and into the military preparations up to the occupation of Pretoria.' Haig was one of those called to give evidence. It will be observed that the terms of reference dealt with operations only up to the capture of Pretoria, but, both in the preliminary *précis* which he gave to the Commission and in his oral evidence, Haig dealt with his experience throughout the campaign. His views on the tactical handling of the various arms are worth recording. He thought cavalry would have a larger sphere of action in future; in fact, he said 'as now armed, it is a new element in tactics'. By this he was referring to the arming and training of cavalry for dismounted action. He had, however, only slightly modified his views on mounted infantry. Here he said:

> The ideal cavalry is that which can fight on foot and attack on horseback, and I am thoroughly satisfied from what I have seen in South Africa that the necessity of training cavalry to charge is as great as it was in the days of Napoleon.
> Cavalry (though in a few situations it may be strengthened by the support of mounted infantry) will be able to act successfully without it, but mounted infantry cannot act strategically alone and independently of cavalry. For horsemen armed with firearms

only (even though highly-trained as cavalry) cannot cope success-fully with cavalry either in attack or defence. . . .

To take away from cavalry its power of assuming the active offensive by mounted action, by depriving it of the *arme blanche*, is to withhold from it a very considerable advantage without any compensating gain. We must conclude therefore that cavalry must be armed with the best firearms available, and with either the lance or sword.[4]

Haig's views accorded with those of French, but not with those of Roberts or Ian Hamilton. Roberts did not attach much importance to shock tactics, he wanted to abolish the lance but thought the cavalry should still be trained with the sword. Hamilton compared the sword to a mediaeval toy,[5] although he left it as part of the cavalry armament 'for the same reason as infantry have the bayonet'.

Haig thought artillery 'only likely to be really effective against raw troops, possessing a low morale and feeble manœuvring power, while the process of "wearing out" an adversary requires an enormous expenditure of ammunition'. He thought infantry likely to remain the backbone of every army but, as it was the most easily improvised arm, he thought 'the bulk of the money should be spent in maintaining the more "technical" services efficient; namely, artillery and cavalry'. He emphasized the importance of training infantry in concealment and said, 'thus a given number of men will not only hold the same extent of front as formerly, but a larger reserve will be available for counter-stroke, which is the soul of a successful defensive action'.[6]

Questioned on the regimental spirit, local recruiting and the undesirability of posting a man away from his own regiment, Haig replied: 'I am not in a Highland regiment, but I fancy there are a good many Highlanders in them; anyhow, they get the traditions, and Englishmen joining get to believe they are Scotchmen. There is a little leaven of Highlanders that leavens the lot.'[7]

# 5

# 'THE EDUCATED SOLDIER'

Much as Haig enjoyed being in Edinburgh, he did not regard it as a good station for cavalry and tried without success to get it changed to Aldershot or York. Haig knew that both Kitchener and French were trying to get him under their command. Kitchener had become Commander-in-Chief in India and wanted him as Inspector-General of Cavalry, whilst French at Aldershot wanted him to command the cavalry brigade there. Haig told French that he would prefer the cavalry brigade but he was not prepared to do anything to affect the decision. As he said in a letter to Henrietta, he was not anxious about early promotion but was more interested in doing the tasks that fell to him. For the moment he put his heart and soul into the training of his Regiment. He seems to have taken the 17th Lancers more to his heart than he ever did the 7th Hussars and he made friends who remained close to him for the rest of his life. No doubt some of the older officers found his high standards irksome, but his enthusiasm was an inspiration to the younger officers and it was from these that his friends came, among them Alan Fletcher, Bertie Fisher and Osborne Beauclerk, afterwards Duke of St Albans.

Duff Cooper was able to talk to them about their commanding officer,[1] and it seems that a week of six days' work was demanded. Each Sunday Haig, with three of his officers, would go to Muirfield (which involved a three-mile drive, half an hour in the train and a four-mile walk). There, they would play two rounds of golf before returning by the same means. Surprisingly, there is no talk of church in this routine, but the Sabbath was observed to the extent that they did their own caddying. Haig bore all expenses of the outing. And golf was not their only sport, for Haig set out to bring his regimental polo team to the standard of excellence he had attained in the 7th Hussars. He himself played back and, breaking the long run of successes of his old Regiment, the 17th Duke of Cambridge's Lancers won the regimental trophy. The delight of the Duke, who was now eighty-four years old and who watched the final, may be imagined – indeed, it was obvious to all as he drank the health of the team in champagne from the large trophy.

Kitchener had his way and, on 15 October 1903, Haig embarked for India, where he took over the appointment of Inspector-General of Cavalry. He was made substantive Colonel and given the local rank of Major-General, thus becoming the youngest officer of that rank in the British or Indian Armies. Kitchener was just beginning the controversy with Curzon, the Viceroy, that caused a deep personal rift between them and eventually led to Curzon's resignation. Kitchener expected to command the army in India in fact as well as in name, but the system then in being did not allow this. The Viceroy had his own military department. The head of it was a major-general who not only advised the Viceroy independently of the Commander-in-Chief, but who also controlled the expenditure. Frontier defence and internal security were in the province of the Viceroy and, as Kitchener said, the army seemed to be intended to hold India against the Indians. This system thwarted Kitchener's every effort to organize the army as a field army capable of the defence of India against an external enemy. (There was at that time a Russian 'scare'.) Although Haig was certain that Kitchener was right, he avoided becoming personally involved in the quarrel. However, he described the existing system as 'a pair of horses in double harness without a coachman'. The Commander-in-Chief was so engrossed in the problem that Haig was left free to concentrate on the task of training the cavalry. He made it his business to get to know every regiment and would stay with them for three days at a time to teach, advise and supervise their training. He took special pains to ensure that these visits of inspection were not the source of irritation that they could have been. Instead he made them an opportunity for the exchange of ideas and the kindling of enthusiasm. It was unusual for India to take the lead in training methods, but a system of Staff Rides had just been introduced. Haig eagerly accepted and developed the idea, the precursor of the 'Tactical Exercise Without Troops', which became such a feature of

British Army training methods. These Staff Rides were so important to him that his only published book *Cavalry Studies* was based on the five Staff Rides that he held whilst he was Inspector-General of Cavalry in India. A young officer of the Guide's Cavalry, Philip Howell, helped him in a junior capacity as camp commandant for these Rides and became a friend and protegé of Haig's and the recipient of correspondence to which reference has already been made.[2]

However, the most important event of this tour of duty in India occurred while Haig was on leave at home in the summer of 1905. He was invited by King Edward VII to stay at Windsor Castle for the Ascot races. Duff Cooper has given a graphic account[3] of Haig's meeting on the Thursday with Miss Dorothy Vivian, one of the Maids of Honour to Queen Alexandra, and of his proposal of marriage and acceptance on the Saturday. The King and Queen were delighted, but the King introduced a note of seriousness into his congratulations to Miss Vivian when he asked her to ensure that nothing should be done which would interfere with the career of his 'best and most capable general'. The happiness and permanence of the ensuing marriage might well have been foreseen by those who knew Haig's character, but could hardly have been predicted from a remark which he made to a friend who commented on the speed of his courtship. He replied that he had made up his mind about far more important things in half the time. The marriage took place in the private chapel of Buckingham Palace on 11 July 1905. Haig, accompanied by his wife, returned to India at the end of August.

One of the keenest and most influential advocates of army reform at this time was Viscount Esher. He had been a member of the Elgin Commission, and Balfour, who was then Prime Minister, had wished to make him Secretary of State for War. But Esher preferred to work behind the scenes where he had great influence with Crown and Cabinet. He did, however, agree to become Chairman of the Prime Minister's Committee on War Office Reform out of which came the replacement of the office of Commander-in-Chief by an Army Council and the creation of the General Staff. During the hearings of the Elgin Commission, Esher had written to the King commenting on the capable way Haig had given evidence and adding: 'In him your Majesty possesses a very fine type of officer, practical, firm and thoughtful, thoroughly experienced not only in war, but in military history.'[4]

The fall of Balfour's Government and the advent of the Liberals did not lessen Esher's influence. In his own words, Haldane, the new Secretary of State for War, had agreed 'to be "nobbled" by our committee'. Esher had previously written to Haig in India saying that the Army Council 'are not "fliers" but they are hard-working, average sort of men, who are employed in settling the groundwork of an administrative plan, which, in the hands of a strong Chief of the General Staff, may, one of these days, become a very highly efficient machine. . . . When you have finished your work in India, and when Lord K. has finished his, you will both find the soil here well tilled and ready for your sowing.'[5]

Esher had hoped that Haig would be made Director of Staff Duties, but this appointment was filled by Lieutenant-General Hutchinson. After the change in government, Esher worked continuously on Haldane to replace Hutchinson with Haig. As a temporary expedient, it was agreed that Haig should be given the appointment of Director of Military Training, which was shortly becoming vacant, and later transfer to Director of Staff Duties. Haig returned to London in June and was almost immediately struck with a fever which led him to take a 'cure' in Switzerland.

He took up his appointment as Director of Military Training in August and remained in it just over a year before becoming Director of Staff Duties. This had certain advantages because the former appointment, in addition to responsibility for training, was concerned with home defence and, as such, with the reorganization of the Militia and Volunteers. Haig was therefore immediately plunged into the problem of raising the Territorial Force, one of the most sensitive with which Haldane had to deal. The Militia and the Volunteers both existed as home defence forces with no higher organization than the unit. The logical requirement was that the Militia should become a draft-finding organization for the regular army, whilst the Volunteers should become the second-line army of all arms, organized in brigades and divisions. This would require cuts in the regular army and a reduction in the number of volunteer units in order to pay for the reorganization, and a change in character in the Militia, the old 'Constitutional Force'.

All these changes were strenuously resisted. The Militia was strongly represented in the Lords and the Volunteers as strongly in the Commons. Military opinion opposed the reduction in the regular army and ridiculed the idea of a division completely found from part-time soldiers. Roberts, Ian Hamilton and Henry Wilson were among those who thought it impracticable to provide a divisional artillery from territorial units. Haig thought differently and was adamant that the Territorial Force had to be an army of all arms and in every way the counterpart of the regular army. There was, however, one point on which Haldane and Haig were not to get their way; that was the Militia. Haig attended a meeting at Knowsley, where Lord Derby had invited a number of Militia commanding officers to meet Lord Haldane. Lieutenant-Colonel Ellison (secretary of the Territorial Forces Committee) was the only other regular officer there. The Militia were offered the alternatives of becoming the senior units in the new Territorial Force or of training drafts for units of the regular army. They would accept neither. As a result, the Militia was replaced by the Special Reserve. Although many officers and men and some complete units opted to transfer, the Militia as such wasted away as those who refused to transfer came to the end of their service.

On 8 March 1907, Haig wrote to Howell in India: 'You will have seen Haldane's scheme before this. I was astounded at the ignorance displayed by those who spoke after him in the Ho. of Commons. The people's representatives seem to play a game called politics! I gather that Balfour is favourable to the scheme but opposes the Bill in order to delay the introduction of other Bills on other contentious subjects. I wonder if the Members are as ignorant on other questions such as Education as on War organization!'

When Haig became Director of Staff Duties in November 1907, Haldane's Territorial and Reserve Forces Bill had already received the Royal Assent. By this time also the regular reductions were agreed. They affected some artillery batteries, two battalions of Foot Guards, and eight line battalions, all from regiments that had four battalions. The King was much displeased at the reductions, especially in the Guards. It will be observed that there were no reductions in cavalry. By his reductions and reorganization, Haldane was able to make a saving in the Army Estimates of two million pounds and yet to build out of the scattered units of the army an Expeditionary Force of six divisions and one cavalry division backed by a Territorial Force of fourteen divisions and fourteen yeomanry brigades. It is his share in this great work, more perhaps than any other, that earns for Haig the title 'The Educated Soldier' which John Terraine gave him in his book,[6] and which has been used for this chapter.

Duff Cooper, who knew both Haig and Haldane, has given this account of their working together.

The work was more arduous and fatiguing than any to which Haig had been accustomed. Long hours at his desk in the War Office were interrupted by luncheons and followed by dinners at Haldane's house in Queen Anne's Gate, sometimes alone with his chief and sometimes attended by other workers from the War Office or Haldane's colleagues from the Cabinet. Too often, also, when the dinners were over and the guests had left, a further consultation would take place in the Secretary of State's study, and the weary Director would not get home until the small hours. To Haldane such work was the breath of life, such hours were habitual and the discussion of difficult problems to the accompaniment of continual cigars was the pleasantest way of passing the time. But Haig did not talk easily and did not smoke at all. He was accustomed to early hours, fresh air and much exercise.

Two more different types it would be difficult to conceive than Haldane, the subtle-minded philosopher with the smooth flow of words, and the ponderous ungainly body, and Haig, the man of action, alert and vigorous physically and mentally, swift in decision, almost tongue-tied in debate. Two things they had in common, the vision of what was coming and the determination to be prepared for it.[7]

What this was is clear from an entry in Haig's diary one night after they had dined alone together. 'We discussed objects for which Army and Expeditionary Force exist. He in no doubt – viz. to organize to support France and Russia against Germany, and perhaps Austria. By organizing war may be prevented.'

Apart from these serious discussions, there was one somewhat amusing extra-mural conference. Henrietta was apparently interested in spiritualism and took Douglas to a seance where she persuaded him to consult the medium. Haig records the event in his diary, but does not suggest any scepticism on his own part or surprise on hers when he asked the medium whether the Territorial Force should be based on a company or a battalion system. Whether the spirits got it wrong or the medium misinterpreted them is not known but the answer advocated the company system.

First as Director of Military Training and then as Director of Staff Duties, Haig had made the General Staff a reality and, in Haldane's words, gave the British a staff which was 'thinking out military science with a closeness which is not surpassed in the great military schools on the Continent'. But there was for Britain a wider context and Haig's last major work in the War Office was the blossoming of the General Staff into the Imperial General Staff. His work was consummated by the unanimous adoption of the conception by the Colonial Conference of July 1909. The conference, at which Haig was present, confirmed the organization of the Imperial General Staff and accepted 'the standardization of the Military Forces of the Empire without impairing the autonomy of the self-governing Dominions'.[8] As a result, the first military member of the Army Council was, by order in Council on 22 November 1909, styled Chief of the Imperial General Staff.

Haig looked outside to the Royal Navy too. He wrote a paper on the need for a reform of their staff system similar to that which had been effected in the army. His paper was put before the Cabinet and, although no action was taken at the time, it made a deep impression on Winston Churchill and stimulated his later reforms. On that later occasion Haig wrote to Howell (4 January 1914): 'I now have a report on the Naval War Staff Training which Winston has sent me. He asks for my views! They won't train a staff officer *of any kind* in four months at a *College*! but the Sailors have made a great advance in admitting that any training at all is necessary beyond the practical work on board.'

One of the General Staff officers who worked most closely with Haig on his army reforms was Colonel Lancelot Kiggell. Haig had a great admiration for his ability and never forgot the help he had given him. It was no doubt for this reason that Haig later took him as his Chief of Staff. That there was also a close friendship is shown by their correspondence. Haig almost always used the surname formally and seldom Christian or nicknames, even to his close associates like Edmonds, but letters to Kiggell almost always began 'My dear old Kigge'. Kiggell helped Haig in many of his works. One was the preparation of the new training manual for operations – *Field Service Regulations*. Another was to assist in running a Staff Ride to test its doctrine while it was still in draft. Haig was anxious to establish this new training method in the home commands on which the new Expeditionary Force was based. The rôles of 'Military Training' and 'Staff Duties' seem to have been very flexible, and the golden rule seems to have been that what was important was done by Haig. When he had been DMT, he dealt with the war organization, now that

57

he was DSD, he was putting the training methods right. So realistic was the scenario for Haig's Staff Ride that the Director of Military Operations objected that it gave away too many military secrets, and Haig had to modify it. He took immense pains in the preparations and running of the exercise. Two preliminary War Games were held in the War Office and the main exercise for sixty-nine officers of War Office Staff, Home Commands and one representative from Australia, lasted five days. Nicholson, who had become Chief of the General Staff in April 1908, directed, and Haig's labours were rewarded by the enthusiasm which the Staff Ride aroused.

The arduous work and the unaccustomed sedentary life had its effect on Haig's health. He had suffered a breakdown, probably a recurrence of malaria, in April 1908 and had been away from the War Office until mid-June. It might have been expected therefore that he would welcome release when General Sir O'Moore Creagh, who had succeeded Kitchener as Commander-in-Chief in India, asked him to become his Chief of Staff. But Haig's heart was still in his work in the War Office, and he was worried about who might succeed him to carry on his policies. On 24 April 1909, he wrote to Kiggell, who had just gone to Edinburgh as Brigadier-General in charge of Administration:

> This is just a line to tell you very confidentially that Sir O'Moore Creagh has asked me to go to India as his Chief of Staff. At first I refused, but as he pressed me and on thinking the matter over, and looking at the importance of starting a General Staff in India, weeding out Simla and developing the Imperial General Staff, I thought it best that I should go. . . . *Please do not mention this.* But it is so important to get a suitable man to replace me here, that I am anxious to have your ideas as to likely officers, so I have disobeyed Sir O'M's injunctions! Please let me have your opinion soon in order that I may be prepared to recommend a good officer to the CGS.
>
> Personally I would rather stay at home, besides it means leaving the children at home and my wife coming out and visiting them each winter [*sic*]. . . .[9]

The correspondence between them continued for some time. They seem to have decided that, as Haig put it, 'Colin Mackenzie is the man. He was a year at the Staff College with me . . . and I thought him an honest fellow with much common-sense. For several reasons

I would strongly oppose Rawley [Rawlinson].' In this same letter Haig gave his views on the coming struggle with Germany and it seems that, even then, he was thinking of a war of attrition. Thus he wrote:

> As regards meeting the storm which we all foresee, it seems to me that it will last a long time, we will win by wearing the enemy out if we are only allowed 3 more years to prepare and organize the Empire. And it is of vital importance to have the machinery available in India trained as soon as possible to turn out staff officers who may be of use when the time comes, and the resources of that country organized for *Imperial* needs, instead of only for India's as at present. It was this idea that made me accept Sir O'M's offer, and I honestly think I can do more good with him than here during the next 3 years.

A month later, Haig was writing to Kiggell telling him that he was the man to succeed him. Kiggell replied by return of post, being modest about himself and pointing out that he was junior to Henry Wilson, Commandant of the Staff College, one of the establishments he would have to control as DSD. Haig replied:

> I don't agree with your views on Brigadier Kiggell! Nor do you correctly value the importance of 'continuity' in this directorate for the success of the Imperial General Staff. Wilson should go to a Brigade. His being senior to you must not be allowed to interfere with the relationship of the DSD to Comdt S. Coll. If it does that latter must be unfit for his position. I agree that it would be well that the DSD sh'd be a Major-General but then the officer who is selected sh'd be promoted – not a less well-qualified man selected because of his rank. However, the decision will rest with the S of S advised by CGS. I merely state my views and I have done so strongly and hope that I may get my way.

He did; and Kiggell was appointed DSD. In his letter of congratulation, Haig said: 'This is a triumph for ability and honesty over incapacity and intrigue – so I have great hope for the future and the General Staff.'

The Haigs sailed for India in October. Before they left, they stayed with the Royal Family at Balmoral. By the special invitation of Queen Alexandra, they were accompanied by their two daughters, born in March 1907 and November 1908. The King was well enough to be out regularly with Haig on the moors, but these were their last meetings as six months later he died. It was not only his daughters that Haig left behind; his thoughts were still very much with the War Office. His correspondence with Kiggell went on by almost every mail (a weekly sea mail in those days, a letter costing one penny). After only a year as DSD, there was talk of moving Kiggell to be Commandant of the Staff College. On 14 July 1910, Haig wrote:

> *On no account* sh'd you go to the Staff Coll. The development of the Gen'l Staff will be thrown back for many years if you leave your present job now. Besides with so many *talkers* at W.O. – Aldershot – Camberley & elsewhere who know not what war really is, nor Clausewitz's fundamentals, the whole show may be wrecked unless you are in a responsible position and ready to put stopper into the windbags' mouth! I already see from your discussions at the Staff Coll Conference a tendency to split hairs, and a desire for *precise* rules to guide officers in every conceivable situation in war. This wants watching. Only a man of character like yourself can produce the right corrective.

In India, the old quarrels between Viceroy and Commander-in-Chief were over, but the dual system had not been removed. It had only been moved down one step. Now the Commander-in-Chief had two separate rôles, each with its own staff. He was both Commander-in-Chief and Military Member of the Viceroy's Council and it is said that, like Pooh Bah, in one capacity he sometimes officially disagreed with himself in the other. Haig described this as 'the canonization of duality' and tried hard to get rid of the system. He did not succeed. Instead he directed his energies to the more important matter of making the army in India an efficient part of the Imperial forces which must be made ready for the war which he thought inevitable. This meant looking outside India, a policy which found favour neither with the Viceroy, Lord Hardinge, nor with Lord Morley, the Secretary of State for India. On the discovery in Whitehall that such plans were being made, orders were sent that the studies should be abandoned and the existing papers destroyed. Happily the orders were not strictly obeyed. The plans were hidden away in a secret file and, when the time came, they were of use in the despatch of the Indian Corps to France.

Whatever the political direction it could not interfere with Haig's efforts to see that the army was trained on modern lines. By Staff Rides he ensured the promulgation of the teaching of Field Service

Regulations and he took a special interest in the Staff College which Kitchener had set up at Quetta. He sent a copy of the report on one of his Staff Rides for Kiggell's comments, saying:

> You will see that I have tried to preach 'the doctrine' as laid down in FSR Vol. I and have quoted chapter and verse so that the General Staff here may interpret the Reg'ns in the way in which I believe is intended. . . . You will see I rubbed in the absolute necessity for having the *will to conquer!* Since I carried out this staff tour *your pal* Repington produced some articles in the *Times* criticizing the tactical principles of our FSR and saying that the Germans only are wise. I have looked over what we did in the light of his instructions and I can only feel thankful that *his* Training Manual was not in the hands of our army because we must undoubtedly have achieved disaster by trying to turn a position with its flank resting on a river. . . .

Haig's comments on his visits to the Staff College show he was not the dry old stick some people imagine him to have been. Of the annual dinner, he said: 'We tried to make it more convivial and less official than when K. used to make use of it as an advertising medium and published in the papers a speech re his scheme of reforms before it had been delivered!' The next year, on 22 October 1911, he wrote more fully:

> I was much struck with the friendly feeling existing between Braithwaite and his staff, and the officer students. This was not the same last year. In fact there was a gulf between Tommy Capper and the lads so that I was taken off to bed last year soon after we left the dining room, from very boredom! Yesterday . . . I saw each of the senior term individually after the manner of Camberley. Capper gave me a terrible bad report of this lot last year when I was here . . . I am glad to say Braith has found merit in a good many of them, & turned them into quite an average term. I then made them an address. I felt rather like the 'amateur' addressing the 'professional'. But as Tommy Capper frequently told me, 'the great merit of having outside lecturers at this College is that the officer is shown how much better our own instructors can lecture'. . . . I must add how thoroughly Braith has justified our selection of him for the post of Commandant. T. Capper did well but he was too full of nerves and too much of a crank to get the best out of

61

officers. In my opinion things are on a much more satisfactory footing than they were a year ago. Professors and students seem now a happy family party which augurs well for a *united* staff in years to come.

On 12 May 1911, Haldane asked Haig if he would accept the Aldershot Command which was shortly to be vacated by Smith-Dorrien. He gladly did so with the proviso that he should, as the Viceroy wished, stay on in India until after King George v's visit for the Durbar in December. On 5 April just before he had received Haldane's telegram, Haig had written to Kiggell commenting on a rumour that French was to succeed Nicholson as Chief of the Imperial General Staff:

> If French does become GIGS I expect he will accept your advice on all matters and drive things through on whatever lines you consider right. His little peppery ways will be useful to you in tackling the QMG and establishing a moral superiority over the other military members. . . . I am really proud of the confidence which *you* place in me when you know you did all the hard work *for me* when I was DSD. As to going to Aldershot there are too many applicants I expect for that billet, for the powers that be to think of me. In any case I have never asked for an appointment and I don't intend to begin now – besides I am full of work here and could not leave those who have loyally supported me in difficult times for another year at least – I should then have done 3 training seasons out of my allotted four! . . . What a suggestion that I should succeed that great officer Miles as QMG. You mean to have me murdered by the ASC I suppose. However I am ready to go anywhere in a good cause, provided you help and support me and don't go making yourself ill by overwork.

This last theme was one to which Haig often referred. He was always telling Kiggell to take leave and advised him to keep out of 'that place from *noon* Friday to Monday *every week*'. He also invited Kiggell to visit him in India. The warmth of the invitation can be judged by 'you must try to run out to see me for the winter – I'll arrange everything for you – Rawly wrote to me wanting to come but I can't find room for him'.

Haldane followed up his telegram with a letter saying that it was his own strong wish that Haig should go to Aldershot where there was a great deal to be done. This drew a comment to Kiggell: 'I am glad of this as I sh'd feel nervous at taking over the command in "absolute efficiency".' In his last months Haig did not abate his efforts to ensure that India maintained an army which would be a valuable Imperial contribution. He resisted the calls for reductions, saying to Kiggell: 'It is just as well I am here at present as the AG [Barrett] is ready to disband units and reduce numbers without a murmur! I suppose because he *thinks* his future advancement to command of a division depends on being obedient to the wishes of the powers that be.'

Germany had recently resumed work on the railway from Anatolia to Baghdad, for which she had obtained a concession while Britain was engaged in the Boer War. Haig saw this as a danger to India. 'She can now threaten Egypt when the time comes. The next step will be to squeeze Persia and so threaten Afghanistan and India.' He thought few of our diplomats realized what German power was and how she was squeezing out Britain in the Middle East. The Viceroy did not agree with these views and feared Russia rather than Germany. In one of his letters before he left India, Haig wrote: 'I appreciate your wanting to see me as CIGS. I fear I am not sufficiently "accommodating" for the post. Indeed I expect both the Viceroy and the C-in-C will be glad when I cease to be CGS.'

On 5 October, he wrote to Howell to the same effect: 'I expect some of them will be glad when I leave the country! But I like our old C-in-C and hate to see the way Fleeter tries to get at the old gentleman, so we do our utmost for him. But unfortunately he does change his mind when he gets out of range, and perhaps forgets! All the same he knows India very thoroughly, and is therefore very valuable at the present time.'

One of the most delicate questions that Haig had to deal with was the possibility that commissions should be granted to Indians. Two letters show that he was more liberal and forward-looking than most officers of his generation. On 26 January 1911, he wrote to Philip Howell giving his views on a proposal that certain officers of 'position and status' might be given commissions for duty with the Viceroy's Bodyguard and with certain Indian Princes. He said that was 'no real solution to the problem. The capable Indians will not be satisfied with that; they look to a time when they will hold commissions like you or me and can command you or me. My reply would be, "Certainly, provided you are qualified." The question is what is qualified. In my opinion it must vary according to rank, but in the first place it must be an axiom that theoretical knowledge or examination tests alone are not a qualification for commissions of any sort. . . .

Six months later he wrote to Kiggell:

As regards the granting of commissions to Indians, the Government have not yet decided to give them commissions, but they are being pressed by various influential sections of the community and there are many thoughtful officers of the civil service who think that the Indians really suffer under a grievance. . . . Personally I feel that there are only two ways of treating India; either we must look forward to the time when India will be in the same position as one of the Dominions, and we must prepare for it gradually, looking forward say another 100 years; or the other way is to treat India entirely as a vassal state and keep it entirely under control. For this we shall want a very much larger army than we have now, and it seems scarcely possible, having started to give people a voice in the Government to retrace our steps. There is thus, in my opinion, no other course than to give the sons of the fighting class an opportunity of becoming officers; only those however who show that they are morally and intellectually fit for such appointments. . . .

Haig left India two days before Christmas, and, on 1 March 1912, he took over the Aldershot Command. He brought with him from India two officers, Captain Charteris, an officer of the Royal Engineers as his Assistant Military Secretary, and Captain Baird of the 12th Cavalry as his ADC. Charteris tells of the leave-taking in India when his Chief Clerk said to Haig lugubriously, 'Many a man who has been successful in India has come to grief at Aldershot.'[10] Although only one of the three was Indian Army, the arrival of Haig with his two staff officers was regarded as 'The Hindoo Invasion'. Charteris has written an interesting account of Haig's life at Aldershot and has recounted a number of amusing stories which still remain current.[11]

Apart from devoting his military energies to the training and efficiency of his command, earmarked as I Corps in any expeditionary force, Haig had time for sporting and social activities. Golf had replaced polo as his own physical exercise and he strongly objected to what he regarded as a growing tendency, the preference of the young officer for dancing rather than outdoor sports. He did not approve of the introduction of *thés dansants* in the Officers' Club. But there was a more positive social outlook too. He went carefully into the financial difficulties which young married officers suffered and he urged the authorities to introduce a marriage allowance. His method of entertainment too was sensible. He avoided the large parties which had been customary and, in order to get to know the officers under his command, he held small dinner parties of twelve three times a week.

At the end of his first training season, in which he had taken a great personal interest in all the field exercises, he was faced by large-scale army manœuvres in East Anglia. He commanded a force consisting of the two Aldershot divisions and a cavalry division under Allenby, and was opposed by a force of two divisions and one cavalry and one yeomanry brigade under Grierson. Haig's part in the manœuvres was not a success. He was generally considered to have been defeated by Grierson, but worse was his showing at the final conference. This was held in Trinity College, Cambridge, and was attended by the King and by many University dignitaries as well as all the heads of the army. Haig had written out a clear account of what he intended to say but he did not refer to it. Instead, he embarked on an improvised speech which, besides being unintelligible, was exceedingly dull. Those present who did not know Haig could have had no inkling of his military ability or his clear and incisive mind, but there might justly have been foreboding of the difficulties he would have in explaining his strategy to busy and perhaps impatient politicians.

In early 1914, the British Army suffered its most serious, perhaps its only political crisis of modern times. Put simply, the matter at issue was whether officers would obey instructions from the Government to force Ulster into accepting the proposed Home Rule Bill. The trouble arose out of a casual and hypothetical question as to future action, but, owing to political and military mismanagement, it grew into a question of principle, whether the army should be entitled to strike a bargain with the Government over the terms on which they would carry out the orders of that government. The course of events has often been recounted[12] and need not concern us here except in so far as it affected Haig. He could not fail to have been concerned indirectly in an incident which led eventually to the resignation of the Secretary of State for War, Seely, the CIGS,

French, and the Adjutant-General, Ewart, but he was brought in personally only because his Chief of Staff, John Gough, wanted to resign in sympathy with his brother Hugh Gough, Commander of 3rd Cavalry Brigade at the Curragh. Haig refused to forward Gough's resignation and went to see Haldane, now Lord Chancellor, in the hope that the Cabinet would settle the matter in a way which would not involve the loss of many valuable officers at such a time. That the problem involved some equivocation even in so single-minded a soldier as Haig is clear from his letter of 27 March to Philip Howell. Howell had transferred from the Guide's Cavalry to the 4th Dragoon Guards.

We are I believe all united in this command as regards the following: that we will go to Ulster or anywhere and do anything required of us, short of coercing our fellow citizens in Ulster or elsewhere to submit to an Irish Parliament against their wishes.

At a meeting I had with my GOC Divns. & Brigadiers 4 days ago I pointed out the terrible results of disintegration in the Army – our status as a Gt. Power is imperilled to put it briefly – and I begged them to induce all regimental & other officers to keep aloof from politics. I urged this y'day also at the War Office. All agreed *the army must have nothing to do with politics.*

I don't agree that the army has ever left its proper position in the State. Some politicians have tried to put us in a false position for their party purposes but I trust they have failed. You at the Curragh must put yourselves in the hands of the Army Council & leave it at that.

We must trust the Army Council now to carry out what I know to be the real intention of the Cabinet, namely not to use the Army in any way which can be interpreted as bringing coercion upon the Ulstermen. The AC will also do their utmost to get the Army taken out of the political arena. I feel that it is intolerable that the Army sh'd be made a political tool of each party in turn!

The resignations of the three members of the Army Council were made as a point of honour and of dignity and not as a protest. French wrote to Haig: 'We should not have taken the step if we had not been confident that the officers, NCOs and men would continue to carry out their duties in the same loyal and wholehearted manner which has ever characterized the Army.'

# 6

# SUBORDINATE COMMANDER

On 4 August 1914, the day that war was declared, Haig wrote a letter to Haldane asking him 'even at great personal inconvenience, to return to the War Office for as long as the war lasts and preparations are necessary'. He went on to give his idea of the course of the war and the part that the BEF should play:

> This war will last many months, possibly years, so I venture to hope that our only bolt (and that not a very big one) may not suddenly be shot on a project of which the success seems to me quite doubtful – I mean the checking of the German advance into France. Would it not be better to enlarge our expeditionary force by amalgamating less regular forces with it? In three months' time we should have quite a considerable army, so that when we do take the field we can act decisively and dictate terms which will ensure a lasting peace. I presume of course that France can hold out even though her forces have to fall back from the frontier for the necessary time for us to create an army of 300,000.

In a postscript, he added: 'What I feel is that we have such a mass of undeveloped power which no one knows better than yourself how to organize and control. This will be impossible if the bulk of the highly-trained officers are at once carted off to France and a Secretary of State appointed who is new to the existing system. I do hope you will set to work to complete the organization you started in 1906.'

On neither count did events turn out as Haig hoped. Asquith decided to make Britain's most eminent soldier, Kitchener, the

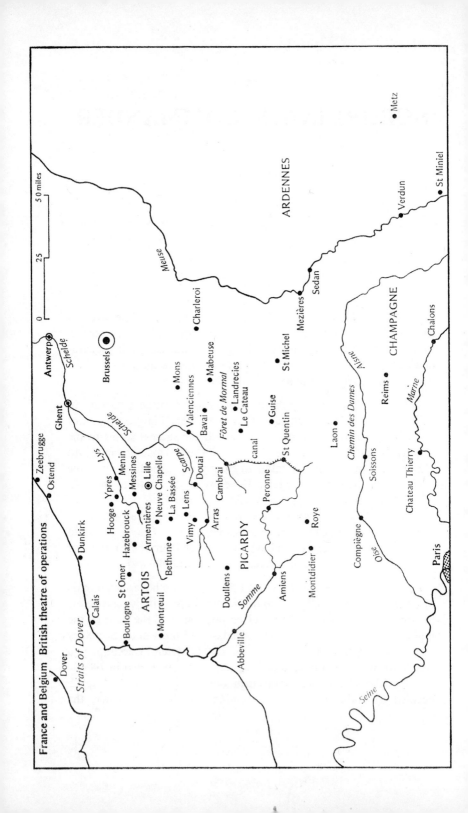

**France and Belgium  British theatre of operations**

0 · · 25 · · 50 miles

Dover
Straits of Dover
Zeebrugge
Ostend
Dunkirk
Calais
Boulogne
St Omer
Hooge
Ypres
Menin
Messines
Hazebrouck
Armentières
Neuve Chapelle
Lille
Bethune
La Bassée
Vimy
Lens
Arras
Douai
Cambrai
Scarpe
Scarpe
Montreuil
ARTOIS
Doullens
PICARDY
Somme
Abbeville
Amiens
Montdidier
Roye
Peronne
canal
St Quentin
Guise
Le Cateau
Landrecies
Fôret de Mormal
Bavai
Valenciennes
Mons
Mabeuse
St Michel
Charleroi
Mézières
Sedan
ARDENNES
Verdun
St Miniel
Metz
Brussels
Antwerp
Ghent
Schelde
Schelde
Lys
Meuse
Laon
Chemin des Dames
Aisne
Soissons
Compiègne
Oise
Reims
Marne
Chalons
CHAMPAGNE
Chateau Thierry
Paris
Seine

Secretary of State for War. Great as some of Kitchener's achievements were, the experiment of having a soldier, and such a headstrong and self-sufficient soldier, as the political head of the War Office was not a success. So far from Haldane returning as Secretary of State, he was kept in the background and later forced to leave the Cabinet. He remained out of office for the whole of the war. His sin was that he had been a student of German philosophy and had confessed openly that Germany was his spiritual home. Like Prince Louis of Battenberg (father of Mountbatten of Burma), the First Sea Lord, he was unjustly put on one side in deference to the popular anti-German feeling.

On psychological and political grounds, it would not have been possible for the British to hold back from participation in the war on the Continent until she had organized a larger expeditionary force. Such a course would have been a question for discussion between the British and French Governments in the years before the war. But the British Government had been concerned with other affairs and, without committing itself, had allowed the two General Staffs to co-ordinate plans. As a result, the British had had no influence on the French plans while all the essential preliminaries, such as shipping and rail movements, were based on the French plans for mobilization and concentration.

Haig saw all this when he attended Asquith's first war council on 5 August. Reports were given of the Belgian resistance to the German advance and he 'trembled at the reckless way Sir J. French spoke about the "advantages" of the BEF operating from Antwerp against the powerful and intact German army'. When it came to his turn to speak, he emphasized the danger of defeat in detail if we allowed ourselves to be separated from the French at the outset of the campaign. He also made the point that the war was bound to be a long one and urged that a considerable number of officers and NCOs should be withdrawn from the Expeditionary Force to become instructors in the expanding army. French strongly disagreed with this view and held to his orders that only three officers per battalion should be withdrawn from units earmarked for the Expeditionary Force. The idea of going to Antwerp was shot down, both by Winston Churchill, who said the navy could not protect the convoys, and by the CIGS (Douglas) who said that the movement arrangements could not be altered at this stage. It is surprising that Haig, as former DSD, should not himself have realized this last point. After the meeting Haig drove to the War Office with Kitchener and was struck by his ignorance about the Territorial Army and the progress that had been made in raising and training a volunteer second-line army. Thus, because of Haldane's exclusion and the refusal of Kitchener and French to listen to him, the full fruits of Haig's work in the War Office were not gathered.

We have seen the regard which French had for Haig and how well the two had been matched as commander and staff officer. But in the years since the South African War, the two men had developed in quite different ways. French had rested on the reputation he had made and had gone for the easy life. Haig had devoted himself to preparation for the task which he saw clearly ahead. Haig wrote in his diary of 11 August the assessment of French which he gave to King George v. The King had continued the association with the Haigs, which had begun with his father, and on this occasion the King was visiting his troops at Aldershot to wish them God Speed on their departure for France. There was ample opportunity for conversation as they drove round the garrison in an open car and afterwards as they lunched together. Haig wrote:

> The King seemed delighted that Sir John French had been appointed to the chief command of the Expeditionary Force. He asked me my opinion. I told him at once, as I felt it my duty to do so, that from my experience with Sir John in the South African War, he was certain to do his utmost loyally to carry out any orders which the Government might give him. I had grave doubts however, whether his temper was sufficiently even or his military knowledge sufficiently thorough to enable him to discharge properly the very difficult duties which will devolve upon him during the coming operations with Allies on the Continent. In my own heart, I know that French is quite unfit for this great command at a time of crisis in our nation's history. But I thought it sufficient to tell the King that I had 'doubts' about his selection.

Haig repeated his doubts to himself in his diary of 13 August, writing: 'His military ideas often shocked me when I was his Chief of Staff during the South African War.' He added doubts about French's Chief of Staff, Murray, who had until recently been one of the divisional commanders under him:

> Recently during certain divisional exercises I had had occasion to criticize Murray's handling of his division. . . . So I had a poor

opinion of his qualifications as a General: and in some respects
he seemed to be an 'old woman'. For example, in his dealings with
Sir John. When his own better judgment told him that something
which the latter wished putting in order was quite unsound,
instead of frankly acknowledging his disagreement, he would
weakly acquiesce, in order to avoid an outbreak of temper and a
scene. With all this knowledge of the Chief and his CGS behind me,
I have grave reason for being anxious about what happens to us in
the great adventure upon which we are now to start this very
night. However, I am determined to behave as I did in the South
African War, namely to be thoroughly loyal and do my duty as a
subordinate should, trying all the time to see Sir John's good
qualities and not his weak ones. For certainly both French and
Murray have much to commend them although neither, in my
opinion, are [*sic*] at all fitted for the appointments which they
now hold at this moment of crisis in our country's history.

Two divisions were temporarily retained in England for home
defence so the BEF crossed to France in the strength of one cavalry
division, four divisions and, in addition, a cavalry and an infantry
brigade. The force was organized in two corps with Grierson in
command of II Corps. Grierson died of a heart attack in the train on
the way to the concentration area and was replaced by Smith-
Dorrien. The British force was so small in relation to the two main
opposing armies that it was hard to imagine that its action could
affect the outcome. The Germans had since 1905 been committed to
a plan of mass envelopment of the French left or northern flank,
although Schlieffen's original plan had been somewhat watered down
by the more cautious Von Moltke. The French knew broadly the
German intentions, but they believed the German attack could be
delayed by the Belgian forts and their own detachments long enough
to allow their own offensives in Alsace and Lorraine to win the day.
In the outcome, the French attacks failed and the British contingent
found itself on the critical flank where the main weight of the German
attack fell.

Haig was right in his opinion that Murray would have little
influence with his chief and that it was rather on Wilson, the Deputy
Chief of Staff, that French would depend. Wilson had been the
Director of Military Operations and had taken the leading part in
the Anglo-French staff talks. He was a pronounced Francophile and

believed wholeheartedly in the competence of the French generals and looked to the success of their offensive. He was in every way the opposite of Haig, a persuasive talker, witty, quick-witted and not unduly conscientious in the methods by which he got his way. We have already seen some indications in the earlier chapters of Haig's near-distrust of two brilliant and not dissimilar generals, Wilson and Rawlinson, with whom he was to be closely associated during the war.

I Corps detrained just south of Le Cateau and, on 21 August, began the advance into Belgium. Haig's diary for that day shows that he saw some of the dangers ahead. He did not like the fact that his corps was advancing into the Charleroi–Mons valley, a difficult area where they could be held up by small parties of enemy and he was apprehensive that great masses of the enemy seemed to be marching unopposed towards the left flank of the BEF. His apprehension was heightened by a conference on 23 August when it became clear that French had not discussed the situation with Macdonogh, his most capable Head of Intelligence, and that little account was taken of air reconnaissance reports which showed that at least three corps were within striking distance of Mons. Wilson still trusted in the success of the French offensive. On the day before, Haig had visited the commander of the French corps on his right, the outside corps of Lanzerac's Fifth Army, but no inkling had been received of the French disasters which were even then taking place further south.

On 23 August, the leading troops of the First German Army came in contact with the BEF. The weight of the attack fell on II Corps on the left and Haig's corps was hardly engaged, except to send one brigade to assist Smith-Dorrien. GHQ had already issued orders for the resumption of the advance on 24 August but, late on the 23rd, French heard that the three French armies on his right were in full retreat and that the BEF was dangerously exposed. The Chiefs of Staff of the two corps were summoned to GHQ to receive orders and, at two am, Haig was wakened to receive a message from Gough that both corps were to withdraw in the direction of Le Cateau and that I Corps was to occupy a rearguard position to cover the withdrawal of II Corps. Haig immediately dictated orders to the staff officers on duty and organized the rearguard under Horne, his artillery commander. He then drove off in his car to give orders personally to the divisional commanders and the brigadiers. In his diary he noted: 'I was back ... before 4 am. Thanks to the motor I was able to give

72

personal orders to the chief commanders concerned in the operations in the space of an hour and enabled them to cancel the orders which the troops were on the point of carrying out for a forward movement.'

25 August was an eventful day. I Corps took up their rearguard position at Bavai, but II Corps, more closely engaged, found great difficulty in extricating itself. By evening, the troops had struggled back to Le Cateau and Smith-Dorrien told French that he must stand and fight next day as his corps was unfit to march again without a halt. Further away, Joffre, the French Commander-in-Chief, had realized the gravity of the situation. Aged sixty-two, he was an officer of Engineers who had risen to his position by colonial service, a sound military knowledge and the accidents of seniority rather than by outstanding ability. But he had the advantage of a cool head and an unruffled spirit so that, unlike the French Command in 1940, he took the immediate steps which would make salvation possible. He realized that the fall of Paris and the defeat of France could be avoided only if he had an effective force which could act against the northern flank of the German advance. He therefore set in motion the arrangements which would give him his Sixth Army to operate on the outer flank of the BEF. There were to be anxious days before he could reap the fruits of this wise and timely move.

On this eventful day Haig was not at his best. After dark on the evening before, he had returned to the farm where he was billeted and had been violently sick. Charteris came in and saw him. Despite protests, he insisted that his chief should be seen by the corps medical officer, Colonel Ryan. Charteris wrote in his diary, 'D.H. was at his worst, very rude but eventually did see Ryan, who dosed him with what must have been something designed for elephants, for the result was immediate and volcanic! But it was effective, for D.H. got some sleep, and in the morning was better though very chewed up and ghastly to look at. He wanted to ride as usual but Ryan insisted on his going in a car that day.'[1] Although Haig had had some nasty bouts of illness during his service, this is the only occasion during the Great War when he is reported as being ill.

Before the onset of the sickness on 24 August, Haig had seen French and Murray at Bavai. Smith-Dorrien had already begun to report the exhaustion of his corps and recommend a day's halt. However French and Haig agreed that such a halt would expose the

BEF to the danger of being surrounded. Murray and Haig had discussed the roads for the continued withdrawal and the direct route to Le Cateau had been allotted to II Corps while I Corps would move by roads to the east of the Forêt de Mormal. The routes of the two corps thus diverged. So little was Haig aware of the true state of II Corps that on that same evening of 25 August, when his own corps suffered quite a small attack at Landrecies, Haig had called on GHQ for reinforcement from II Corps. Haig had set up his headquarters at Landrecies, where a considerable alarm was started by the local population who cried that the enemy was upon them. Haig himself, just arrived by car after his night's sickness, took command of the local situation and sent out mounted patrols to reconnoitre. The enemy attack materialized just after dark against a company of the Coldstream at the entrance to the town and against a troop of the 13th Hussars a few miles away. The gravity of an attack which had penetrated as far as the corps headquarters can be imagined and it shows the dangers to which the BEF was exposed. But the episode was of little importance in relation to that which faced II Corps and there is no doubt that Haig's reports to GHQ were grossly exaggerated. These reports acted on a Commander-in-Chief and staff already rattled and prevented the proper co-ordination of the two corps during the withdrawal.

Smith-Dorrien decided, despite French's views, that he had no alternative but to stand and fight. In ignorance of this decision, and in accordance with the orders of his chief, Haig issued orders in the early hours of 26 August to continue the withdrawal. Communication between the two corps was thus lost and was not regained until 1 September. This was certainly not the fault of Haig. Twice on the day of Le Cateau he sent word to GHQ that he had no news of II Corps. In the second signal, he asked for information which would enable him to decide how he could help and asked for his message to be sent on to II Corps. Neither message received an answer. But the battle of Le Cateau had at least one important effect. The check to the German advance allowed the BEF to get clean away and Kluck, Commander of the German First Army, lost touch and swung to the south-west, thus creating a gap with the Second Army on his left and passing across the front of the BEF and the French Fifth Army.

On 28 August, after some rearguard fighting in which one battalion was almost completely lost, I Corps had marched almost twenty-two miles. Haig wrote: 'Staff Officers as well as troops were so dead tired it was most difficult to get orders understood and delivered to troops and then carried out. . . . The men were daily becoming weaker from want of rest and from not having sufficient time properly to prepare their food, and the strain of the daily skirmishes and of the continual retirement was beginning to be severely felt. Anxiety and fatigue were also telling on the minds and bodies of Commanders as well as on their Staff Officers.'

Yet on that same day Haig saw the possibility of some offensive action if only his infantry could get one day's rest. He was in close touch with the French Fifth Army, whose commander, Lanrezac, was being stirred to action by Joffre. Colonel Helbronner, from Lanrezac's staff, was at I Corps Headquarters. He describes how Haig had just received a report from an air reconnaissance. Haig marked the information on Helbronner's map and said, 'Go quickly to your General and give him this information. Let him take advantage of it without delay. The enemy is exposing his flank as he advances. Let him act. I am anxious to co-operate with him in his attack.'[2] Haig said that he could support the French attack with heavy artillery and that, after twenty-four hours' rest, his infantry would be able to participate. He also made the reservation that he would have to get formal approval from GHQ. This he failed to get. Joffre had visited French on 27 August and told him of his preparations for a counter-stroke, but had added that some days' further withdrawal would be necessary. A spirit of pessimism, not shared by either of the corps, seems to have prevailed at GHQ. Murray had collapsed at his desk on that day from strain and lack of sleep and French seems to have made up his mind that the BEF would not be fit to fight before it had eight or ten days' rest. He therefore refused two requests by Haig to participate in Lanrezac's action, forbidding even the heavy artillery support and ordering that 'no active operations of any arms except of a defensive nature will be taken tomorrow'. Thus I Corps was unable to take any part in the Battle of Guise, an important step in creating the situation necessary for Joffre's coming counter-stroke.

On 1 September, the inner flanks of the two corps were again in contact and, on that day, Kitchener met French at the British Embassy in Paris to insist that he should co-operate in every way possible with Joffre's plans. The retreat continued for four more days, but henceforth the movements of the BEF were directed to ensuring a reduction of the gap with the French Fifth Army and ensuring a junction with the Sixth Army concentrating east of Paris. On 5 September, Haig received the welcome news that the retreat was over and that on 6 September the BEF would advance eastwards.

The Germans played into Joffre's hands when Kluck, in order to lessen the gap with Bulow, wheeled south-east to leave Paris on his right flank. The whole of Joffre's command from Verdun to Paris turned to the attack, but the Marne was not a battle of bitter fighting. The Germans quickly realized that their offensive had, for the moment at any rate, failed and retired to take up strong positions overlooking the Aisne. Their withdrawal was well executed, but there was a period of danger to them when bolder action by the BEF, which was opposite the gap between Kluck and Bulow, might have undermined the German hold on the position which they were to maintain until 1918.

Haig's attitude of cautious realism was lightened by his under-standing of the opportunity and contrasted strongly with French's extreme pessimism. It was in his misuse of the cavalry that French failed to take the opportunity which Haig could see only too clearly. Instead of sending the cavalry division ahead to seize the ground which would later be occupied by the infantry, French used it passively to cover the gap with the French Fifth Army. Haig had had early doubts about the Fifth Army, but Lanrezac had now been re-placed by the more resourceful Franchet d'Esperey. Haig had sent Charteris to ascertain his intentions and to observe the condition of his troops and Charteris had reported favourably. Haig was not rashly optimistic but he believed that, if the French did advance and if they were not forestalled by a counter-attack, there was the opportunity for success.

When the advance did come, Haig was ready. He impressed on his two divisional commanders, Monro and Lomax, 'the necessity for quick and immediate action'. Of a brigade commander, who was later to become one of his most trusted and effective divisional and corps commanders, he wrote: '. . . made difficulties and seemed to lose spirit which seemed to be so noticeable at Aldershot in peace time!' In a letter to Lady Haig he commented on this change in some between peace and war: 'You would be surprised to see how the hard work of the last fortnight has shown up the hardy plucky ones and brought them to the front. Some of the thin ones, the man-eaters, are like jelly fish nervous and jumpy!' In the same letter he showed his feelings for the French people whose homes were ravaged by war and, in his diary for 7 September, he wrote: 'The Germans billeted here a few nights ago. . . . A German General slept in this room. . . . What a situation! German and English alternately occupy the house without any permission. The inhabitants are much upset and they are powerless. . . . What an argument in favour of an adequate national defence.'

That same day Haig regretted the slow progress 'in view of the fact the enemy was on the run'. He had seen Allenby and deplored the fact that the cavalry bivouacked that night behind his right flank. On the next day he observed what was to be the outstanding characteristic of the German conduct of defence and withdrawal throughout the war: 'The enemy guns and cavalry did not long remain in action, but the machine guns were handled with great skill and resolution. . . . Whenever our infantry advanced, fire was opened from some unexpected direction.'

The advance continued northwards until 11 September when, by Joffre's orders, the BEF and the Sixth Army pivoted on Haig's right to swing north-eastwards. Haig thought this was a mistake and lost the opportunity of cutting off a large part of Kluck's Army. On 13 September, I Corps forced a crossing over the Aisne and was then faced with fighting its way up the steep slopes on the north bank and the long wooded rise to the Chemin des Dames ridge four miles beyond. But on 13 September also, the German Seventh Army was arriving in strength to occupy the ridge. In pouring rain the attack was continued on the 14th and, although the results were disappointing, the right division of Haig's corps and the Moroccan division on his right gained a footing on the Chemin des Dames. That was the full extent of the success. The Chemin des Dames remained in German hands until its capture at great cost in Nivelle's offensive in 1917. Joffre's counter-offensive was over.

Haig had felt the growing strength of the German resistance since 12 September, but at GHQ optimism was just returning and Wilson was talking of being in Germany in four weeks. Haig felt that a few fresh troops thrown into the fight might have tipped the scale, but he had none. French, who visited I Corps on 14 August, had no reserves either. He was well pleased with the position of the corps and Haig had no doubt that the effort to get on to the Chemin des Dames before nightfall had been worthwhile. But the cost was, for those early days, heavy: 160 officers and 3,500 men on that day alone.

Haig went forward to both his divisional commanders and found them tired, but confident and in good heart. Lomax was distressed by the casualties. Three out of four commanding officers in one brigade had been lost, but Haig comforted him, taking the responsibility on himself and saying, 'what a splendid action they had fought, after so many trying weeks retreating and marching. They had indeed given their lives to save our fatherland. It will be hard to find a finer example of endurance and discipline in all the annals of British arms.'

In reviewing these days of fighting, Haig thought the enemy infantry no match for our own troops and reckoned that the feat of the BEF coming immediately after a long and exhausting retreat showed that 'the short-service regular army of today has nothing to fear from comparison with the long-service army of the last century'. Writing to Lady Haig on 19 September, he said: 'our troops held their trenches with great determination in spite of cold and wet weather and difficulties in the matter of cooking their food. I sent 10,000 rations of bully beef to the French troops who are on my right and who had nothing but wet bread and raw meat for 4 days. ... I was afraid if the troops were starving they might leave their trenches and so uncover my right. So my gift was not altogether disinterested!' Incidentally Haig did get a most grateful letter of thanks from the corps commander, followed a few days later by a gift of a case of champagne.

It is a mark of Haig's deep affection for his wife that during this critical period, and indeed throughout the war, he wrote to her almost without exception each day. The letters are not full of endearments but they breathe a loving confidence and a complete unity of spirit. Although they accompany the latest instalment of the diary they contain full military comments and remarks on those with whom he had dealings. That was the life he was living and which he wished to share. In this letter of 19 September she was told that, although the diaries were otherwise strictly private, they might be shown to Lord Stamfordham for the King.

French gave Haig full credit for the part he had played in the retreat and in the advance to the Aisne. He sent several congratulatory letters to Haig and reported favourably to Kitchener. It is doubtful if the high opinion was reciprocated. Certainly Haig annotated his copy of French's despatch of 7 September with the remark, 'A most misleading document. D.H.'

Although Joffre had achieved a complete reversal of the situation, he had succeeded neither in exploiting the gap between Kluck and Bulow nor in enveloping Kluck's outer flank. The German disenchantment may be judged by the decision to replace Moltke by Falkenhayn and now both sides strove to outflank the other in what was wrongly called the race to the sea. The Allies were already at the sea as the Belgians still held Antwerp. French suggested, and Joffre agreed, that there were advantages in having the whole of the British contingent on the left of the French Army as had originally been intended. The BEF now consisted of three corps and, by the time the move was completed, it had risen to four. IV Corps was commanded by Rawlinson. Haig had often been doubtful about this brilliant officer, so different from himself, but that he realized his good qualities is shown by his diary when they first met as brother corps commanders: 'His bright joviality is of great value to an army when on active service and things are not going too well.' I Corps was kept in the trenches above the Aisne until last, and it was 19 October by the time it was in position on the left of the new British line. The situation then was fluid as the Germans had captured Antwerp nine days before. Among the first objectives of I Corps was a village called Paschendaele, a name which was ever to be associated with Haig's own.

The move of the BEF to the left had much to commend it, particularly because of the importance to Britain of the Channel Ports. But during the retreat, the British lines of communication from Boulogne and Le Havre to Amiens had been shifted to the Loire ports and St Nazaire. The move of the BEF at this juncture caused considerable disruption of the French rail communications and prevented Joffre, whose decision it was, from moving French troops quickly to the north. Thus, neither the aim of outflanking the Germans, nor the aim of getting the BEF on the left of the French Army, was achieved. Gallieni, the Governor of Paris, to whom some of the credit for the Battle of the Marne is due, had some justification for his remark that the Allies were always twenty-four hours and an army corps behind the enemy.

The first battle of Ypres started as an encounter battle not unlike the situation in which the BEF advanced to Mons. Both sides were unduly optimistic and vague about the movements of the other and each was trying to outflank the other. The French armies on the British left were grouped under Foch, whose views, always favourable

79

to the offensive, were no doubt fully interpreted to French by his disciple Wilson. On 19 October, when he saw Haig, French was certainly optimistic and, estimating the enemy strength on his front as one corps, he talked of an advance to Bruges. Haig had learned to question French's intelligence assumptions – it was not that the GHQ had a bad intelligence staff, but the interpretation that was put on the information they provided. Haig had promoted Charteris from ADC to be his Intelligence Officer and on this occasion Charteris did well. By information gleaned from GHQ and the Belgians, he deduced that there were in fact two German corps in the offing in addition to the one mentioned by French. So Haig had some idea of the opposition he was to face. I Corps did not get the few days' rest they were hoping for, and for a week the British and French attacks continued, interrupted from time to time by the necessity to fight a fierce defensive battle. Every new French unit arriving at the front was ordered by Foch to the attack and he implored the British to conform. But during the last days of the month, the inexorable German pressure was increased as Falkenhayn put into the attack a freshly-grouped army intended to drive down the Menin road through Ypres to the sea.

John Terraine has written a graphic description of the battlefield of Ypres and the historic significance of the old fortress town which he calls 'the outlying fortification of Dunkirk'.[3] He points to the Flanders ridges which form the rim of an irregular saucer dominating the town in the centre from a distance varying from three to six miles away. Although First Ypres was in every way an Allied battle with French, Belgians and British all taking a full share, it was along the rim of the saucer that Haig with his corps played the dominant rôle. On 26 October, Haig began to feel the pressure as the 7th Division of IV Corps on his right began to give way. He ensured that Lomax took command of the situation and allowed a battalion to be used in support of the 7th Division at the expense of his own attack. He went out himself to see the situation and commented, 'It was sad to see fine troops like the 7th Division reduced to inefficiency by the ignorance of their leaders in having placed them in trenches on the forward slope where the enemy could see and so effectively shell them.' Haig had equally critical remarks to make about the in-experienced French and German troops who took part in this battle.

It is significant that in these last days of mobile warfare, he was always forward to get the feel of the battle, to see the troops in action and to give confidence and counsel to his divisional, brigade and battalion commanders. That he thought of their comfort too is shown by his diary for 29 October: 'I move the Reporting Centre back to 'White Chateau' near level crossing on Menin Road to enable Lomax to make himself comfortable in Hooge Chateau. I found him living with his divisional staff in small cottages of two rooms.' Alas, the kindness did not have the result that was intended! Two days later while the two divisional commanders and their staffs were in conference, the chateau was hit by four large shells. Lomax was mortally wounded, Monro was stunned and three senior staff officers killed. Lomax was a sad loss to Haig. Militarily he trusted him implicitly and he always had an affectionate word for him in his diary.

The catastrophe occurred at a moment of crisis in the battle. 7th Division had now been put under Haig's command and in addition to his three divisions, he had two cavalry brigades. The main weight of the German attack was directed at Gheluvelt and the thirteen battalions in the attack were inspired by the presence of the Kaiser himself. Gheluvelt fell, although it was later recaptured and lost again before the battle was over. At the moment of its first fall, Haig traced on his map a line little more than a mile in front of Ypres to which the corps must fall back if necessary and where it must fight to the end. Then, as Charteris recounts,[4] 'he rode out with his personal staff and escort up the Menin Road through the stragglers, back into the shelled area, his face immobile and inscrutable – saying no word, yet by his presence and his calm restoring hope to the disheartened and strength to the exhausted troops'. Then when he heard of the disaster at the White Chateau, he went up to take personal command of the situation and appoint Brigadier-General Landon temporarily to command 1st Division. When, a little later, news of the recapture of Gheluvelt was brought to him he showed no more outward sign of emotion than he had at the disasters.

The crisis passed and the struggle went on. Foch was insistent to French that the Ypres salient must be held. He promised that only a few days' desperate fighting would be necessary and that fresh French troops would make the resumption of the offensive possible. Some French reinforcements had already come into the line on the British front and I Corps was now sandwiched between two French corps, IX on the left and XVI on the right. On 6 November, one of the French battalions on the right gave way, allowing the Germans to drive a wedge on Haig's flank within two miles of Ypres. Haig's relationship with the XVI Corps Commander was not nearly as good as with Dubois, commanding IX Corps. He wrote: 'The ignorance of the French Commander 16th Corps of the position of his own troops is alarming. Few French Generals or Staff Officers ever seem to go forward to visit their troops in advanced positions.' A few days later, he described the corps commander: 'He is a very fat man, never rides a horse and seldom walks. He has a great reputation for fearlessness and disregard for personal danger. He recently had an armchair placed for himself to sit in on the high road near Dixmude which was under hot shell-fire, in order to encourage his troops.'

The last and most severe crisis of the battle occurred on 11 November. After the heaviest bombardment British troops had yet suffered, I Corps and the French on their left were subjected to a savage attack to cut off the salient and capture Ypres. The Germans penetrated at many points and there is little doubt that they would have attained their objective had it not been for Haig's defensive precautions. With Rice, his Chief Engineer, he had organized heavily-wired strong-points in depth and had insisted that all command posts should be prepared for defence. By the stout defence of these points and by the use of his scant reserves, the enemy attacks were finally held and at some points thrown back by counter-attack. By the end of the day the last reserves had been used and Haig reported that, unless reinforcements were sent up, both his own and Dubois' corps would be cut off. But the Germans had had enough; they were incapable of pressing their attack further. That evening the weather which had been changeable and threatening finally broke. Several days' heavy downpour reduced the battlefield to a quagmire and then nights of hard frost increased the discomfort.

Ypres was the deathbed of the BEF, which Haig had done so much to create. Indeed, it was the deathbed of the whole regular army. I Corps alone with an establishment of 18,000 was reduced by the battle to a mere 3,000 officers and men, or less. Haig had proved himself as the master of the defensive battle. By the skilful thinning-out of troops where risks could be taken and by the use of his cavalry as a mobile reserve – albeit as mounted infantry – he had almost to the end been able to maintain a reserve for counter-attacks or to plug the gaps. He was way ahead of others in discovering how, by making the best use of scant engineering resources, a partial trench system could aid the defence. On the moral side he was a rock. He was always at hand where the strain was greatest. He had the gift, common to many great soldiers, of being able to sleep properly. He could be roused to deal with an emergency, quickly take in the information, issue the orders necessary and go to sleep again at once. He thought always of his men and did everything he could to ensure that they got what comfort and rest was possible. But on questions of true discipline there was no relaxation. The will to fight and to obey orders was paramount. The straggler and the deserter received no sympathy and little mercy. And he demanded the highest standards from officers in command of units.

On 17 November, the relief of I Corps began and they were back in general reserve by the 21st. The next day Haig went home on five days' leave. Lady Haig came up from Empress Eugénie's hospital in Farnborough, of which she had charge, and they stayed at Henrietta's house in Prince's Gate. Their two daughters, who were living in Wales with their aunt, joined them. There was only one way in which Haig wished to spend his leave and that was quietly with his family. There were however some calls of duty and on three mornings there were meetings; with Lord Kitchener, with the Prime Minister, and at the War Office. He was also received by the King, who was very complimentary about the work of I Corps and Haig's own conduct of the battle. Haig went down with Lady Haig to the hospital, and was most impressed with the organization and comfort. He was surprised to find there were so few patients – as well he might be, for he saw only three, and there were five nurses! The last afternoon of his leave was spent taking the children to the zoo. Unfortunately they were so late that, to the great disappointment of 'Xandra and Doria', the monkey-house was shut before they got to it. However, all the other animals were seen and the day enjoyed.

In a generous tribute which epitomized Haig's part in the battle, French had written 'The success of this great defence, like those which preceded it, was due in the first place to Sir Douglas Haig, who so skilfully handled the scant force at his disposal, and economized the few reserves with such soldierlike foresight'. As a result, Haig was promoted General on 20 November and when, at the end of the year, the British contingent expanded into two Armies, Haig was the obvious choice to command the First Army. The Second

Army went to Smith-Dorrien, despite the recent failure of his corps in an attack which Haig attributed to the fact that 'the higher leaders did not mean business'. The new organization took effect on Christmas Day. Haig had spent Christmas Eve tying up and addressing the gifts which Lady Haig had sent for all his staff and servants, thirty-six in all. In his task he was assisted by Secrett, his servant, and by his two ADCs, Straker, and Alan Fletcher, who had recently arrived from India with the 17th Lancers.

Haig's army consisted of his old corps, now commanded by Monro, Rawlinson's IV Corps and the Indian Corps under Willcocks. Soon after his return from leave, he had paid a courtesy visit to the Indian Corps headquarters in a large château near Béthune.

It was a very cold November day, foggy and dull. I was very pleased to see the Indian soldier again, because I had many happy memories of my life in India with them in manœuvres. But I frankly felt a thrill of surprise at the air of dejection and despondency which met me all round the chateau; both outside (where orderlies and others were hanging about numbed with cold) and inside where all ranks, Staff Officers, British and native clerks, seemed to be working together in three or four rooms on the ground floor. There was one particularly large room in which there were three large and long tables arranged for a meal. I was told that three officers' messes (including the Corps Commanders) were accommodated in this room, and that all cooked in the same kitchen! All the windows were shut and the atmosphere was, of course, very close. I came away feeling that things were not altogether in an efficient state in the Indian Corps and certainly very different from what I had expected to see at the Headquarters of an Indian Expeditionary Force on Active Service.

# 7

# THE FIRST ARMY OFFENSIVES:
## Neuve Chapelle to Loos

Haig's promotion brought him into the higher sphere of strategy: he would no longer be involved in the close control of battle. One of his first tasks was to support French in representations about the employment of the New Armies. Kitchener had ideas of sending out six armies, each of three corps. Haig agreed with French and Smith-Dorrien that it would be a mistake to send out large formations 'under rather elderly commanders and inexperienced staff officers'. They thought it much better to send out battalions or brigades to be incorporated into existing divisions. Another of Kitchener's proposals was even more strenuously resisted. This was that the New Armies might be better employed outside France, in co-operation with Italy or Greece. Haig said that 'we ought not to divide our Military Force, but *concentrate on the decisive point* which is on this front against the main German Army. With more guns and ammunition and more troops, the Allies were bound in the end to defeat the Germans and break-through.'

Repington, *The Times* correspondent, came to see Haig to find out whether he thought there was any possibility of advancing on the Western Front. According to Haig, he seemed to think the British people would not stand heavy casualties and that we should not get a general sufficiently fearless of public opinion to incur the losses which must result from an attempt to pierce the German fortified front. Haig replied that as soon as we had ample high explosive ammunition 'we could walk through the German lines at several places'.

Repington also brought up the possibility of Murray being re-placed as Chief of Staff. He thought Wilson was working on the French Mission to get Joffre to suggest himself taking Murray's place. Haig expressed astonishment at the idea of such intrigue, but the idea was not new to him. A month before, on 19 December, he had written to Lady Haig: 'Henry Wilson has been intriguing to get poor Murray moved on, so that he might take his place. H.W. is very cunning but has no military knowledge for such an appointment and I am sorry that he should have succeeded in his disgraceful plotting.' In fact, Repington was behind the times because, on the day they spoke, Haig already knew that Wilson was being moved from GHQ to become French's Liaison Officer with Joffre. Murray was replaced. It is possible that Asquith, remembering the Curragh, would not approve Wilson's appointment but it is certain that Haig advised French to take Robertson, as he did. Robertson had been a most capable quartermaster-general of the BEF and had the con-fidence of all the senior officers. In differing spheres, Haig and Robertson were to continue a close association until 1918.

In his letter of 20 January in which he told Lady Haig that she would see that 'the wicked intriguer' had not flourished this time, Haig ended on a more personal note: 'How you have reduced the loan account: £6,000 is nothing: it was £16,000 not long ago, when we went to India. But I wish you would not stint yourself in any way. After the war we'll have more money than you and I can spend *comfortably*! For we both like simplicity and unostentatious ways. . . .'

Early in 1915, the French had taken over the whole of the Ypres salient with the British to the south. Haig's First Army was on the right on a front of eighteen kilometers from the Béthune–La Bassée canal to just north of Armentières. Joffre's plan was that he should make his main effort in Champagne with a subsidiary offensive in Artois. He asked French if, as soon as the ground had dried out, he would carry out an attack to assist the Tenth Army in Artois. The Tenth Army was commanded by Maud'huy, who incidentally was the corps commander who had sent Haig a case of champagne during the fighting on the Aisne. French decided to entrust the attack to First Army and Haig chose as his objective the Aubers Ridge, an almost imperceptible rise overlooking Lille. The resulting battle of Neuve Chapelle is important because it was Haig's first attempt to break an organized German position. It is possible to say that the Battle of Neuve Chapelle ought not to have taken place. Joffre had insisted before the Artois offensive that the British should take over the Ypres salient so that IX Corps could join Tenth Army. However, Kitchener held back the troops earmarked by French for this purpose in case they were needed for the Dardanelles, and Joffre accordingly postponed his Artois operations. French had the impression that the British Army was not taken seriously by his Allies and he thought his largely-increased force required offensive experience. He decided therefore that Haig should go ahead on his own.

The keystones of Haig's plan were careful preparation and surprise. Rawlinson's corps had the principal part, and, within that corps, Davies' 8th Division. Haig gave Rawlinson his ideas in good time and let him work on the details, but he kept a close watch on all the planning and, by discussion with Rawlinson, Davies and Mercer, the Commander Army Artillery, he saw that his ideas were put into effect. Mercer originally suggested a bombardment lasting four days and Rawlinson's idea was for an attack on different sectors on successive days, but both were overruled because they would forfeit surprise. The bombardment was to be continued only long enough to cut the wire and, to gauge the time this would take, experiments were carried out behind the lines. It was considered that shrapnel was best for the purpose because the instantaneous fuse had not then been perfected and it was realized that high explosive would churn up the ground and the wire to make an even more effective obstacle. As a result, it was decided to have a bombardment of only thirty-five minutes after which the infantry would advance 2,000 yards to the ridge before the enemy had recovered his equilibrium. Guns were brought up gradually and registered unobtrusively. Commanders were carefully briefed and infantry rehearsed in their tasks. For this, great use was made of aerial photography of the German trench system. Haig was always conscious of the help which aircraft could give to the land battle and he had as his Royal Flying Corps Contingent Commander no less a person than Major Trenchard. This was the first meeting of the two men.

During the preparations for the battle, Haig suffered a great personal blow. His Chief Staff Officer, John Gough, who was shortly going to command a division, was killed by a chance bullet while paying a farewell visit to his own Regiment. There was a close friendship between the two. The only disadvantage of the partnership was that Gough felt Haig did not need him and that he would be better employed looking after a lesser man. When Haig was sent to command at Aldershot, he had tried to get Kiggell as his Chief Staff Officer, but Kiggell had been needed as Commandant of the Staff College. It is interesting to surmise what might have happened if Gough had been spared. He might well have gone on to be Chief of Staff when Haig became Commander-in-Chief and might have been a more decisive occupant of that position than was Kiggell.

The attack went in on the morning of 10 March. At first all went well, except on the left of the 8th Division where two batteries had arrived late and had not been able to register. There, launched against uncut wire covered by machine guns in enfilade, the 2nd Scottish Rifles and the 2nd Middlesex suffered grievous casualties. Nevertheless, in under two hours, Neuve Chapelle and a mile of the first objective were captured and this was soon extended to 4,000 yards at a depth of 1,200 yards. The battle continued for three days but this was almost the full extent of the gains. Haig had moved forward his cavalry to exploit success, but the opportunity to use it did not arrive.

The battle was a lost opportunity. Haig had chosen his objective well, he had made a successful initial plan and he had surprised the enemy. The Germans were comparatively weak here and a position might have been gained which would have saved many subsequent casualties. Haig worked hard to discover what had gone wrong and to learn lessons for the future. The first obvious point was the shortage of artillery ammunition and this strengthened Haig's conviction, not to be borne out by future events, that if only he had ample ammunition success must follow. The more important lesson, that success and not failure must be reinforced and that units must not stop while those on their flank are held up, was only partly appreciated.

Haig's investigation of this last aspect caused some unpleasantness. Rawlinson at first blamed Davies and recommended that he should be relieved of command of his division. Haig had a high opinion of Davies. He had been his first Chief Staff Officer at Aldershot and had gone from there to command a brigade in I Corps with which he had fought at Mons and the Aisne. Nevertheless, Haig accepted Rawlinson's recommendation which he forwarded to GHQ. Shortly afterwards Rawlinson sent Haig a representation from Davies, together with his own admission that it was he, Rawlinson, who had delayed the advance from Neuve Chapelle. Haig immediately withdrew his recommendation to GHQ and rode over to see Davies. French and

Robertson thought Rawlinson ought to be sent home, but Haig opposed this course. He considered that although Rawlinson had behaved badly in lack of loyalty to his subordinate, none the less he had 'many other valuable qualities for a commander on active service'. Haig saw Rawlinson and told him what he thought of him, but he was retained in command of his corps.

Haig wrote his own account of the battle and of some other matters to Kiggell on 2 April:

I went to Folkestone for 4 days last week but limited my journeys inland to a motor drive daily to Sandwich to play golf. I thoroughly enjoyed it but wd. much have liked a talk with you. I think things go on here all right, but if they wd. only give me gun ammunition we wd. clear the Germans out of France in 6 weeks!

Compared with the French efforts in Champagne we did very well at Neuve Chapelle, but if Rawlinson had only carried out his orders and pushed on from the village at once we wd. have had quite a big success. As a matter of fact, in the preliminary arrangements, I went so far as to interfere with the dispositions of the 8th Divn. and ordered the troops (2 Battns.) holding the 'starting trench' to be found from the 2 attacking Brigades instead of from the third Brigade of the Divn. as ordered in the Divn. orders – and I gave as my reason the necessity for the Divn. Comr. to have a complete unit under his hand in readiness to push forward the moment the village was in our hands. Still, our troops did well even though tacticians on the spot were not in evidence. And the fighting spirit of the 4th Corps and the Indians is now first rate: quite up to that of the First Corps! The Indian Corps suffers from too many *old* officers. I had really to drive them to undertake the operations at N. Chapelle by pointing out to them that it wd. mean the end of the Indian Army if their officers said they could not undertake an offensive strike, and I had to replace them with a Divn. of the 1st Corps. Now that the operation was a success Sir Willcocks is as pleased and as proud as can be!

I hope we may soon see you out here in some capacity. When is this New Army to take the field? I can't understand why the fleet was allowed to bombard the Dardanelles forts before troops were on the spot to reap the fruits of the bombardment! I suppose there is some Winstonian subtlety in the plan which has not appeared yet.

The Second Battle of Ypres which lasted from 22 April to 25 May did not directly concern Haig because the British share in the fighting was taken by the Second Army. Two episodes however demand notice. The German offensive opened with the use of poison gas for the first time. Almost the whole weight fell on the French and, despite some warning, the gas came as a complete surprise. Haig was not very generous to the French in his comments on the event, but he got at once to the heart of the matter. The lesson seen by him was that the early success of the new weapon caused the Germans as much surprise as the French and their plans did not allow them to reap the advantage.

The other episode concerned the command of Second Army during the grim defensive battle. Neither French nor Haig had appreciated Smith-Dorrien at his full worth and, during this battle, French did not give him a free hand. It is not unjust to say that the entries in Haig's diaries at this time show a rather small-minded satisfaction in French's criticism to him of Smith-Dorrien and the comparison of his expressed satisfaction with Haig. French appears to have been trying to get Smith-Dorrien to resign but, on the very day that Smith-Dorrien wrote to French referring to the obvious lack of confidence in him and saying that it might be better if someone else should command the Second Army, he received a peremptory order to hand over to Plumer. No reasons were given.[1]

Joffre now felt able to go on with his project of a two-handed blow in Champagne and Artois. He again asked the British to help by attacking to the north of Tenth Army, which was now commanded by d'Urbal. Haig had not had the same happy relationship with Joffre as he had had with Maud'huy. At Ypres he had described him as 'a tall, suave, elderly gentleman – rather an actor, the type of man seen on the stage playing the part of "the respectable uncle" – and unpleasantly polite'.

French readily agreed to fall in with Joffre's plan and it was again the First Army that had the task of attacking over much the same ground as at Neuve Chapelle. It would be pointless to follow in any detail the three offensives carried out under Haig's orders; Aubers Ridge, Festubert and Givenchy. The plan for Aubers Ridge was a repetition of that for Neuve Chapelle. But the Germans, as well as the French and the British, had learned lessons from Neuve Chapelle and the wire obstacles and entrenchments were stronger, the machine guns even more cunningly placed and hidden and, above all, the counter battery fire most effective. The attack on 9 May was held without the Germans having to use any of their reserves, and the British casualties on that day of some 500 officers and 11,000 men almost equalled those of the three days of Neuve Chapelle. The failure was accentuated by the early success on the same day of the French further south, especially by a corps commanded by a certain General Pétain. The British attack had been intended to help the French, but instead the Germans had been able to move reserves from their front to hold the French advance which petered out for want of well-placed reserves and failed to take Vimy Ridge.

The French had plenty of artillery ammunition and their preliminary bombardment lasted six days as against the forty minutes of the British. On the credit side this had given the British some element of surprise, but in fact the bombardment did little more than raise both the dust and the alarm and the infantry went in against unbroken obstacles. Joffre wanted the British attack renewed and French instructed Haig to try again. This time Haig arranged a bombardment of thirty-six hours, the longest allowed by the ammunition available, and, to effect surprise, there was to be a night attack, the first by the British in this war. Bad weather prevented the observation necessary for an accurate bombardment and the attack was put off twenty-four hours, thus prolonging the bombardment to sixty hours at the expense of ammunition for the later stages. The night attack by 2nd Division, commanded by Horne, one of Haig's protegés, was successful in forcing the Germans out of a position they had taken months to prepare. The dawn attacks which followed also achieved a measure of success. This time the German reserves were drawn and there was hope of further advance but, with the shortage of ammunition and the absence of fresh reserves, tired divisions could not succeed. In the ten days during which fighting continued, the casualties were 700 officers and 16,000 men, proportionately much lighter than in either of the two earlier battles. Haig was more convinced than ever that he was on the right lines and that all he needed was more ammunition and enough divisions to give him an effective reserve. Givenchy was a much smaller battle, confined to IV Corps, and with limited ammunition. Although it achieved nothing, it did not lessen the prevailing conviction.

One by-product of these attacks was an outcry in the British press against the munitions shortage. It was started by an article by Repington in *The Times*, but both Asquith and Kitchener attributed it to French. French indeed had something to complain about. In December 1914 he had estimated his requirement of 18-pounder ammunition as fifty rounds per gun per day. By May 1915, the number supplied had gradually crept up to eleven rounds per gun per day. Other ammunition was deficient on a similar scale. The uproar about the shortage was one of the things which caused Asquith to form a Coalition Government in May 1915 and, in that Government, Lloyd George, the former Chancellor of the Exchequer, became Minister of Munitions. It must be said that Kitchener had not been complacent about the ammunition situation and the measures that he had taken began to bear fruit by September, while the efforts of the Ministry of Munitions did not show until well on into 1916.

The First Army offensives and the hopes they raised for the future brought a number of important visitors to Haig's headquarters. At the end of May, Joffre came and said he had long wished to come because the troops under Haig's command always fought so well. Asquith came on 1 June, Ben Tillett on 13 June, and Kitchener on 8 July. Ben Tillett was the leader of the Dockers' Trade Union and a noted firebrand of those days. Haig seems to have been most friendly and treated him with sympathy and tact. They discussed the attitude of Socialists in France and Germany and the relations between officers and men in the British Army. On this point, Tillett confessed he had completely changed his views since he discovered that his docker friends who were now soldiers had unbounded trust in their officers.

Both Asquith and Kitchener were losing what confidence they had in French and it is fairly apparent that they were eyeing Haig as a possible successor. Asquith was shown everything at the headquarters and given a thorough briefing on staff work and procedure in battle. He also visited the troops and the trenches, including the 7th Division, commanded by Hubert Gough. Haig, recalling the Curragh incident, was interested to see Asquith and Gough happily taking tea together. Naturally the position of French was not mentioned but, significantly, Asquith told Haig to write to him whenever he could spare the time.

Kitchener was less reticent about French. It was partly through Haig's influence that French had invited Kitchener to come over; he had previously been firmly against such visits. Kitchener told Haig that in bygone days French had listened to his every word, but that now he could not get him to comply with a single suggestion. Now 'K. was ready to do anything "to black French's boots" if need be, in order to obtain agreement and win the war! He wanted me to assert myself more, and to insist on French proceeding on sound principle'. Haig replied that this was easier said than done and 'in any case it was more his affair to control Sir John French than mine. I had really to do as I was ordered by Sir John, and French had more self-confidence now than when I was with him in South Africa.'

The meeting ended with the inevitable request by Kitchener that Haig should write to him. From his earliest military days Haig seems to have drawn those in authority to suggest that he should confide in them his views about his superiors. Some may feel that he responded too readily to such invitations.

In fact, Haig's relations with French had improved since the Aisne. There had been a little anger on the part of Haig's staff because French, in his communiqué, had claimed the credit for Neuve Chapelle, whereas in fact he had left everything to First Army. But Haig was too big a man to indulge in such petty jealousies. His view is best shown by his conversation with the King when he went over to Buckingham Palace to receive the collar of the GCB on 14 July. The King was frank about the friction between Kitchener and French and indicated that he had lost confidence in French. Haig pointed out that the time to have got rid of French was immediately after the Retreat and that 'now the army was stationary and could practically be controlled from London'. Again came the request to write to Wigram 'and no one but he and W. would know what I had written'.

Through all these visits and through the confidence which these august persons showed in Haig, he was brought into the strategic discussions. The Cabinet was disturbed by the failure to force the Dardanelles where, at the end of April, the Gallipoli landings had succeeded only in gaining a footing. On the Western Front, on the one hand they deplored the static situation, on the other they feared the Germans might break through. There was some difference of opinion about what would happen if the Allies had to withdraw. The Channel Ports were of paramount importance to the British, but there might be a choice between defending them and conforming with a French defence of Paris. At GHQ French was in favour of concentrating on holding the Channel Ports; Robertson, who wrote to Haig about it, believed the British must keep in touch with the

French. On both campaigns Haig's views are clear from his correspondence. His letters also show some concern at the lack of strategic direction in the Government and at the War Office. On 27 June he wrote to Wigram:

> I still think it is folly to pour more troops and ammunition down the Dardanelles sink. The whole BEF here if added to the force now there cannot clear the two sides of the Dardanelles so as to make the Straits passage safe for ships and ensure the fall of Constantinople. By going on in the way in which the Cabinet is now acting great risk is run of the French making peace by the winter. . . . To the onlooker here there seems no supreme control exercised over the war as a whole. I attribute this to the failure to make use of the General Staff in London. You allow our policy to be dictated by whoever is the ablest speaker. Fundamental principles of strategy seem daily to be ignored. This is the decisive point: bring all the strength of the Empire to this point and beat the enemy. Then all else will be ours for the picking up.

In his views on the importance of the Channel Ports, Haig not only foresees the problems which will arise in 1918 but also gives a vision of the fate of the Allies in 1940:

> . . . if the enemy inflicts a decisive defeat on the French, the British could not fight on land without Allies. In my opinion, therefore, the important thing is for the British Army to remain united with the French. When the German Army was much more efficient than it is now, it failed against the two Allies united. If, however, the British were to separate and to take up a position in front of Calais and Boulogne, it would certainly mean defeat in detail, because the enemy could contain us with a comparatively small force, while he massed in great strength and defeated the French.

Neither Kitchener nor French wanted another offensive in 1915, but Joffre thought otherwise. The French Army was now at its peak and the whole nation burned to throw the Germans out of France. A short advance would bring their army into the plain of Douai where vital German communications were only twenty miles from the front. Success here would endanger the whole German position north of Verdun. Joffre wished therefore to try again before the end of the summer with his double attack in Champagne and Artois. He asked that the British should attack as close to his left as possible.

French felt bound to agree and, on 20 June, he instructed First Army, which was to be reinforced and consist of four corps, to prepare a plan for an attack on a front from Lens to the La Bassée Canal. Haig made a full personal reconnaissance and in a report which later proved to be only too true said that the area was not suitable for an attack.

> The German defences were so strong that until a greatly increased establishment of heavy artillery was provided, they could only be taken by siege methods. . . . The ground, for the most part bare and open, would be so swept by machine-gun and rifle fire both from the German front trenches and the numerous fortified villages behind them, that a rapid advance would be impossible.

He commented also on the excellent facilities for German artillery observation and the difficulty in the chalk area of hiding trenches in the assembly area.[2] He would have preferred no attack at all until the artillery situation had improved but, if an attack had to be made, he thought it should be made astride and north of the La Bassée Canal and he still believed the capture of the Aubers Ridge would give the best tactical results. Not only was the ammunition situation precarious but the British Army had too little heavy artillery for an attack on organized defences. The proportion of heavy artillery (six-inch and over) to field guns and howitzers in the German Army was one in three, in the French one in four and in the British one in twenty. The Germans were producing 250,000 rounds of gun ammunition a day, the French 100,000 and the British still only 22,000.

Despite Haig's report, French felt that he had to comply with Joffre's wish for an attack as close to the Tenth Army as possible. Haig was not surprised at the decision because his own liaison officers had reported the doubts in French minds about the determination and ability of the British Government to prosecute the war in France. The feeling was largely caused by their misgivings at the despatch of four British divisions and a quantity of ammunition to the Dardanelles when both were so much needed in France. Moreover Kitchener, who came over again in August, told Haig privately that the Russians had been severely handled and that the Allies must act urgently in the west to ease the pressure on them.

On 14 September, French attended a conference with Joffre and Foch, who was to direct the attacks of the British First and French Tenth Armies, and the other two army group commanders. After many delays in the planning date, it was decided that the attacks would go in simultaneously on 25 September. Haig was to attack on a front of twelve kilometres with I Corps, now under Gough, and Rawlinson's IV Corps, each of three divisions. In each corps, one of the divisions was a New Army division (9th Scottish and 15th Scottish) in action for the first time. Haig also had a cavalry division in reserve, but French retained under his own control the General Reserve: XI Corps consisting of the newly-constituted Guards Division – experienced troops – and two new divisions, 21st and 24th. Foch had been to see Haig on 12 September and Haig sensed that he had come to find out whether the British really meant to fight. Leaving him in no doubt on that point, Haig told him, 'Joffre's orders were the same to me as those of Marshal [*sic*] French'. Haig was worried by French's decision to keep the reserve corps under his own control. His experience in his own earlier battles and that of the French one in May at Vimy told him that the critical stage of the offensive was the exploitation of the first break into the enemy defences. The opportunity must be lost unless the reserves were properly placed and under the control of the commander fighting the battle. He discussed the point with Foch and asked him to use his influence with French.

Haig had another tactical worry. He had not sufficient artillery for an attack on a two-corps front. He hoped to make up the deficiency by the use of gas. After the German use of gas at Ypres, Kitchener had ordered the preparation of retaliatory measures and Haig had been impressed by a demonstration of 'the chlorine wave' which he had attended in August with his corps and divisional commanders. The German respirators were known to be ineffective and the gas would enable Haig to make his first attack with all six divisions instead of the two for which he had sufficient artillery support. The gas had two disadvantages, it depended on a favourable wind and it could be used only in the first phase, leaving subsequent stages to the scant artillery support. He thought the prevailing southwest wind made it likely that conditions would be favourable, but it was desirable to have a variable date for the attack. However, the French were not using gas and Joffre insisted on a firm date for his widespread attacks. His only concession was that, if necessary, the attack on the first day would be limited to two divisions, leaving Haig to put in the main attack on one of the succeeding two days.

The release of the gas from cylinders was to take place an hour before the infantry advance and two and a half hours' notice was required before the gas release. On the eve of the battle the wind was blowing from the German trenches but at nine pm the meteorological forecast was that the next morning the wind would be west or south-west, possibly reaching twenty mph. Haig therefore issued orders that the arrangements for the attack would stand and that zero hour would be decided later. Despite some less favourable reports during the night, Haig decided at three am, after discussion with his meteorological officer, that zero hour for the release of gas would be at sunrise, that is five-forty am, and that the infantry would attack at six-thirty.

Haig's diary for the 25th reads:

I went out at 5 am. Almost a calm. Alan Fletcher lit a cigarette and the smoke drifted in puffs towards the NE. Staff Officers of corps were ordered to stand by in case it were necessary to counter order the attack. At one time, owing to the calm, I feared the gas might simply hang about our trenches. However, at 5.15 am, I said 'carry on'. I went to top of our wooden look-out tower. The wind came gently from SW and by 5.40 had increased slightly. The leaves of the poplar trees gently rustled. This seemed satisfactory. But what a risk I must run of gas blowing back upon our own dense masses of troops.

The Germans had two strongly-defended lines, and on IV Corps front there was also an intermediate line. The Germans were surprised by the gas but its progress was somewhat uncertain and in places it hung about No Man's Land or even drifted back. However, the British infantry fought well and, except for the 2nd Division on the left, where the gas was least effective, all captured the first line. By noon IV Corps had also captured the intermediate line, including Loos, but not the dominant Hill 70 beyond it. Although the second line had nowhere been breached, the Germans were in some disarray and this was the moment foreseen by Haig when he wanted fresh divisions to exploit his success. But they were not at hand.

Haig had asked GHQ that two divisions of the reserve should be ready and rested not more than 4,500 yards behind the front line at the time the attack went in. French assured him that at daybreak on the 25th the 21st and 24th Divisions would be where he wanted them. He did so order XI Corps, but he delayed the forward move until after dark on the 24th. Moreover, the move was not specially organized as a priority operational move but took its chance on an ordinary supply route. The marching columns suffered delays at the numerous level crossings and were hampered by indifferent traffic control and, as a result, the rear units did not arrive until six am. Far from being ready and rested, the divisions were tired, strung-out and unfed. Much of this can be attributed to bad staff work for which French was not immediately to blame, but he was obviously wrong in not putting the reserve under Haig in the first place, and, as he did not do this, he ought to have ordered the move forward twenty-four hours earlier and given special supervision to the move of the raw divisions. The handling of these two divisions was in marked contrast to the careful nursing of the two new divisions under Haig's command which had been enabled to put up a fine performance in their first action.

In addition to his failure with the move of the reserve, French was also at fault in his own command arrangements. He rightly wanted to be well forward in the battle but he separated himself by twenty miles from his Chief of Staff and headquarters without special communications and relying only on the civil telephone. For most of the time he was out of touch both forward and back. As soon as he had reports of his first success, Haig sent a staff officer to French to ask XI Corps to be ready to advance at once. Even then, French did not put the two divisions under Haig and it was two hours before he ordered their move. It was dark by the time the divisions reached the original front line and they were committed to a night advance over ground they had never seen. By this time the German position had been restored and the attack was called off. The divisions spent a second night on the move and on the 26th were put into the attack, not against a shaken and disorganized enemy as they had been led to expect, but against a determined enemy protected by deep and intact wire defences. After the failure of this attack, the battle went on for seventeen days with little success either for renewed British attacks or for German counter-attacks.

The case against French for mismanagement of the battle is so strong that care must be taken not to overlook grounds for criticism of Haig. It can be said that he wastefully used the two new divisions after the opportunity had passed. Surprise had gone and it might have been better to use them in the two established corps in a carefully-prepared attack. But it must be remembered that Haig was acting in support of the French Tenth Army. They had been less successful than the British and the enemy still held the Vimy Ridge; Haig, with two uncommitted divisions in hand, felt he had to do something to exploit his success. The Tenth Army, despite ample artillery and ammunition, did not make up for its original neglect of surprise. Ironically, its lack of success was attributed to the reserves being too far forward so that they could not be used where they were needed.

Another ground for complaint against Haig is highly controversial since it involves that most difficult of all issues, a conflict of loyalties. The Battle of Loos convinced Haig that French was not fit to remain in command. He did not hide his opinion. He must obviously have known that he was a possible successor to French, indeed the most likely one. These two facts have led some critics to condemn Haig as an intriguer and to say that he deliberately supplanted French. Anyone disposed to accept such criticism should first ask himself what Haig should have done in the light of his conviction and the knowledge that the future of the British Army was at stake.

Before the battle was over, on 29 September, Haig wrote to Kitchener, the member of the Government to whom the Commander-in-Chief was responsible:

You will doubtless recollect how earnestly I pressed you to ensure an adequate reserve being close in rear of my attacking divisions and under my orders. It may interest you to know what happened. No reserve was placed under me. My attack, as has been reported, was a complete success. The enemy had no troops in his second line, which some of my plucky fellows reached and entered without opposition. Prisoners state the enemy was so hard put to it for troops to stem our advance that the officers' servants, fatigue-men etc., in Loos were pushed forward to hold their second line to the east of Loos and Hill 70.

The two Reserve Divisions (under c-in-c's orders) were directed to join me as soon as the success of First Army was known at GHQ. They came on as quick as they could, poor fellows, but only crossed our old trench line with their heads at 6 pm. We had captured Loos 12 hours previously, and reserves should have been at hand then. This, you will remember, I requested should be arranged by GHQ and Robertson quite concurred in my views and wished to put the Reserve Divisions under me, but was not allowed.

The final result is that the enemy has been allowed time in which to bring up troops and to strengthen his second line, and probably to construct a third line in the direction in which we are heading, viz., Pont à Vendin.

I have been given some fresh divisions and am busy planning an attack to break the enemy's second line. But the element of surprise has gone, and our task will be a difficult one.

I think it right that you should know how the lessons that have been learned in the war at such cost have been neglected. We were in a position to make this a turning point in the war, and I still hope we may do so, but naturally I feel annoyed at the lost opportunity.

Public opinion in Britain was disturbed by the comparative failure and the heavy casualties, just over 50,000 men, in the first battle in which the New Armies were engaged. Haldane was sent out by the Government to discover why things had gone wrong. On 9 October he lunched with Haig, who expressed to him freely his opinion on the handling of the reserves and of French's command arrangements during the battle. He added one more criticism: he did not think it right that two such inexperienced divisions should have been used as reserve. The Guards Division, also in xi Corps, which came into the battle later, and some other divisions found by interchange within one of the two armies less actively engaged should have been used for this vital rôle. Here Haig may have been unjust to French. This was not a thoughtless decision of convenience. Divisions already in France were much watered down by inexperienced reinforcements and French thought that divisions fresh from their training at home might show more thrust in an exploitation rôle. Obviously there was something in French's idea. Later experience in the Second World War bore this out when the newly-trained divisions often performed better than the veteran divisions brought home from the Mediterranean.

Robertson, who was faced with an even more serious conflict of loyalties because he was French's Chief of Staff, felt as strongly as Haig that French was unfit to continue in command. Matters were made more complicated by the fact that there was a move, one in which Haig had a hand, to get Robertson made cigs in place of Murray. Murray had done excellent work in restoring the General Staff to its proper function, but he was not strong enough to guide so headstrong a Secretary of State as Kitchener. Robertson had been summoned to London to discuss the strategy of the war and the future of operations in the Mediterranean where, in August, the Suvla landings had failed to break the deadlock and the Allies had just made their first landings in Salonica.

Two days after his return, on 17 October, Robertson came to see Haig. In addition to telling him of the discussions in London, Robertson told him that Lord Stamfordham, on the orders of the King, had asked him whether he did not think the time had come to replace French. Robertson had refused to answer and had not committed himself to the King at his subsequent interview. Robertson wanted Haig's opinion.[3]

Haig said:

> . . . up to date I had been most loyal to French and did my best to stop all criticism of him or his methods. Now at last, in view of what had happened in the recent battle over the reserves, and in my view of the seriousness of the general military situation, I had come to the conclusion that it was not fair to the Empire to retain French in command on this the main battle front. Moreover, none of my officers commanding corps had a high opinion of Sir J.'s military ability or military views; in fact, *they had no confidence in him*.

The King visited the troops in France in October and, during the visit, he suffered an unfortunate accident when a mare, lent him by Haig, reared up in front of cheering troops and fell, pinning the King below her and bruising his leg. Before the accident, on 24 October, Haig had dined with the King, who asked him what he thought of French's leadership. Haig told him exactly what he thought and it is this which has led to accusations of intrigue. But it must be remembered that the King had no executive authority. He was using his privilege as Sovereign and titular head of the army to keep himself informed. Among Haig's statements was one which said: 'French's handling of the reserves in the last battle, his obstinacy, and conceit, showed his incapacity, and it seemed to me impossible to prevent him doing the same things again.' He said therefore that he thought, for the sake of the Empire, French ought to be replaced and he expressed himself willing to serve under anyone 'chosen for his military skill to be c-in-c'. The King said that two of the corps commanders, Gough and Haking, had given him 'startling truths of French's unfitness for the command' and that Robertson had complained of the difficulty of dealing with French's frequent changes of mind.

Despite Kitchener's opinion, no immediate change in the command took place. The campaigning season was over and Kitchener was more concerned with the Mediterranean where Monro, the Third Army Commander, who had been sent out to Gallipoli to report, had recommended evacuation. Kitchener, not satisfied, went out himself at the beginning of November and recommended only partial evacuation. Haldane, after his discussions with French and Haig, had used his judicial mind and his political discretion to balance the evidence and report to the Government that no blame for the failure at Loos could be attached to French. With the publication of French's despatches on 2 November a new storm arose. The despatches gave timings for the release of the reserves to First Army which Haig was able to show to be untrue by producing orders and messages. An acrimonious correspondence between Haig and GHQ ensued, in which GHQ maintained that the despatches were substantially correct. The GHQ side of the correspondence was carried on by Robertson, who knew the facts but had to work on French's instructions. The controversy ended with a meeting between French and Haig (at which Haig told his wife that French was very uncomfortable), but he finally agreed to send the whole correspondence to the War Office.

Haig had unburdened himself in his letters to Lady Haig. On 3 November he wrote: 'But he has distorted the facts in a surprising way in several cases. The truth is bound to come out in time, when no doubt he will be despised in the way he deserves. I have however more important things to think about at present.' The next day he wrote: 'Don't trouble yourself at all about Sir J. French's despatch. It is full of lies ... TRUTH *will out in* TIME.' A week later, in response to a suggestion by Lady Haig that he was being too kind to French, he said: 'So long as I am under Sir John, the army will only suffer if there is friction between us.' On wider affairs he wrote: 'I am greatly concerned at your account of your visit to the House of Commons. I agree that a dictator is wanted, but the difficulty is to find one!' And Haig even turned against his old chief when he said: 'I was sorry to see that Lord Haldane did not quite speak the truth about Sir John French not being responsible for the absence of the Reserves. He alone was responsible. However we must forget these petty questions and look to the future. . . .'

Among the more important things to which Haig was devoting his mind was the control of war strategy. Esher was still influential behind the scenes and he came to lunch with Haig on 14 November. The two of them agreed that Esher would recommend that Robertson should become CIGS. The position of Kitchener was seen to be a difficulty and Haig's solution was that the Imperial General Staff should be separated from the War Office, which would remain responsible only for administration and the provision of men, supplies and ordnance. The CIGS would then be responsible for advice to the War Council direct and not through the Secretary of State for War. Haig suggested that Kitchener should become Viceroy of India. He strongly advised against a proposal that he should become Commander-in-Chief Mediterranean, because 'where he is, by his masterful action he will give that sphere of the operations an undue prominence in the strategical spectre.' When, in December, Robertson did become CIGS, he achieved a more logical solution of the problem than that proposed by Haig. The CIGS remained Head of the General Staff at the War Office, but Kitchener with magnanimity and common sense agreed that all military advice to the War Council would be given through CIGS, who would also sign all orders to execute their policy under the authority of the Secretary of State. Kitchener thus fell into the same position as any other member of the Cabinet who was also a member of the War Council.

While Kitchener was in the Mediterranean theatre, Asquith himself had taken charge of the War Office and it was he who made the decision to replace French with Haig. He more than once affirmed that the decision was his alone and that he was not influenced by any outside pressure.[4] Haig had lunch with Asquith on 23 November, but neither mentioned the question of command. Asquith must however have told Robertson, with whom he was having frequent discussions, because it was from Robertson on 25 November that Haig first heard of the decision. Robertson may have told French also because, on 4 December, French wrote to the Prime Minister tendering his resignation. He recommended that Robertson should succeed him. Kitchener had apparently not been told of the decision because, on 3 December, just after he had returned from the Mediterranean, he told Haig that he had written to the Prime Minister recommending the change in command and saying that if Asquith did not settle the matter that day he would press for a decision on the next. He told Haig he would see him again when he was in the saddle and he urged him to keep friendly with the French and to regard Joffre as Commander-in-Chief in France.

On 10 December, Haig received a letter from the Prime Minister offering him the command, subject to the King's approval, and telling him that Robertson would probably come home to become CIGS. Haig at once accepted the appointment.

It is fruitless to suggest changes in the past and then to rewrite history, but it is worth considering whether French was right and that Robertson should have succeeded him, leaving Haig to become CIGS. Robertson's own comment on the recommendation was 'this would not do either from the point of view of seniority or experience in the command of troops'.[5] Both men had the calibre for either task, with the one important weakness that neither could express himself verbally to politicians. Both had the knowledge and ability to take in the conflicting pulls of strategy and, once they had made up their minds, both were unshakeable. There might have been two advantages in the reversal of rôles. In the relationship of two strong men, Haig, for reasons of background and experience, was the stronger. The CIGS should be the superior will to the Commander-in-Chief of one theatre of war. The advantage of this was seen in the Second World War when there was no doubt that Brooke, as CIGS, was paramount. The other advantage might have lain in the fact that Robertson was more of a realist than Haig. He would have been equally determined to defeat the enemy, but he might have been wiser in choosing the moment to break off the offensive.

Among the letters of congratulation which Haig received was one from the King, and there was also one from Haldane. The King expressed his complete trust in Haig and asked him to write freely in the knowledge that any information would be treated in the strictest confidence. Haldane said:

It was with mingled feelings that I read the news – sadness about Sir John – whom I like much – and rejoicing over the chance that has come to the brilliant soldier whom I have known and admired for so long. I have for months past wished that you had been in London from the beginning – with the supreme direction of the war and the opportunity of playing chess against the Great General Staff of Germany. I know which I should have backed. You have a great strategical mind – a rare gift in this country.

But now you have a great task and responsibility with which you are admirably fitted by gifts and by training to deal. . . .

Haig had a number of questions of command and appointments to settle. He said that he wanted no change for change's sake and that appointments proposed by French should go ahead. He had however to replace Robertson as Chief of Staff and find his own successor with First Army. Kitchener offered Murray as Chief of Staff. Haig refused but said he was willing to give him command of a corps. He asked for Butler, who had replaced John Gough and gone on with Haig to First Army. Butler was considered too junior and so Haig took his old friend Kiggell, with Butler as deputy. Of Kiggell, Haig wrote at this time: 'I have the greatest confidence in him as a soldier also as a gentleman.' He said in a letter to Lady Haig: 'I took Gen Kiggell as my CGS because I wanted to get him out to the front. We can't afford to lose an officer like him. After he has been with me three or four months he will be able to get command of a corps and Butler will then take his place. We are quite a happy family.' For command of First Army, Haig recommended Rawlinson, writing in his diary 'though not a sincere man, he has brains and experience'. Robertson agreed with the choice, but Rawlinson only got the command temporarily. Monro, who had been replaced in Third Army by Allenby, returned from Gallipoli after the evacuation and took over First Army. Three months later, Rawlinson got the newly-constituted Fourth Army.

Haig showed some magnanimity towards Wilson when his close friend Rawlinson told him that he was feeling frustrated and wanted to go on half-pay. Wilson's own diary shows that his frustration was caused by the feeling that he had missed his second opportunity of becoming CIGS and that, with the accession of Haig and Robertson, he had little hope of advancement. Haig said it was unthinkable for a man of Wilson's standing to go on half-pay and authorized Rawlinson to offer him command of a division. Haig was better than his word because on the day French left France, Haig told Wilson he was to take over IV Corps from Rawlinson. There may have been some pressure from above because both Asquith and Kitchener had promised Wilson a corps.[6]

One more appointment is of interest. French told Haig he had promised Winston Churchill command of an infantry brigade. Haig told French that this was impossible until Churchill had proved himself in command of a battalion. A week before, Haig had seen Churchill on duty in the trenches in the Guards Division and his commanding officer had spoken highly of his keenness. But Haig said, 'his knowledge however is where we were 15 months ago'. Haig gave his decision personally to Churchill, and arranged that he should take command of the 9th Battalion King's Royal Rifle Corps. Later, Haig found that this battalion was shortly leaving France and Churchill took command of the 6th Battalion Royal Scots Fusiliers.

On 16 December, a few days before he became Commander-in-Chief, Haig unburdened himself to his wife:

> I can honestly say that no Commander in our Army has been so highly tested as I have been in this war. The retreat after engaging the enemy towards Binche; then the advance, including the fights at Le Petit Morin and the Aisne – (all with no orders from GHQ) – then at Ypres – and since then all the fighting of this year – indeed the only fighting which has been done by the British Army in the theatre of war. I can write this to you . . . I always feel how fortunate I am to have you in whom to confide.

On 18 December before going to his farewell interview with French, he wrote again to his wife: 'At 3 pm I go to see Sir J. French. As you can imagine I don't look forward to it. He has been so deceitful for a long time and all the time has made the most of me as a friend.'

# 8

# COMMANDER-IN-CHIEF:
## Strategic Considerations and Allied Dialogue I

Haig took over as Joffre was preparing his plans for 1916. The instructions of the British Government, conveyed by Kitchener, were clear. The mission of the British Expeditionary Force in France was to support and co-operate with the French and Belgian Armies against our common enemies and to drive the German Armies from French and Belgian territory. One paragraph detailed Haig's position as Commander-in-Chief:

> The defeat of the enemy by the combined Allied Armies must always be regarded as the primary object for which the British troops were originally sent to France, and to achieve that end the closest co-operation of French and British as a united Army must be the governing policy; *but I wish you distinctly to understand that your command is an independent one, and that you will in no case come under the orders of any Allied General further than the necessary co-operation with our Allies above referred to.*

It would be possible to tell the story of Haig as Commander-in-Chief by continuing with a history of the war on the Western Front and by leaving the reader to make his own judgment. But that history, in short and in long versions, has often been told and there is the danger that the conclusions to which it leads may be tainted by well-justified horror at the type of war that it was and not so well-justified ideas of what it might have been. To put it brusquely, it was a bloody war, but the question is whether if Haig, or anyone else, had fought it differently victory could have been won at less bloody cost. It is proposed therefore to set out in this chapter and the next the main phases of the campaign and the relations between Haig and his Allies, and in succeeding chapters to study the separate themes which may throw a light on Haig's character and achievements.

The principal stages of the war in so far as they directly concerned Haig can be easily held in the mind in six stages. First, came the great German offensive against the French at Verdun from 21 February to 29 April 1916, followed by the series of British attacks on the Somme from 1 July to 18 November 1916. At the end of the year, Lloyd George replaced Asquith as Prime Minister and Nivelle became Commander-in-Chief instead of Joffre. Early in 1917, the United States entered the war against Germany and Russia began to collapse. The second stage is the German withdrawal to the Hindenburg Line, the abortive Nivelle offensive and at the same time, in April, the British attacks at Vimy Ridge and Arras. The third stage begins with the British attack on Messines Ridge in June and then the long Third Battle of Ypres from 31 July to 12 November. It is only the last two phases of this battle that properly have the name of Passchendaele. Towards the end of Third Ypres, the Italians suffered disaster at Caporetto and Haig was called upon to send a contingent to the Italian front. The fourth short stage, the Battle of Cambrai from 20–30 November, ended the campaigning for 1917. In 1917, there had been British successes in Mesopotamia and in Palestine which drew some British eyes towards the eastern Mediterranean.

Early in 1918, Wilson replaced Robertson as CIGS. The fifth stage includes the two German offensives against the British, towards Amiens on 21 March and on the Lys on 9 April, during which Foch became Generalissimo of the Allied armies in the West. In May, the Germans turned their attacks against the French and towards Paris and the stage ends with the French counter-stroke on the Marne on 18 July. The final stage begins with the great British offensive at Amiens on 8 August and the successive defeats inflicted on the German Army leading to the Armistice on 11 November 1918.

The idea of an offensive on the Somme as the main operation for 1916 came from Joffre. There was not the same strategic concept as in 1915 of converging thrusts to push out the German salient north of Verdun, but Joffre believed that French manpower would last for only one more offensive so that this was to be the decisive operation to end the war. There were therefore two requisites, it must coincide with a Russian offensive and the British Army, already thirty-nine divisions strong and still growing, must co-operate to the full. The last was one of the reasons Joffre chose the Somme, it was the main junction point of the French and British forces. The offensive could not take place until July because the Russians would not be ready. Until that time Joffre believed there should be attacks to prepare the way and to wear out the enemy (*Bataille d'Usure*) and the weight of this must be borne by the British.

Joffre came to see Haig at St Omer on 20 January to give him his ideas and seek his co-operation. It was however principally a ceremonial visit to GHQ to welcome the new Commander-in-Chief. Haig describes it in his letter to Philip Howell of 2 February:

> I am pretty busy here, very friendly with Joffre and the French generally ... (Joffre) presented me with the Grand Cordon in front of the 3rd Brigade, and kissed me on both cheeks! It was quite a surprise and I could not help laughing especially when Rawlinson and Henry Wilson's turn came next and they, being tall and thin, had to stoop down for it in cold blood. ...

Haig had time to think about Joffre's ideas before he went, with Kiggell and Brigadier-General Charteris, now Head of Intelligence, to meet Joffre and Castelnau, his Chief of Staff, at Chantilly on 14 February. Haig's ideas for the rôle of the British Army in 1916 were very different from the plan which Joffre had expounded. He had already talked with Admiral Bacon, Commander of the Dover Patrol, who had emphasized to him the importance to Britain, and to the Royal Navy in particular, of the coast from Zeebrugge to Ostend, now in German hands. Haig agreed with Bacon that operations to regain this coast were of great importance, but made it clear that definite plans would have to await Joffre's decision on the Allied offensive. He had, however, instructed Plumer commanding the Second, northernmost, Army to consider alternative plans on his front; the capture of the Messines Ridge or attacks towards Lille or the railway junction of Roulers (see Map 6, page 136). Haig's diary on 14 January shows that he, too, was thinking of wearing-out attacks, although not on the same lines as Joffre. He envisaged them as being of about three weeks' duration to draw enemy reserves, and they must be timed closely with the main offensive.

Robertson had quickly made his weight felt as CIGS and he and Haig had an excellent rapport, with constant correspondence and meetings. Kitchener was now a spent force and the General Staff had properly become the sole source of military advice. Robertson not only discussed the Western Front, but unburdened himself to Haig on the general strategic situation and his difficulties with the Government. On Christmas Day 1915, two days after Robertson became CIGS, Haig comforted him with: ' "All beginnings are difficult [says the Bosche proverb]", so you will very soon find things running splendidly.' He went on to tell of his own good relations with Joffre, relations no doubt enhanced by Haig's fluency in the French language:

> My visit to Joffre last Thursday was quite a success. . . . I went there at 10.15 so as to get finished before 11 a.m. when J. lunches I was told, but it was 11.30 before we finished our talk. No one was with Joffre and me when we had our talk. The old man was quite delighted I hear and when I left he volunteered the remark '*C'est excellent – c'est parfait*' – and as you can imagine the French at once telephoned the result to HQ here.[1]

On 5 January 1916, Robertson wrote: 'I am afraid I am giving you many accounts of my troubles, but I am rather full of them and I also want you to know what I have to contend against so that you may not think I am unduly neglecting matters in France.'

Robertson was present at Chantilly on 14 February when Haig met Joffre for the official discussion of plans for the 1916 offensive. It was agreed that the attack should take place astride the Somme about 1 July. On two points, however, Haig would not give way to Joffre; one the relief of the Tenth Army, the other the timing and nature of the preliminary operations. Haig agreed in principle that he should take over from the French Tenth Army, which was still south of the old Loos battlefield sandwiched between the British First and Third Armies, but he was not going to have his army frittered away before the great offensive and he told Joffre he would not be strong enough to carry out the relief till the next winter. Haig felt he had won an even more important triumph by resisting Joffre's request for a series of preparatory offensives to be carried out by the British Army in April and May – he considered that such battles would be as expensive for the British as for the enemy and that the Germans would have time to replenish their equipment and reorganize their reserves in time for the main battle. He convinced Joffre, as he had already tried to do by letter and in his informal talks, that the preparatory attacks should be made only ten to fifteen days before the main attack.

The Germans were not to wait on the Allied initiative. Exactly a week after the meeting at Chantilly, the German attack at Verdun began. At the end of 1915, Falkenhayn had made a broad appreciation of the situation and had come to the conclusion that Britain was the main enemy. But he thought the British would only carry on the war on the Continent through their Allies. He believed Russia and Italy could, in the long term, be discounted because of their inefficiency and internal difficulties and so the essential step in the defeat of Britain was the elimination of the French Army. Direct action against Britain would, for the moment, be confined to submarine warfare. Verdun was selected as the central objective because Falkenhayn believed that it protected vital areas in defence of which France would be prepared to bleed to death.[2]

On 18 February, three days before the attack began, Castelnau dined with Haig and asked again for the relief of Tenth Army on the grounds that an attack on Verdun was immediately impending. Haig told Robertson of his reply:

I, of course, said that if the Germans did attack, the British Army would support the French to the utmost of its power, and in the best possible manner. That is, either by taking over more line, or by counter-attacking. I preferred the latter as being the soundest method of defence. I also pointed out that so far only some nine divisions were located opposite the Verdun salient, which with eight holding the line makes 17 Divns – not enough for a decisive result. I therefore ventured to think that a blow would be delivered against the British, and that it might even be found to be the main effort.

Haig was wise enough to hide his annoyance at so early a repetition of the demand and, when his own appreciation was found to be wrong, he arranged the relief. He also did more. He placed a reserve of divisions on his right flank where, if need be, they could support the French, and, on 27 February, he telephoned Joffre to tell him he would go over to Chantilly on the next day 'to shake him by the hand, and to place myself and troops at his disposal'.

The intensity of the fighting at Verdun and the difficulty in holding the German attacks made the necessity for a major Allied offensive all the more apparent; the exhaustion of the French Army made it equally clear that it would have to be almost entirely a British effort. Haig wanted to husband his resources and to ensure that he entered the offensive with a fully-trained army. The final evacuation of the Gallipoli Peninsula in January had given him nine more divisions, including five tough and experienced Australian divisions, but he told Kitchener on 29 March that he had not got an army but a 'collection of divisions untrained in the field' out of which he hoped to make a fighting army. Haig and Robertson both wanted the Allied forces in Salonica brought to France, but the French, for political reasons, wanted the effort there to be increased rather than diminished.

When Rawlinson had become free on Monro's return to the First Army, Haig had set him to study possible offensives either on the Somme or at Ypres. Now, in March, Rawlinson was given command of the newly-formed Fourth Army on the right of the British line, next the French, with the task of preparing the Somme offensive. In the months before the Somme, Haig was subjected to pulls in different directions. The French wanted immediate attacks to relieve the pressure on Verdun. Their Government was moving away from the idea of a major offensive to end the war in 1916 because they now thought the risk too great. Clemenceau, not yet Prime Minister but an influential member of the Government, told Haig on 20 May that the French would prefer another winter at war rather than risk an attack before the Allies were at their maximum strength. For his own part, Haig was against wasting effort, except in an emergency to save the French Army from disaster. The British Government was reluctant to face the problem of the manpower necessary to maintain the army in a major offensive; Kitchener and Robertson were pressing for compulsory service, but Asquith was using his political skill to avoid the issue. Robertson told Haig that there were plenty of men, but that there were no intelligent plans for using them. The War Office cannot be held blameless. Kitchener said that in April there were 1,300,000 men under arms in Great Britain, yet in mid-June, just before the battle of the Somme began, the army in France was more than 40,000 men under establishment.

In April, Haig came over to London specifically to tell the Government of his intentions. On the 14th, he saw Kitchener and Robertson at the War Office and asked them whether he had the Government's authority to embark upon a major offensive with the French that summer. Kitchener assured him of that authority. Haig's few days at home gave him little opportunity for leisure. He visited Buckingham Palace, where the King again assured him of his full support. He also saw Esher and visited Leopold de Rothschild, who had become a close friend and confidant since his War Office days. He also tells of an afternoon's shopping with Lady Haig but the next day, Saturday the 15th, as he was leaving to play golf with her, he received a message from Kitchener asking him to attend a meeting at 10 Downing Street at noon. The subject was manpower and, in particular, the problem of the maintenance of the army in France during a major offensive. Austen Chamberlain said that Britain was financing the Allies and that nothing must interfere with the requirements of industry. Asquith, who was himself in country clothes and seemed to Haig anxious to get off for the week-end, did not force the issue but seemed inclined to leave it to the War Office to solve the problem.

Haig now had the full authority of his government to participate in Joffre's offensive, but the part the French could play was now considerably lessened and the Russians, on whose offensive Joffre much relied, began to talk of delays. The advantage which the Germans had from their central position, or interior lines, could only be minimized if the Allies attacked simultaneously on all fronts and the chances of doing that seemed to be diminishing. Haig had begun to lose some of his confidence in Joffre. He wondered 'whether the old man was past his work' and he wondered also who was really Commander-in-Chief and how far the French Government would tie Joffre's hand. Some of these doubts came from his talk with Clemenceau on 4 May. Haig had greatly pleased Joffre by telling him that Clemenceau had asked to see him before agreeing to the meeting. Clemenceau was an outspoken critic of Joffre and Joffre himself refused to see him.

The fears about a delay in the Russian offensive were not realized and, in any case, Joffre thought that the aftermath of the Verdun battle demanded an offensive not later than 1 July. He promised Haig that he would make from twenty to twenty-six French divisions available. The Italians were at this time under severe attack by the Austrians, directed by Conrad, but the Russians were able to take advantage of the consequent weakening of the eastern front and the offensive launched by Brusilov in Galicia on 3 June achieved extensive success, the last Russian victories in the war.

One more dramatic event before the battle opened was to have a long-term effect on Haig. On 5 June, Kitchener, on his way to Archangel, was lost at sea. Haig had, several months before, observed

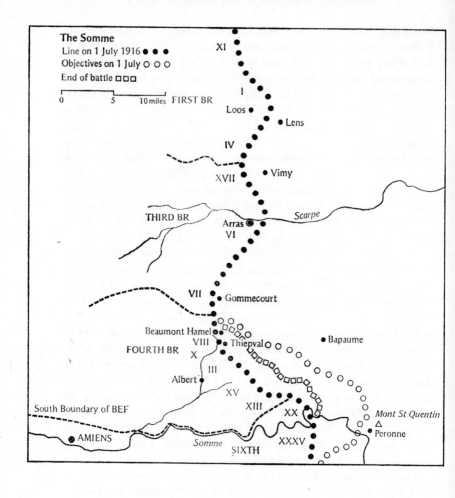

The Somme

Line on 1 July 1916 ● ● ●
Objectives on 1 July ○ ○ ○
End of battle □□□

0        5      10 miles

XI

I

Loos ●

● Lens

IV

XVII

● Vimy

THIRD BR

*Scarpe*

Arras ◉

VI

VII

● Gommecourt

Beaumont Hamel ●

VIII

● Thiepval

● Bapaume

FOURTH BR

X

III

Albert ●

XV

South Boundary of BEF

XIII

XX

● Mont St Quentin △

● Peronne

● AMIENS

*Somme*

SIXTH

XXXV

FIRST BR

that Kitchener had aged and, on 9 February, he had written in his diary: 'I felt pained that his mind should be losing its power of comprehension and decision at this time of crisis in our country's history.' He knew, too, that the politicians had lost their faith in Kitchener, so it was more his replacement by Lloyd George than his removal from the scene that affected Haig. He does not appear to have expressed any feelings of personal loss of a friend as does, for example, Esher.

The Battle of the Somme opened on 1 July after seven days' preliminary bombardment. The initial assault was made by five divisions of the French Sixth Army and eleven divisions of the British Fourth Army, organized in five corps. The French on the right captured all their objectives, but only the right British Corps, XIII, gained all its objectives for the first day. On the left, VIII Corps failed to make any headway. Haig had been round to see all the corps commanders on the two days preceding the attack and, on the day itself, he was with Rawlinson at his headquarters. He supported him in his decision to press the attack again on the next day. Rawlinson, after talking to all his corps commanders, assessed the day's casualties as 10,000. They were, in fact, 60,000.

The first phase of the battle continued for eight days, at the end of which there was still no progress in the two left corps; the other three corps were in possession of most of the German first line. On Haig's express instructions and after some doubts voiced by Rawlinson, part of the German second position had been included in the objectives of the three left corps for the first day. The 36th (Ulster) Division had been the only one to enter the second position and they had later been forced back. Gough, with a small staff, had been placed on the right flank to be at hand to take command of the two right corps, and there were three cavalry divisions from the reserve to exploit the break-through when it came. When Rawlinson saw that it would not come, he sent Gough with his staff to take command of the two left corps. On this embryo, the Fifth Army was eventually built. This is how Gough, chosen by Haig as his thrusting commander of a pursuit force, got bogged down in the sober business of trench warfare.

The tactical conduct of the battle which dragged on for more than four months – until 12 November – will be discussed in a later chapter. Here it must suffice to bring out the strategic issues. The British action had certainly achieved two of its objects; it had effectively drawn off German pressure on Verdun and the French Army generally, and it had prevented German diversion to other theatres. But what had been intended as a decisive break-through which might possibly have ended the war had deteriorated into a battle of attrition. This wearing-out battle, in many ways desired by Joffre, was one of which Haig had often written and always he had emphasized the necessity to ensure that it was the German Army and not the British Army that was worn down. Ludendorff, who in effect took over from Falkenhayn in August, considered that the battle came near to breaking the spirit of the German Army and that 'the German Army had been fought to a standstill and was utterly worn out.'[3] One German writer and psychologist wrote, 'The Somme was the muddy grave of the German field army, and of the faith in the infallibility of the German leading. . . .'[4] Another wrote, 'In its results the first material-battle of the World War turned to the disadvantage of the victorious [sic] Germans, for no art of the commander could give them back the trained soldiery which had been destroyed.'[5]

There has been endless controversy over the relative casualties because of the different systems by which the two sides recorded them. The Germans did not include the lightly wounded, while the British included all who left their units. The Germans often excluded the missing. Edmonds, as Official Historian, tried to balance the figures by a careful analysis of regimental and divisional records and of published casualty lists. He came to the conclusion that the German casualties amounted to at least 660,000 against the total of 630,000 combined British and French casualties.[6] Sir Charles Oman, who was responsible for investigation of German casualties during the war, came to conclusions not very different from those of Edmonds. He also wrote an answer to the scathing criticism of the battle by Winston Churchill, which, like Lloyd George's, had been based on the assumption that the British casualties were only half those of the Germans.[7] Later, Liddell Hart made a detailed study of the subject and came to the conclusion that Edmonds had grossly exaggerated the German casualties. He made his papers available to John Terraine when he was writing Douglas Haig, the Educated Soldier, but Terraine was not convinced.[8] There followed a somewhat acrimonious correspondence in The Times between Liddell Hart and Terraine. To quote one more eminent military historian, Cyril Falls subsequently wrote, 'It is just possible that Edmonds exaggerates slightly, but I prefer his figures to those of Liddell Hart.'[9]

Further study of the conflicting figures is unlikely to lead to any

1 Douglas Haig's mother, Rachael Haig

2 The Haigs' wedding day, 11 July 1905. *Left to right* Douglas Haig and his wife, formerly the Hon. Dorothy Maud Vivian; Queen Alexandra; Captain and Mrs Bell

3 *Above* 17th Lancers polo team which won the Inter-Regimental Cup in 1903. *Left to right* Captain R. Garden (No. 1); Colonel D. Haig (Back); Major A. Tilney (No. 2); Lieutenant A. Fletcher (No. 3), later Haig's ADC

4 *Left* Generals Sir Douglas Haig and Sir Charles Monro, Brigadier-General J. Gough, Colonel Perceval, Western Front, 1914

5 *Opposite above* The Somme, 1916: Allied troops advancing through the wire. Their vulnerability to enfilade machine-gun fire is apparent (*see* Chapter 10)

6 *Opposite below* Aerial view of the Somme offensive in the French sector. Captured German trenches are occupied by Allied reinforcements during the attack on Vermandovillers, 17 September 1916

7 *Opposite above*
Lloyd George, Haig,
Joffre and Thomas at
the 14th Army Corps
Headquarters,
Meaulte, 12
September 1916

8 *Opposite below*
King George V with
General Joffre,
President Poincaré,
General Foch and
General Sir Douglas
Haig at Château Val
Vion, Beauquesne, 12
August 1916

9 *Above* Haig on his
charger 'Poperinghe'

10 Brigadier-General
J. Charteris, head of
'Intelligence' GHQ, is
presented to Queen
Mary at Blendecques,
5 July 1917

11 *Above*
Passchendaele, 6
October 1917.
Canadians of the 2nd
Division laying a
duckboard track
over the churned-up
ground while
wounded and
prisoners (in the
background) trudge
from the front line.

12 *Left* Field-
Marshal Sir Douglas
Haig with General
Sir Arthur Currie
and staff looking
towards the German
lines from Bouvigny
Hill, 28 February 1918

13 *Opposite* A war-
time *Punch* cartoon
depicting Haig's
success at Cambrai,
November 1917

## ST. GEORGE OUT-DRAGONS THE DRAGON.

[With Mr. Punch's jubilant compliments to Sir Douglas Haig and his Tanks.]

14 Field-Marshal Sir Douglas Haig with the Army commanders, Cambrai, 11 November 1918: Generals Plumer (2nd), Byng (3rd), Birdwood (5th), Rawlinson (4th), Horne (1st): Lieutenant-Generals Sir John Davidson, Montgomery, Sir Louis Vaughan, and others

15 Haig in his GHQ train, 1918

conclusion other than that the casualties to both sides were grievous and almost intolerable. The question is whether the Battle of the Somme had an appreciably different effect on the capacity of the German, the British and the French armies to continue the war. It has been stated above that the blow to the Germans was the undermining of the belief in the professional skill of their army, a fully-trained national army. The small British Regular Army had already wasted away by the end of 1915. The British soldier, regular or citizen, has always been more than a little sceptical about military expertise and has less faith in his training than he has in dogged courage. The men in the New Armies of 1916 were trained to do little more than follow their leaders or hang on to the end; they were at heart less affected therefore than the Germans. However, the fighting qualities of the German Army in 1917 and the first half of 1918 showed that the effect on it was to produce some cracks in the wall rather than, as Haig considered, to undermine the foundations. This leaves us with the French, who were a professional army more like the German than the British. Here there are grounds for believing that the part the British played in the Battle of the Somme did give the French the opportunity to make a partial recovery from the onslaught at Verdun. Joffre was well satisfied and foretold at the Chantilly Conference of November 1916 that the fruits fought for in 1916 would be gathered in 1917. But it can hardly be said that the prolongation of the attacks under the awful conditions of October and November could be justified on those grounds.

Falkenhayn had called off his offensive against Verdun within ten days of the opening of the Somme battle, and it was the Somme which caused his supersession. Before the end of August, the French had completely regained the initiative at Verdun and were able to make successful attacks there in October and December. Although the Russian offensive had petered out towards the end of August, the Italians were by then having some success. In addition, Rumania joined the Allies on the 27th August, thus raising hopes – though these were soon to be dashed. There was understandably a call for a renewed offensive in the west. On these grounds, Haig's renewed attacks on 15 September may be justified. The objectives were not very different from those of 1 July, but tanks were used for the first time. But when the lack of any important success became apparent, Haig should surely have brought the battle to an end.

Although much has been made above of the relief afforded to the

French at Verdun and of Joffre's position as the author of the offensive, it must not be assumed that Haig's conduct of the battle was directed by Joffre or that Haig's responsibility was passed on to him. Two days after the battle, (at Joffre's request) Haig had received Joffre and Foch. Joffre had talked of the direction in which the British attacks should be pressed. Haig's diary reads:

> Joffre began by pointing out the importance of getting Thiepval Hill. To this I said that in view of the progress made on my right near Montaubon, and the demoralised nature of the enemy's troops in that area, I was considering the desirability of pressing my attack on Longueval. I was therefore anxious to know whether in that event the French would attack Guillemont. At this, General Joffre exploded in a fit of rage. 'He could not approve of it'. He '*ordered* me to attack Thiepval and Poziéres'. If I attacked Longueval I would be beaten, etc, etc. I waited calmly till he had finished. His breath heaved and his face flushed! The truth is the poor man cannot argue, nor can he easily read a map. But today I had a raised model of the ground before us. . . . When Joffre got out of breath I quietly explained what my position is relatively to him as the 'Generalissimo'. *I am solely responsible to the British Government for the action of the British Army;* and I had approved the plan and must modify it to suit the changing situation as the fight progresses. I was most polite. Joffre saw he had made a mistake, and tried next to cajole me. He said that this was the 'English Battle' and 'France expected great things from me'. I thanked him but said I had only one object, viz., to beat Germany. France and England marched together, and it would give me equal pleasure to see the French troops exploiting victory as my own.

Again, in August, Joffre pressed Haig to renew his attack, but Haig said he would not be ready until 15 September. On 1 September, he wrote to Robertson telling him that Joffre, after expressing approval of what had been achieved so far, had pleaded that he never asked Haig to do what he did not believe his army could do. Haig commented, 'I do only what I judge right in the full consideration of all the factors in the problem regardless of Joffre, Castelnau & Co's pressure in another direction.'

Further proof that the Somme was Haig's battle is given by the general review which he had sent to Robertson on 1 August and which Robertson had read to the War Committee. He pointed out that, because of his attacks, pressure on Verdun had been relieved and the Russian successes made possible. The ability of the Allies to drive the Germans from the strongest positions had shaken the faith of the Germans, their allies and neutrals in the invincibility of the German Army and had impressed on the world 'England's strength and determination, and the fighting power of the British race'. He emphasized the heavy losses inflicted on the enemy and said that in one month seventy enemy divisions had been used up, against thirty-five at Verdun in five months. In another six weeks, he believed, the enemy would be hard put to it to find men. He thought we must maintain our offensive which would 'result eventually in his complete overthrow'. On casualties, he said, 'Our losses in July's fighting totalled about 120,000 more than they would have been had we not attacked. They cannot be regarded as sufficient to justify any anxiety as to our ability to continue the offensive.' He expressed his intention of continuing to attack whenever the state of his preparations and the general situation made success probable and saw the battle continuing well on into the autumn. He did not, however, consider it justifiable to calculate that the enemy's resistance would be completely broken without another campaign next year.

Haig was certainly right in his view that another campaign would be necessary, for 1917 was the year in which the failure of the Nivelle offensive undid what had been achieved in the recovery of the French Army and in which the battle of attrition continued in the Flanders mud. The weight was thrown more heavily on the British Army and there was nothing but the transient success at Cambrai to point the way to possible future success.

One unfortunate result of the Somme was that it caused Lloyd George to lose confidence in Haig. During the whole of the battle, Lloyd George was Secretary of State for War and he became Prime Minister on 7 December. The relations between Haig and Lloyd George are discussed in a later chapter. Here it must be stated that possibly it was not so much a lack of confidence in Haig on Lloyd George's part, as a strengthening of his personal conviction that neither side could obtain a result on the Western Front and that Allied victories must be sought elsewhere. The weight of Lloyd George's disapproval fell more directly on Robertson than on Haig, but in strategical ideas the two were one. However, Lloyd George's faith in the possibility of victory in the west was for the moment kindled, not by Robertson or Haig, but by the rise of a new star in

France. Nivelle had established his reputation in the fighting at Verdun where, in May 1917, he had taken over Second Army from Pétain, who had become Army Group Commander. Nivelle devised a system of attack which was most successful, culminating in a formidable counter-stroke in October. Nivelle had imagination and, so different from Haig, he had the gift of tongues. He was fluent both in French and English – no doubt because he had an English mother – and a persuasive talker. In December, he superseded Joffre as Commander-in-Chief on the Western Front and, at the same time, Franchet d'Esperey replaced Foch. This was hard on Foch because, like Haig, he had obeyed Joffre in falling in with a strategic plan with which he did not altogether agree. Joffre was promoted Marshal of France and, for the time being, remained nominally the military adviser to the Government. Haig also received his promotion. On 1 January 1917, he became a Field-Marshal. Among the congratulations he received were letters from the King and from Haldane. Haldane said: 'You are almost the only military leader we possess with the power of thinking, which the enemy possess in a highly-developed form. . . . If I had had my way, you would have taken the place at the head of a real Great Headquarters Staff in London on the 4th of August 1914.'

Nivelle had no intention of carrying out Joffre's plan which was broadly a repetition of the Somme, but with the British making a more northerly thrust towards Douai. Nivelle believed he had discovered the secret of the offensive and that, by his methods, a lightening stroke of twenty-four or forty-eight hours' duration would breach the enemy front and allow reserves to pour through and disrupt his communications. This was an operation for the refreshed French Army, and the British would be required to take only a subsidiary part. Briand and Marshal Lyautey, the new War Minister, readily accepted the plan, an important element of which was Nivelle's promise that if he was not successful he could break off the attack after forty-eight hours. Briand had reason to trust Nivelle's promises because, before his counter-attack at Verdun, Nivelle had told him that at a certain time on a certain day he would tell him that Fort Douaumont had been recaptured. Precisely at that hour and that day, Nivelle did ring him up from Verdun to give him the splendid news.[10]

Haig's first meeting with Nivelle was on 20 December. Haig was impressed and wrote in his diary:

We had a good talk for nearly two hours. He was I thought a most straightforward and soldierly man. . . . He is confident of breaking through the enemy's front now that the enemy's morale is weakened, but the blow must be struck by surprise and go through in 24 hours. The necessity for surprise is after all our own conclusion. Our objective on the Somme was the relief of Verdun, and to wear out the enemy forces with a view to making the decisive blow later, when the enemy's reserves are used up. Altogether I was pleased with my first meeting with Nivelle. He is in his 61st year. Is alert in mind and has had much practical experience in this war as a gunner, then in turn Divl, Corps, and lastly, Army Commander. . . . He also mentioned that Lloyd George had said to him at Verdun that 'the British are not a military people'. I said L.G. has not studied our military history.

Nivelle followed up his visit by a letter on 2 January giving his ideas to Haig in more detail. In the light of what happened later, Haig's reply is most important. He had every intention of co-operating in Nivelle's bid for a quick and decisive victory, but he kept in mind that, whatever else happened, the Germans must not be left in possession of the Belgian coast. On 6 January he wrote to Nivelle:

I have already agreed to launch such an attack as you describe, but not to an indefinite continuation of the battle to use up the enemy's reserves. Such continuation might result in a prolonged struggle, like that on the Somme this year, and would be entirely contrary to our agreement that we must seek a definite and rapid decision. . . . You will remember that you estimated a period of 24 to 48 hours as sufficient to enable you to decide whether your decisive attack had succeeded or should be abandoned.

The third phase . . . will consist in the exploitation by the French and British Armies of the success previously gained. This is, of course, on the assumption that the previous successes have been of such magnitude as will make it reasonably certain that by following them up at once we can gain a complete victory and, at least, force the enemy to abandon the Belgian coast. . . . I must make it quite clear that my concurrence in your plan is absolutely limited by the considerations I have explained above, on which we have already agreed in our conversations on the subject. It is essential that the Belgian coast shall be cleared this summer. I hope and believe we shall be able to effect much more than that. . . . But it

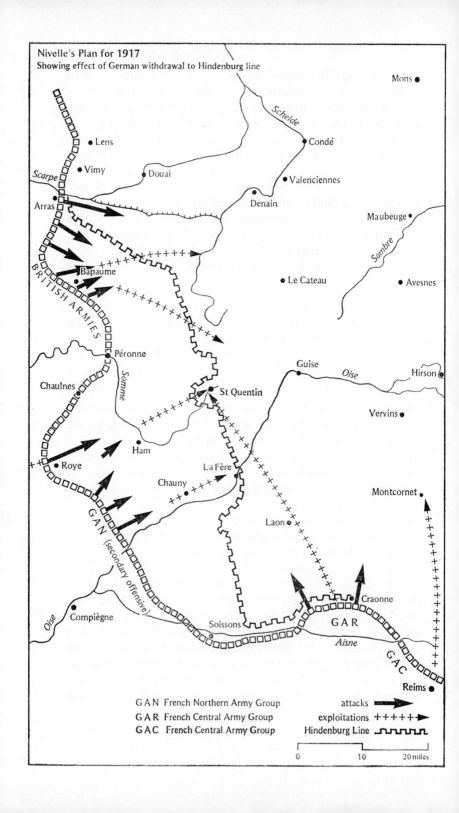

Nivelle's Plan for 1917
Showing effect of German withdrawal to Hindenburg line

Mons

Schelde

Lens
Vimy
Douai
Condé
Valenciennes
Scarpe
Denain
Arras
Maubeuge

Sambre

BRITISH ARMIES
Bapaume
Le Cateau
Avesnes

Péronne
Guise
Oise
Hirson

Somme
St Quentin
Vervins

Chaulnes
Ham
La Fère
Roye
Chauny
Montcornet

GAN (secondary offensive)
Laon

Oise
Compiègne
Soissons
Craonne
GAR
Aisne
GAC
Reims

GAN  French Northern Army Group                    attacks
GAR  French Central Army Group          exploitations  + + + + +
GAC  French Central Army Group          Hindenburg Line

0            10           20 miles

must be clearly understood between us that if I am not satisfied that the larger plan, as events progress, promises the degree of success necessary to clear the Belgian coast, then I not only cannot continue the battle but I will look to you to fulfil the undertaking you have given me verbally to relieve on the defensive front the troops I require for my northern offensive.

Nivelle's answer giving general agreement reached Haig in London a few days later, after he had gone for a week's leave. His whole household was already asleep when, at midnight, the loud knock on the door of a special messenger from the War Office aroused them to deliver the letter.

Haig and Nivelle seemed to be in agreement, but the politicians still had ideas outside the Western Front. Briand decided to send two divisions to Salonica and wanted the British to do the same. Lloyd George had his own ideas and thought salvation lay in assisting an Italian offensive. His project was put forward, without reference or warning to his own General Staff, at an inter-Allied conference in Rome in the first week in January. The Italians were pleased, but, since any such plan would run counter to the Allied agreement for the Western Front, no action could be taken then. It was on the way back from this conference that Nivelle met Lloyd George for the second time. He presented himself to the British delegation at a wayside station, asked for support for his ideas and was invited to come to London to discuss them.

The result of the meeting in London was Lloyd George's whole-hearted conversion to the Nivelle plan. (See map, p. 122.) Forgotten for the moment was the search for an easy victory elsewhere; Italy, Salonica, Jerusalem, Baghdad, anywhere. On the morning of 15 January, Lloyd George, with Hankey, met Robertson and Haig. The discussion was not so much a preparation for the meeting with Nivelle as a dissertation by the Prime Minister on how much better the French Army had performed than the British in 1916. Haig patiently explained how the prolonged British fighting had enabled the French to recover, but Lloyd George was not convinced. He was disposed only to show his opposition to any repetition of an offensive like the Somme. That afternoon Nivelle, Haig and Robertson met the War Committee. Nivelle explained his plan, but the discussion centred on his requirement that the British should, as a necessary preliminary, take over part of the French front. Haig and Robertson had already explained to the Government that this extension of the British front, involving ten divisions, could only be achieved either by sending more troops to France or by a reduction of the offensive capacity of the British Army. No decision was taken, the soldiers withdrew and the War Committee continued the discussions alone. Before the resumed meeting next day, Haig was told that the War Committee had decided he must accede to Nivelle's request for the relief of French troops. Nivelle gave a draft in French of the conclusions to which he wanted the War Committee to agree and Haig translated this for the Committee. Apart from requiring a delay in the relief from February to March, Haig was able to agree and all signed the document. The attack was to take place not later than 1 April.

On the day after the meeting, Lloyd George caused Robertson to send Haig a special instruction stating that the War Committee had approved Nivelle's plan and required him to carry it out both in letter and in spirit. Haig was already prepared to do this in the same way that he had always played his part in Joffre's plans, that is to say with the normal discretion which a commander is allowed for the methods employed and with due regard for his national responsibilities. Friendly relations with Nivelle continued and there seemed to be only one difference between them – whether or not Vimy Ridge should be included in the British objective. Nivelle wanted the British attack to extend only as far north as the River Scarpe. Haig believed that if he was to avoid getting his force into a pocket between the Hindenburg Line and Vimy Ridge, he must direct his attack far enough north to include the Vimy Ridge. Nivelle gave no indication that he had any serious objection to Haig's plan. On another point, the reluctance of the French to give the full use of railways which Geddes, Haig's movements expert, considered necessary, Nivelle also seemed inclined to support Haig.

On 22 February, Haig heard from Robertson that the Prime Minister wished to hold a conference at Calais on 26 February to discuss the railway problem. Lloyd George, Robertson, Haig, Briand, Lyautey and Nivelle were to attend. Haig was a little surprised that such a high-powered meeting should be required to settle such a technical matter but he agreed and asked only that Geddes should attend and that terms of reference for the conference should be drawn up. The last request, which was not observed, shows how far-sighted Haig was in these matters.

On the day before the meeting, Haig received a most important intelligence report which said that the Germans were preparing to withdraw to the Hindenburg Line, which ran from south of Arras through St Quentin to Cambrai and Laon (see map on p. 122). Haig believed the information but wrongly assumed that such a withdrawal would 'have great disadvantage for the enemy'. That it did not do so was due in part to the fact that Nivelle at first refused to believe it and when, in March, it actually took place refused to alter his plans to meet the new dispositions.

Before the conference, Lloyd George sat next to Haig at lunch and agreed to see him with Geddes before the first session. After lunch, however, Lloyd George hurried off with Briand and later sent a message to say he could not spare the time. The conference had been in progress for less than an hour when Lloyd George dismissed the railway experts, telling them to settle the matter on their own, and said he wished to discuss Nivelle's plan. Nivelle went through the plan (which had already been heard by all present) and Lloyd George then pressed Nivelle to emphasize the differences with Haig, despite the fact that the two had already virtually resolved them. After Haig had had a chance to speak, Lloyd George washed his hands of strategy and asked about the command arrangements. He suggested that the French should draw up a paper to be discussed after dinner.

The resultant French paper handed to Robertson gave Nivelle direct authority over the commanders of British armies and reduced Haig to an administrative and disciplinary rôle. It asked that a British staff should be set up at Beauvais, the French GQG, reporting not to Haig but to the War Committee in London. Robertson and Haig, both men of few words, were speechless and aghast. Robertson brought Hankey, and Haig brought Kiggell, to a private discussion. Haig records 'we agreed we would rather be tried by Court Martial than betray the Army by agreeing to its being placed under the French.'

Hankey was regarded by Robertson and Haig as being on Lloyd George's side, but, in his own words, the proposals took his breath away[11] and he determined to convince Lloyd George that they were impossible. He set about drafting an acceptable compromise that night. Next morning he saw Robertson, who for the first time in the war had passed a sleepless night, but found he was still so angry that it was impossible to do anything with him. He then went to Lloyd George, who had also had a bad night and who expressed himself determined not to be thwarted. Hankey 'warned him he could not fight on the basis of the outrageous French document' so Lloyd George accepted Hankey's compromise as something on which he could stand.[12]

The new proposal which, after some heartburning, was accepted by Robertson and Haig and by Briand and Nivelle was that the British Army should fight, as before, as a single command under Haig, but that for the period of preparation and for the forthcoming operation alone Haig should be directly under Nivelle's command. Haig returned his right of appeal to the British Government if he considered Nivelle's instructions imperilled the safety of his army.

Haig did not believe that Nivelle had had anything to do with the instigation of the plan to bring him under command. He was deeply hurt by the whole proceedings, but assumed it to be a political plot by Lloyd George and Briand. He could not conceive that a responsible soldier like Nivelle could have been privy to such duplicity. Nevertheless, as is shown by President Poincare's diary, Nivelle was certainly closely concerned and possibly the author of the plot.[13] Had Haig known this, it is doubtful if he would have agreed to the Hankey compromise. Haig sent a very full account of the Calais Conference to the King, saying that he had signed the document 'as indicating that I would loyally do my best to carry out its provisions, *not* that I thought such a paper to be desirable or necessary!' Haig concluded his letter:

> Your Majesty will observe that in my dealings with Mr Lloyd George over this question, I have never suggested that I would like to resign my command but, on the contrary, I have done my utmost to meet the views of the Government, as any change at this time might be a disadvantage to the Army in the Field. It is possible, however, that the present War Cabinet may think otherwise, and deem it necessary to replace me by someone else more in their confidence. If this is so, I recommend that the change be made as soon as possible, because of the proximity of the date fixed for the commencement of offensive operations. At this great crisis in our history, my sole object is to serve my King and Country wherever I may be of most use, and with full confidence I leave myself in your Majesty's hands to decide what is best for me to do at this juncture.

Stamfordham's reply on behalf of the King showed that His Majesty fully appreciated Haig's feelings and believed that he would be able to clear all difficulties with Nivelle. He also asked Haig to dismiss from his mind any idea of resignation.[14]

Nivelle's tactless assumption of unquestioned authority made it certain that the controversy was not yet over. On the very next day, he sent peremptory orders to Haig asking for a copy of his orders to his army commanders. He also required that the British Mission should be set up at Beauvais as soon as possible and that Wilson should be appointed as its head. Haig's comment in his diary was that it was 'a type of letter which no gentleman could have drafted, and it also is one which no c-in-c of this great British Army should receive without protest.' He accordingly protested to the Government through the cigs on the interpretation Nivelle had put on the Calais agreement. His reply to Nivelle brought in the French Government, as did his reception of the next instructions sent in equally peremptory terms. Haig's remarks on this instruction were perfectly proper and courteously expressed. He referred to the German withdrawal which had already begun and said that it would set free German reserves for an attack – possibly on the Flanders front – the security of which was so vital to Britain. One of Nivelle's comments written on the letter is especially illuminating. Haig said that his action was subject to his responsibility for the safety of his armies. Nivelle wrote in the margin: 'That responsibility is mine, since the British Government has so decided.'[15]

Briand wrote indignantly to Lloyd George, saying that Haig's attitude showed both determination not to accept the decision of the Calais Conference and his opposition to the proposed offensive. Accordingly a new conference was held in London on 12 and 13 March. This time the British Government was firm; all members of the War Committee and the Cabinet, except Lloyd George, saw that Haig had been right and that they should have heeded Robertson's warnings. The soldiers came to a mutually-acceptable agreement in which Nivelle conceded that his control over the British Armies could only be exercised through Haig, and in which Haig accepted Nivelle's instructions for the forthcoming offensive and undertook to do his utmost to further them, subject only to his national responsibilities. Even so, Haig felt it necessary to append to his signature the following note, which expresses perfectly his idea of the agreement.

I agree with the above on the understanding that, while I am fully determined to carry out the Calais agreement in spirit and letter, the British Army and Commander-in-Chief will be regarded by General Nivelle as allies and not as subordinates, except during the particular operations which he explained at the Calais Conference.

While I also accept the agreement respecting the functions of the British Mission at French Headquarters, it should be understood that these functions may be subject to modifications as experience shows to be necessary.

On the plea of Robertson, who said that it would please the British Government, Haig accepted the nomination of Wilson as Head of the Mission at GQG. Possibly for some devious reason, Wilson tried to refuse the appointment. He said that whatever he did he would be accused of intrigue against Haig. Haig, with Kiggell present, received him and told him that he would have his complete confidence in military matters. Haig added that it would be an advantage to have at Nivelle's headquarters a senior British officer trusted by the French.

At the time of this controversy, world-shaking events were happening elsewhere. On the very day of the London conference, the Russian revolution broke out and less than a month later, on 6 April, the United States declared war on Germany. Between the two events, the Briand Government fell. The new War Minister was Painlevé, who did not trust Nivelle. Haig's relations with Nivelle returned to their former warmth, but Nivelle was now beginning to lose the confidence, not only of his Government, but of his own senior generals.

Haig and Franchet d'Esperey, commander of Northern Army Group, had different reactions to the German withdrawal. Haig was cautious, but he had constructive ideas. He thought the whole plan should be recast and the offensive carried out where, because of their communications system, the Germans could not withdraw. This would have been an offensive on the lines of Third Ypres starting at a time when the weather and ground conditions were favourable. Franchet d'Esperey, who, on earlier orders from Joffre, already had an attack mounted, thought the beginning of the German withdrawal offered the opportunity for immediate attack. Pétain proposed a revised plan with an attack east of Reims but that, like Haig's, would have meant delay. Nivelle listened to no one, but proceeded with his plans almost as if nothing had happened. The follow-up of the Germans was inept and they were given the opportunity to lay waste the evacuated area and to ensure that the French attack beat the air.

As harmful as his failure to modify his plans was Nivelle's disregard of security and his failure to do anything to surprise the enemy. His plans were sent to the Government and were the subject of open discussion. Pétain, as well as Franchet d'Esperey, voiced his doubts and the Third Army Group Commander, Micheler, who was to command the spearhead attack, also did so continually and critically to Painlevé. At a conference on 6 April, Painlevé faced Nivelle with his three army group commanders, who were asked to voice their doubts. Nivelle, rightly furious, offered his resignation, which was refused.

On 4 April, Nivelle issued his final instructions.[16] He emphasized the nature of the offensive, which was to destroy the hostile forces on the Western Front. There were to be two phases, first a battle in which the opposing front was to be broken and then the reserves defeated; second, the exploitation in which all available Allied forces would take part. In the preliminary phase, the British were to break the enemy front from north of the Somme to the Scarpe and then push their reserves towards Cambrai and Douai. The principal French effort would be that of Micheler's Reserve Army Group on the Aisne. Because of the German withdrawal, the subsequent operations would develop well to the east of St Quentin and the direction earlier intended (see map, p. 122) towards Guise and Hirson. For similar reasons, the Northern Army Group would be confined to an attack astride St Quentin and the Centre Army Group to a one-army attack east of Reims.

The attack of the British Third Army at Arras protected on its left by the attack of First Army on the Vimy Ridge, went in on 9 April, that of Micheler a week later. The Canadian Corps captured Vimy Ridge, a great triumph after Foch's several earlier attempts to take it. At Arras, Allenby's Third Army started with a considerable success, capturing a substantial part of the German second position and breaking into one sector of the third. But the opportunity was allowed to slip.

On 8 April, Haig had written to Robertson thanking him for his 'eve of the battle wishes'. He said:

Y'day I was all round the Corps in 1st and 3rd Armies who are attacking. I have never before seen commanders who are so confident and so satisfied with the preparations and wire cutting. . . .

I hear Nivelle has had trouble. Some of the French govt. wanted to forbid the French offensive altogether. But Nivelle has gained the day. I think this indicates the instability of purpose of our French Allies and if anything goes wrong Nivelle will disappear.

The grave question I have to decide in the next few weeks is whether the present operations are likely to result in freeing the Belgian ports by the late summer. If, say at the end of May, we are still before the line Lille–Valenciennes–Hirson–The Meuse, the preparations should be begun for the switch elsewhere.

Neither the French main attack, nor the two subsidiary attacks, made any substantial progress. Only in one small sector north of the Aisne was the German second position reached and only a footing was retained on the Chemin des Dames. The losses in tanks from artillery fire were catastrophic. Nothing like a break-in had been achieved and the casualties were grievous. It must not be assumed that the Germans did not suffer in the battle. Against their own total casualties of 96,000, the French took 20,000 prisoners and 147 guns and the Germans suffered heavily in their frequent counter-attacks. The tragedy to the French lay in the terrible shock of disappointment, and it was this disappointment which caused the later disciplinary troubles. Happily the Germans did not realize the seriousness of the mutinies; but it was a long time before the French Army recovered its morale. The collapse of the French Army was a possibility that Haig had to take into consideration from now until August 1918. As Haig had foretold, Nivelle was removed. In the latter stages of the battle, he could do nothing without being contradicted from below or overruled from above. On 29 April, Pétain became Chief of the General Staff, a new appointment in Paris, and a fortnight later Foch replaced Pétain, who then superseded Nivelle as Comman-der-in-Chief.

Haig cannot be accused of having any part in Nivelle's downfall. Both he and Robertson were sceptical of Nivelle's idea that deep defences could be penetrated in a single day and Haig had told him so. But he loyally complied with Nivelle's plan and in no way blamed him – as in justice he might have – for the political machinations which had tried to subordinate the British Army to a foreign general untried in higher command. It was not so much the command posi-tion that Haig regretted, rather it was the undue subordination of the

British Army to a hastily-conceived French plan. Most of all, he resented the orders of his own Government to accept an extension of his front which, in his view, vitiated the effectiveness of his army for the task allotted to it. On 13 April, with hopes of exploiting the success at Arras fading, he wrote to Robertson:

> While touching on the error of the Calais Conference you should indicate the serious results which have accrued to our case through the War Committee's decision at London Conference of Jany. by which I was ordered (against my better judgment and protest) to extend my Right to the Roye Road. But for that I should now have at my disposal a large reserve of well-trained divisions with which to exploit our success. As for Italy! Will History ever forgive the War Cabinet for declining in Jany. 1917 to have any confidence in the power of the British Army to play its *part* with credit on the Western Front. Almost every week gives me fresh indications of the *decisive* effects of the Somme battle on the German Army and the German plan. But you and I have always agreed on this.

Haig was quick to see that, from this time forward, the British Army would have to bear the main burden of the campaign on the Western Front. He told Robertson on 29 April that he was sure the French policy would be based on avoiding losses whilst waiting for American reinforcement. He added pithily: 'Pétain calls this system the "aggressive defensive" and doubtless in his mind he imagines the British Army will do all the "aggressive" part while the French "squat" on the defensive.'

# 9

## STRATEGY II:
### Mud, Blood and Disaster,
### but by Faith to Victory

Haig had wanted to attack towards the Belgian coast in 1916, but had been drawn away to the Somme by Joffre. Joffre himself, before his supersession, had agreed to an attack for 1917 which would have led in that direction, but Nivelle's plan had changed all that. Haig had left Nivelle in no doubt that he must be left free to switch his offensive to the north in the early summer; now that he was likely to be the senior partner, there was no doubt as to where his efforts would lie. He looked to the Northern front because he saw that success there offered the greatest strategic advantage, since it gave the opportunity of rolling up the whole German right wing. But naval reasons for clearing the Belgian coast were now even more pressing. The beginning of the German unrestricted submarine campaign in February had critically increased the strain on Britain's maritime communications. In April, more than half a million tons of British shipping was lost. In June, Jellicoe stated at a meeting at which Haig was present that Britain could not continue the war in 1918.[1] It is true that the cross-channel route was less in jeopardy than the more distant theatres and the essential imports to Britain, but the clearance of the Belgian coast would nonetheless give considerable relief to the Royal Navy.

Lloyd George appears to have been in chastened mood after the failure of the Nivelle offensive. He went over to Paris on 3 May, while Pétain was still CGS and Nivelle nominally still in command. Haig was most pleased with his attitude and with two speeches which he made at the conference between the two Prime Ministers and their military advisers and Commanders-in-Chief. Lloyd George said that he did not want to enter into strategic discussions or to know the plans; he hoped that the French Government would take the same line and leave it to the military advisers and the Commanders-in-Chief to decide where and when to attack. Haig said: 'The conference passed off in the most friendly spirit and all stated that they were united in the determination to attack vigorously, and carry on the war *"jusqu' au bout"*.' Before he returned to London, Lloyd George stayed with Haig, who observed that he seemed to have changed his ideas about the British Army. The Prime Minister felt he had 'heartened the French' and congratulated Haig on the success of his operations which he contrasted with the French failure.

It is apparent that Haig judged his Vimy–Arras operations a considerable success from his answer to Lady Haig's suggestion that Lloyd George's changed attitude was due to the King's influence. Haig thought it more likely that Lloyd George liked to keep in with those who had been successful. Although Lloyd George had given unequivocal consent to an offensive while he was in Paris, when he got back to London he caused Robertson to send a message saying that such approval was on the express condition that the French played their full part. Haig accordingly again saw Pétain, who gave him to understand that he recognized that the main effort would be British, but undertook the French would play their full part in support. Haig found Pétain 'businesslike, efficient and brief of speech'. He commented that this last was a rare quality in Frenchmen.

Since the failure of Nivelle, Wilson had lost grace in French circles and he got on less well with Pétain than with the other French generals. He suggested to Haig that he would like Pétain to acknowledge more fully that the French position was now subordinate to the British. Haig showed his wisdom here by saying: 'I think it would be a serious mistake for me in any way to indicate to the French c-in-c that he is playing "second fiddle". As a matter of fact he knows it and has promised to support me in every possible way. Besides, it was Nivelle's adoption of such an attitude towards me which caused so much friction between our respective staffs.'

Although Haig was thus wise in his dealings with Pétain, he misjudged the purport of Wilson's advice and wrongly thought that Wilson had lost his understanding of the French command. In fact,

Wilson's diary[2] shows that he understood very well that the French were only playing for time. To both Pétain and Foch, the idea of an offensive with a view to such distant objectives as Ostend and Zeebrugge was as absurd as Nivelle's vision had been. Lloyd George makes much of the fact that Wilson's views of the French attitude were not passed on to him or the War Cabinet.[3] One of Haig's demands on the appointment of Wilson had been that the Mission reported direct to him and not to the Government. It was not so much that Haig wanted to deceive the Prime Minister, it was simply that he preferred to accept Pétain's own undertaking to him, limited as it was, rather than Wilson's interpretation. Incidentally, Wilson, who gave up his appointment on 26 June, had a long talk with Lloyd George on his return to London and it is inconceivable that the 'Welsh Wizard' did not get out of him what he really thought. It would not be right to think either that Pétain deceived Haig. As he told Wilson, he could not contemplate telling Haig what he thought of his plan. He gave only an indication of the dates he would attack and the number of divisions involved. This apparently satisfied Haig.

A week later, on 1 June, Haig received indications that all was not well with the discipline of the French Army, and he was told officially that Pétain's remedial measures included a proper leave system for French soldiers which would involve the cancellation of their attack timed for mid-June. There could be no French offensive before that already projected for late July.

Haig's own plans were in two phases. First, in early June, a deliberate operation for which preparations were already far advanced to clear the Messines Ridge and so obtain observation and protect the right flank for further operations; second, several weeks later, a larger operation aimed at clearing the Belgian coast. Haig said that the second phase would not be launched 'unless the situation is sufficiently favourable when the time comes'.

The Messines Ridge attack was entrusted to Plumer. Planned and executed with great skill as a siege operation, it was a striking success. The objectives were strictly limited and almost a million tons of explosive were used so that the infantry advance was almost a walkover. The casualties were under 11,000 for nine divisions on a nine-mile front and more than 7,000 prisoners and forty-eight guns were captured. (The total British Army casualties for the whole battle, which lasted a week, were 21,000.)

On the day of the attack, 7 June, Haig went to congratulate

Plumer and then went straight on to see Pétain at Cassell. After a satisfactory talk about six French divisions which were to be placed under Haig's command for the Flanders operations, there was some disturbing news. Haig wrote in his diary:

> Pétain and I then had a private talk. He told me that two French Divisions had refused to go and relieve two Divisions in the front line because the men had not had leave. Some were tried and were shot. The French Government supported Pétain. . . . The situation in the French Army was serious at one moment, but is now more satisfactory. But the bad state of discipline causes Pétain grave concern.

Although Haig did not pass on this information to Lloyd George, the Prime Minister had become sceptical about the support which the French would give to a new offensive. He himself attributed this to the impression he had received from Pétain's demeanour – not his words – in Paris,[4] but he had not given any inkling of this to Haig before he left. On his return to London, however, his mind turned again to the possibility of switching the British effort to Italy. Robertson opposed this idea because he said that if they wished, the Germans could always beat the Allies by concentrating superior forces on the Italian front.[5] Moreover, he thought the Germans might take advantage of the weakening of the Western front to defeat the French. Robertson therefore remained a convinced 'Westerner'; although this did not mean that he was an unequivocal supporter of the Flanders offensive. On 9 June, he had gone over to see Haig and warned him of the dangerous situation the country would be in if large-scale attacks were carried out without full co-operation by the French. Britain might then face the winter without an army. Haig dismissed Robertson's fears, saying he thought the Germans were nearly at the end of their resources and that the only sound plan was to send every available man, aeroplane and gun to France without delay. The fact that the Germans were no longer in a position to land on the British coast should make it possible to release every trained soldier. Robertson's reservations were not completely removed, but he decided he must continue loyally to support Haig. His biographer considers this inward tussle of convictions to be the beginning of Robertson's downfall.[6]

Haig had entrusted the early planning of his Ypres offensive to Plumer and it was intended to entrust the attack to him with Rawlinson

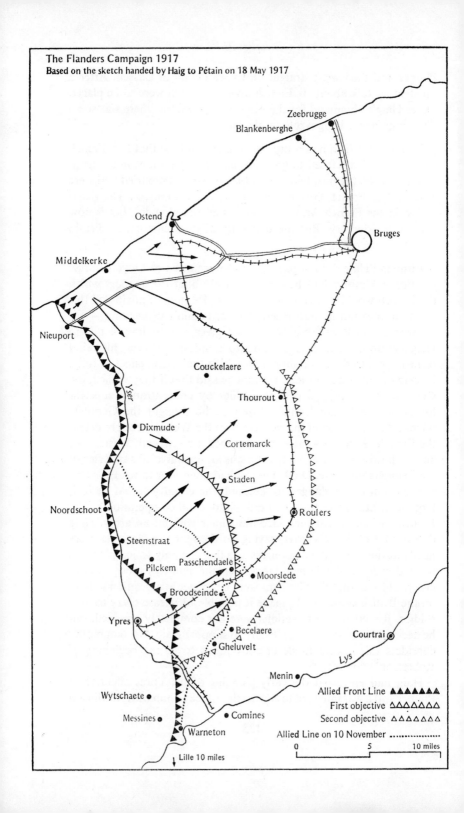

The Flanders Campaign 1917
Based on the sketch handed by Haig to Pétain on 18 May 1917

Zeebrugge
Blankenberghe
Ostend
Bruges
Middelkerke
Nieuport
Yser
Couckelaere
Thourout
Dixmude
Cortemarck
Staden
Roulers
Noordschoot
Steenstraat
Pilckem
Passchendaele
Moorslede
Broodseinde
Ypres
Becelaere
Courtrai
Gheluvelt
Menin
Lys
Wytschaete
Messines
Comines
Warneton
Lille 10 miles

Allied Front Line ▲▲▲▲▲▲▲
First objective △△△△△△△
Second objective △△△△△△△
Allied Line on 10 November ........

0        5        10 miles

working on his northern flank, including in his plan a landing from the sea. Later, he had given Plumer only the preliminary task at Messines, while the main attack was to be entrusted to Gough. This was a significant change. Plumer had planned a step-by-step advance; Gough was chosen because he was a thruster. He arrived with his Fifth Army staff in Flanders on 30 May and Gough went forward with Plumer to the Messines Ridge the day it was captured. Before the battle, Haig had considered the exploitation of Plumer's siege operation and discussed it with both army commanders. Gough had not wanted to participate in another commander's battle so soon after his arrival, and Plumer felt that plans for exploitation would alter the whole character of his attack, particularly in the deployment of his artillery. Haig had not pressed the matter.

Haig's plan can best be visualized from the map on page 136, which is based on the sketch he gave to Pétain on 18 May. On the same day, a file of papers covering all the studies of the Ypres offensive so far was handed to Gough and the final orders to him were evolved in a series of conferences held by Haig. Briefly, the orders were that Fifth Army and Anthoine's First French Army, which was under Haig's command, were to capture the Passchen-daele–Staden Ridge and the railway from Roulers to Thourout. The object was to facilitate a landing near Ostend and to gain possession of the Belgian coast.[7]

Although Haig was thus necessarily going ahead with all the plans and preparations for the battle, he still did not have the full authority of the War Cabinet for his offensive. They were still hovering between Haig's plan and a transfer of force to Italy or to Palestine or even a landing at Alexandretta – possibly all three. In Italy, an attack launched on 10 May had shown promising early signs of success. Haig undoubtedly emphasized the importance of his offensive plans because he knew that if they did not come off, many divisions would be withdrawn from his command. In the light of the French weakness, he believed this might lead to a serious defeat. On 12 June he wrote out his appreciation of the situation and sent it to Robertson for the War Cabinet. In it he said:

I feel justified in saying that continued pressure with as little delay as possible certainly promises at least very valuable results; where-as relaxation of pressure now would strengthen belief that the Allies are becoming totally exhausted and that Germany can outlast them. . . . Waning hope in Germany would be revived. . . . The depressing effect in France would be especially grave and especially dangerous. At the present crisis of the war French hopes must have something to feed on. The hope of American assistance is not sufficient for the purpose. It is still too far distant and the French at the moment are living a good deal on the hope of further British successes. They can and will assist them by keeping the enemy on their front fully employed, wearing him down and preventing him from withdrawing divisions to oppose us. But they feel unable at present to do more than this, and it is useless to expect it of them – although any considerable British successes and signs of a breakdown of the German powers of resistance would probably have an electrifying effect.

It is my considered opinion, based not on mere optimism but on a thorough study of the situation, guided by experience which I may claim to be considerable, that if our resources are concentrated in France to the fullest possible extent the British Armies are capable and can be relied on to effect great results this summer – results which will make final victory more assured and which may even bring it within reach this year. On the other hand, I am equally convinced that to fail in concentrating our resources in the Western Theatre or to divert them from it would be most dangerous. It might lead to the collapse of France. It would certainly encourage Germany. And it would discourage our own officers and men very considerably. The desired military results possible in France are not possible elsewhere. Given sufficient force, provided no great transfer of German troops is made in time from east to west, it is possible that the Belgian coast could be cleared this summer, and the defeat of the German troops entailed in doing so might quite possibly lead to their collapse.

Without sufficient force I shall not attempt to clear the coast and my efforts will be restricted to gaining such victories as are within reach, thereby improving my position for the winter and opening up possibilities for further operations hereafter if and when the necessary means are provided.

It will be observed that, in some places, this reads as an appreciation by a CIGS rather than by a theatre commander, and it thus emphasizes the wrong balance in the otherwise most profitable relationship between Haig and Robertson.

Robertson was able to agree with most of the appreciation; but the Intelligence summary, prepared by Charteris and sent as an appendix by Haig, was more than he could stomach. Its purport was that Germany's resources in men and material were so stretched that Germany might have to accept peace on Allied terms before the end of the year. This view was completely at variance with that of Macdonagh, Charteris's predecessor and now Director of Military Intelligence at the War Office. Macdonagh's report, which had just been put before the War Cabinet with Robertson's support, gave a very different picture of German power and emphasized the dangers of the Russian collapse and the ability of the Germans to transfer forces to the west. Robertson persuaded Haig to withdraw his appendix; most pertinently saying:

> It would be very regrettable at this juncture if different estimates of enemy resources were presented to War Cabinet as it would tend to destroy value of your sound appreciation . . . what I do want to impress on you is this:— Don't argue that you can finish the war this year, or that the German is already beaten. Argue that your plan is the best plan – as it is – that no other would even be *safe* let alone decisive, and then leave them to reject your advice and mine. They dare not do that. Further, on this occasion, they will be up against the French.

A Cabinet Committee consisting of the Prime Minister, Milner, Curzon, Bonar Law and Smuts had been convened to study the future conduct of the war and Haig came over to London to attend its meetings on 19, 21 and 22 June. There, for the first time, the ministers heard Haig's plan with its far-reaching objectives. Lloyd George expressed surprise that the British were now decisively to defeat the Germans single-handed and said that he preferred Pétain's plan of wearing down the Germans with a punch here and a punch there, or an attack on the Austrian front.[8] Jellicoe also attended the meetings and made his notorious statement that the Allies could not continue the war into 1918. The members were much shaken by the naval view but were divided in their conclusions. Two supported Haig whilst the Prime Minister and the other two saw no hope of its success. The Committee was reluctant to overrule its military and naval advisers and the discussion was to be continued.

On Saturday 23 June, Haig wrote his own account of the meeting to Kiggell:

On Thursday L.G. made a long speech agst. action on Westn. front & accused 'Old Wull' of having changed his views & advice since Paris on 5 May! R & I were told to reconsider our opinion, & reply on Monday. L.G's oration was of the lawyer type; its object seemed to be to show black is white! . . . I think it best to hand my reply to CIGS and not to Sec War Cabinet because L.G. has tried to divide us as much as possible, and the I'l. Gen. Staff is the advisory body of the govt. not me. R. has written a very long paper. He suggested that I shd. sign it also, but I think my procedure is the correct one; I shall of course support him to the full at the meeting. I hope Monday will finish this discussion so that I can return on Tuesday.

A quite different matter was raised before the resumption. On the Sunday, Derby came to Haig and said he was anxious he should be fully rewarded and wished to recommend him for a peerage. Haig thanked him warmly but said that, as a Field-Marshal, he had already been fully rewarded. He added: '. . . that I and my wife were thoroughly happy in our present position. If I were made a Peer, I would at once have to live beyond my means and get into debt. Again I did not wish to found a dynasty. The Haigs of Bemersyde were now the oldest family in Scotland.'

The Monday did not bring a decision, but Lloyd George said the discussion would be continued in the War Cabinet and with the French, but preparations could go ahead. The message giving approval for the operation was not sent until 21 July and it crossed one from Haig saying that 'it was startling that the War Cabinet had not yet determined whether the attack was to be permitted' and asking Robertson to explain the serious and lengthy preparations involved.[9]

Haig's note of urgency can be understood because the season for his operation was already late – August and October were habitually wet months in Flanders – so that little campaigning weather was left. He received the assurance of the wholehearted support of the War Cabinet on 25 July, only six days before the assault was actually launched.

Haig had wanted his attack to begin on 25 July so that Fifth Army could be approaching Roulers in time for Rawlinson's Fourth Army to catch the high tides on 7 or 8 August for their landing operation. However, first Anthoine and then Gough asked for delay until 30

July. The preliminary bombardment had already begun on 16 July and, since air observation was an essential element of the artillery plan, the Royal Flying Corps under Trenchard, now Major-General, had begun an offensive five days earlier. This was successful enough to enable them to fulfil their programme of artillery co-operation, photography, reconnaissance and bombing.

After one more day's postponement, the attack went in on 31 July. There was no surprise, the Germans were everywhere ready, and yet the first day yielded much better results than the Somme at less than half the cost in casualties. The reason for this was that the infantry were better trained. It is significant that two of Gough's corps commanders, Maxse and Jacob, were probably the best trainers and most thoughtful tacticians in the army, but the tactical aspect is one which will be discussed in the next chapter. By the end of the day, the whole of the Pilckem Ridge and much of the German second position had been captured, but unhappily the Gheluvelt plateau, on which Haig had placed great importance, was still in enemy hands. After the first day, things did not go well. Heavy rain fell for four days and nights and the battlefield became a morass. The 177 tanks which had been engaged were even more thwarted by the cratering of the ground than by the mud. In the first four days, seventy-seven went out of action and forty-two of these were a total loss. In the bitter fighting which continued for most of August, little progress was made and no important penetration made into the German Languemark–Gheluvelt line which had been the final objective for the first day.

On 25 August, Haig changed the weight of the attack to Second Army and moved its boundary north to take in the Ypres–Menin Road, with command of two of Gough's corps. Plumer asked for three weeks for preparation and, with improved weather, delivered three deliberate and well-organized attacks along the Menin Road on 20 and 26 September and 4 October. Many prisoners were captured and a footing was gained on most of the Gheluvelt plateau, although the enemy still held the south-eastern ridge.

Ludendorff has testified how near the Germans came to defeat. Of the battle on 20 September, he said, 'Obviously the English were trying to gain the high ground between Ypres and the Roulers–Menin Line, which affords an extensive view in both directions. . . . The enemy's onslaught on the 20th was successful, which proved the superiority of the attack over the defence. Its strength did not consist in the tanks; we found them inconvenient, but put them out of action all the same. The power of their attack lay in the artillery. . . . We might be able to stand the loss of ground, but the reduction of our fighting strength was again all the heavier.' Of 4 October, he said, '. . . again we only came through with enormous loss'.[10]

While Plumer was preparing his attacks, Haig had to face a crisis of a different kind. This time it was the French who wanted to send assistance to Italy, where the Italians only seemed to lack heavy guns for victory. Foch had asked for a hundred heavy guns to be withdrawn fron Anthoine's army to send to them. Haig went to London to discuss the matter with Robertson and Lloyd George. Foch apparently believed that success in Italy would have more political effect than a victory in Flanders and Lloyd George, who saw Haig alone, told him that he feared the French were trying to supplant Britain in Italian affections. He would not like the French to be able to say that they wanted to send assistance, but the British prevented them. Haig emphasized the importance of heavy guns in his operations and said that to withdraw a single man or gun from Flanders would be a most unsound policy. Nevertheless, he gratified the Prime Minister by saying he would review the whole artillery position with Pétain and would try to spare fifty heavy guns.

The battle of Broodseinde on 4 October was the last fought in the improved weather. On that afternoon, the rain began again in earnest and both Plumer and Gough now wanted to end the campaign. Even Charteris, who always fed Haig with hopeful information and was not above cloaking the darker picture, came to the conclusion that there was no hope of complete success that year.[11] But Haig himself was reluctant to end the battle with his troops bogged down in the low-lying ground dominated by the Passchendaele Ridge. The campaign now entered the stage which has made Passchendaele a pejorative word. Haig moved into Second Army the Canadian Corps who, fighting an isolated battle with First Army further south in August, had added to the glory of Vimy by capturing Hill 70. Plumer hoped the Anzac Corps that had fought so well at Broodseinde could capture Passchendaele, and Canadian Corps could then take the remainder of the ridge to the south and Gheluvelt. Plumer was too sanguine. There were still in front of him two fully organized positions (Flanders I and II) protected by a belt of wire forty yards deep. Nor was Passchendaele the end: it was itself dominated by the continuation of the ridge. Haig was not properly aware of the situation. He told a group of war correspondents on 11 October it was the mud that had caused slow progress and that he was practically through the enemy defences. He said: 'The enemy has only flesh and blood against us, not blockhouses.'

In indescribable weather, II Anzac Corps fought the First Battle of Passchendaele on 12 October and made little progress. In the Second Battle, from 26 October to 10 November, the Canadian Corps achieved the almost impossible by capturing Passchendaele, but still they could not gain the main ridge. Although only the corps making the main attack have been mentioned, in fact all the forward corps of both Fifth and Second Army were engaged.

Before the campaign was brought to an end on 10 November, Haig's attention had been engaged again with the question of re-inforcements for Italy. On 24 October, the Italians had suffered a crushing defeat at Caporetto and were forced to retire to the River Piave. In accordance with a previous arrangement, the British and French each had to send a corps of two divisions. The executive order reached Haig on 26 October and the troops began to leave the Flanders front on the 28th. During the next fortnight, another corps of three divisions had also left Flanders for Italy and, at the end of the Passchendaele battles, Plumer also left to take command of the British contingent. The Second Army was then absorbed into the Fourth Army under Rawlinson.

It is difficult to judge Haig's decision to launch his offensive and his persistence in continuing the battle for more than three months, most of the time in deplorable weather. The evidence against him is telling. It must be remembered, however, that the evidence is more easily apparent than the strong reasons that impelled him and the underlying advantages of his campaign. In retrospect, much has been made of the awful conditions under which his army had to fight. This will be discussed later, in the chapter on morale, but it must be said here that Haig did realize these conditions in which he was asking his men to fight. He demanded of them the sacrifice that, he believed, was the only way to victory.

The benefit which Haig sought in his battle was the freeing of the Belgian coast. Although this was far from being realized, the other reasons for the battle, the husbanding of the French Army and the wearing-down of the German Army, were both achieved. It was not that the French demanded the British offensive, indeed they would have been content with a more passive attitude. But it is clear from all he said and wrote at the time that Haig did not believe that he could contain the Germans except by an offensive, and the remarks of Ludendorff already noted show that he agreed. Even the launching of the offensive without surprise, always militarily unforgivable, had its advantages because the Germans were far too busy preparing to meet the attack they knew was coming to discover that this was the weakest moment for the French Army.

It is less easy to defend Haig for his persistence in the attack after the weather broke again in early October. As on the Somme, he did not know when to stop. His reasons for wanting to gain the Passchendaele Ridge before the winter were all sound, as was his desire to support the French who were mounting a subsidiary attack in Champagne. In addition, he wanted to hold the German reserves while he prepared his last battle of the year at Cambrai. But sound though his reasons were for wanting to achieve so much, he failed to count the cost or, if he did, to realize that it was far too high a price to pay. The total casualties for the period from 4 October to 10 November were 106,000 men against 138,000 from 31 July to 3 October.

The tanks which had been used in Third Ypres were not an essential to the infantry assault, which was overwhelmingly supported by artillery, but it was hoped that their use might bring some small bonus to the attack. Brigadier-General Elles, commanding the Tank Corps, willingly co-operated in the plan, but could see that every shell fired diminished the hope of this bonus: so he searched for a more fruitful operations area for the time when the other forces necessary could be made available. His Staff Officer, Fuller, made a plan for an attack on St Quentin, but, as this would require two British and two French divisions, Elles felt this was not the time to ask Haig to get French co-operation. Fuller revised his ideas by working out a large-scale raid on Cambrai. Elles worked on this with Byng, who had taken over Third Army from Allenby in the sector opposite Cambrai. In his turn, Byng had accepted the conception and increased its scope. He persuaded Haig to adopt it as soon as he could provide the men to bring five of Byng's divisions up to strength. As hopes dwindled in Flanders and on the very day that he was called on for divisions for Italy, Haig gave Byng the orders to go ahead with his preparations.

The attack was launched on 20 November and was an overwhelming success. The German line was pierced on a front of six miles and, in four hours, two positions of the Hindenburg Line were captured and 4,200 prisoners and 100 guns were taken at insignificant loss. Only two cavalry divisions were available for the exploitation, and they were not suitable for the task. The battle lasted until 7 December, but the magnificent victory for which the church bells were rung in England was not sustained; the Germans recovered and, in counter-attacks, not only regained much of the ground they had lost but also took some of the original British line as well. The lessons are almost entirely tactical and, as such, will be dealt with in the next chapter. Suffice it to say that the dashing of hopes after exhilarating news of success did nothing to enhance Haig's standing with the politicians, but that, on the other hand, the lessons were learned and the fruit gathered in the following year.

1917 had been a bad year for the Allies. By its end, Russia had made an armistice, the Italians were stabilizing their position after defeat at Caporetto, the French Army was still weak and the British had little to show for more than four months' bitter fighting. Only in Mesopotamia and Palestine had there been any success. One other ray of hope was the arrival of the first four American divisions in France; it would, however, be months before they were trained and equipped to fight. Lloyd George thought one of the measures necessary for success was to replace Haig, and even more urgently Robertson. He wrote: 'There were several courses open. The most obvious was to dismiss our Chief Military Adviser, who had failed us so badly, and the Commander-in-Chief who had proved himself as a strategist to be unequal to the gigantic task committed to his charge.'[12] Lloyd George did not see his way to replacing Haig because of the confidence which the army and the nation had in him and the high esteem in which other members of the Cabinet held him, but possibly the main reason was that he did not know who to put in his place.

His first move was, therefore, against Robertson and his mind turned to an idea which Henry Wilson had expounded to him in August. Wilson had written in his diary at the time: 'I then disclosed my plan of three Prime Ministers and three soldiers, to be overall CIGS and to draw up plans for the whole theatre from Nieuport to Baghdad. I told him I had had the plan in mind for $2\frac{1}{2}$ years, and I made it clear it was not aimed at Robertson or Haig, or anyone.'[13] Lloyd George partly adopted this idea after the Italian disaster at Caporetto; and the Supreme War Council was set up at Versailles.

Foch was its chairman and Wilson the British representative. Robertson's comment was that, without an Allied Commander-in-Chief, such a staff was illogical. Staffs, he said, 'do not of themselves command or direct anything'.

Lloyd George's criticism of Haig was levelled at him through his intelligence estimates. Robertson reported to Haig on 6 December the gist of the Cabinet discussion. Lloyd George's argument was that Haig had for long said that the Germans were well on the downgrade in morale and numbers and that he had advised attacking even if the Germans brought thirty divisions from Russia. Although they had transferred only a few, Haig was now hard put to it to hold his own. Robertson also reported and supported criticism of Charteris, Haig's Head of Intelligence.

Charteris had few friends in the Intelligence Directorate of the War Office. They thought his estimates of German strength and morale hopelessly misleading and suspected, rightly, that he had misled Haig on both aspects. Haig was not one to shelter behind a subordinate and replied to Robertson: 'I gather that the PM is dissatisfied. If that means I have lost his confidence, then in the interest of the Cause let him replace me at once. But if he still wishes me to remain, then all carping criticism should cease, and I should be both supported and trusted. Whatever happens, however, you must remain as CIGS as it would be folly to make any change at this crisis in the Head of the General Staff.'

Argument could be of little avail, however, when Northcliffe joined in the hunt against Charteris. *The Times* published a first leader on 12 December criticizing the GHQ Intelligence estimates and saying: 'Sir Douglas Haig's position cannot but depend in large measure on his choice of subordinates. His weakness is his inveterate devotion to those who have served him longest – some of them perhaps too long.'

Charteris himself then moved in the matter, and told Haig that he would rather go than be a cause of embarrassment to him. Haig discussed the matter with Kiggell, who said that Charteris did his work well at GHQ, but was disliked by corps and army staffs. The change was therefore made. Lawrence, older than Haig and an acquaintance of Staff College and Boer War days, replaced Charteris. The appointment lasted only a month because Kiggell was also a target for criticism and Lawrence replaced him as Chief of Staff on 24 January. Haig found Charteris an appointment in GHO as Deputy

Director of Transportation, for which his sapper experience fitted him. Brigadier-General Cox, Macdonogh's deputy in the War Office, replaced Lawrence. Marshall-Cornwall, who was then serving on the GHQ Intelligence Staff, has written: 'Haig's blind faith in Charteris had not been shaken, and he continued to seek the latter's advice in Intelligence matters, rather than follow Cox's wiser counsels.'[14]

After Christmas, Haig went home for a fortnight's leave. There was some welcome family relaxation, such as a visit with his children to the pantomime and a few rounds of golf, but much of his time was taken up by the Cabinet and War Office. Derby came to see him on New Year's Day and told him that Lloyd George had decided to replace Robertson but had been somewhat deterred by Derby's intention to resign if either Robertson or Haig were moved. Derby did feel, however, that Kiggell ought to go. He was a tired man and the doctors gave a poor report of his health. Haig said he wanted Butler, the deputy, to replace Kiggell, but Derby would not agree to this. Butler was not liked by the 'authorities' at home. Haig then ensured that Butler could get a corps and chose Lawrence. Haig also had a meeting with the Cabinet on manpower, which was a perpetual source of worry to him. He told the Cabinet that the coming four months would be the critical period of the war. He thought the enemy might attack both the British and the French and use their reserves to exploit wherever they were successful. He saw himself having to use up his reserves either to help the French or to take over more line from them, and it was essential his divisions should be brought up to their proper strength. Unhappily he added to this correct prognostication the unwise and unwelcome advice that the solution was a renewal of the attack in Flanders. Before his return to France, he had a convivial lunch with the Prime Minister at which Derby bet Lloyd George a hundred cigars to a hundred cigarettes that the war would be over before the next New Year's Day. Haig agreed with Derby, thinking that the end would come from internal troubles in Germany.

On his return to France, Haig broke the news personally to Kiggell that he was to go and told him of his efforts for his future appointment. He soon heard from Robertson, and also from Wilson, that the Supreme War Council had decided the British should extend their front to the south to a point to be mutually agreed near the River Oise. Haig's comment was: 'The Government now have two advisers! Will they accept the advice of the Versailles gentlemen (who have no responsibility) or will they take my advice? Wilson has arrived at his conclusion (so he writes) as the "result of a War Game" and "on mathematical calculations". The whole position would be laughable but for the seriousness of it.'

The extension of his front was no surprise to Haig. He had been in negotiation with Pétain for some months and the relief had begun on 10 January three days before the official judgment. But the extension was greater than he had envisaged. In addition to taking over from First French Army in Flanders, by adjustment a loss of six French divisions, he had to put in two corps each of three divisions between St Quentin and the Oise. This, in addition to his loss of five divisions to Italy, left the front thinly manned, especially in the south. The re-organization involved the move south of Gough's Fifth Army, leaving in Flanders only Rawlinson's Fourth Army. Haig's requirements for reinforcements were 615,000 men to bring all his units to full strength. If he could get them, he intended to create new divisions by reducing the number of infantry battalions in each from twelve to nine. Although Haig's recommendations were strongly supported by the War Office, they were rejected by the Cabinet Committee on Manpower of which not one member was a soldier. The decision was that the army could save men by making the reduction in battalions in a division, but that no new divisions could be created. As Haig's willingness to reduce the number of battalions was based on their being at full strength, he was twice-cheated; thus, he had to carry out the reduction at a time when it was already known that the enemy was preparing an attack.

On 18 January, Lloyd George had a new idea in his search for a way to remove Haig. Hankey wrote:

I lunched with Ll. George, Smuts and Reading. . . . The conversation drifted on to the subject of our army leaders and the failure of the War Office to allow any Territorial or New Army officers to reach the higher commands, a deputation of Liberal leaders having waited on the PM that very morning on the subject. Suddenly Ll. G. said to Smuts, 'I wish you would go out to the Western Front and go right round in order to find out who are the rising men, and to see the new defences they are making to meet the forthcoming German offensive.' Smuts agreed to go at once, and Ll. G. then turned to me and said, 'I think you had better go too.'[15]

Smuts and Hankey stayed the night of 21 January with Haig who gave them every facility to visit GHQ and each Army Headquarters.

If Lloyd George hoped for reasons to remove Haig, then Smuts's report after his six-day visit was not what he wanted. Smuts commented on the good morale of the army and the good work being done. The weakness, he said, was that the men were tired. Whenever units were out of the line they had to provide working parties; consequently there was no opportunity for training or for rest. He also said that the infantry was 100,000 under strength. He added: 'It is my deliberate opinion, as the result of a most careful study of the question, that if the Army is compelled at the present time to take over any further portions of the line beyond that already agreed to, and nearly completed, we shall be running serious risks. We shall be straining the Army too far. Either the defences will not be completed in time, or the essential rest will not be obtained, and the Army will not be in the state in which it ought to be able to resist an attack.'[16]

Lloyd George's own account of the Smuts visit tells us more than Hankey's. He said: 'I sent General Smuts and Sir Maurice Hankey around the front to report to the War Cabinet on the condition of affairs generally, and I confidentially asked them to look and see for themselves whether among the Generals they met, there was one whom they considered might with advantage attain and fill the first place. They came back with a very disappointing report. . . .'[17] Lloyd George cleverly conceals the direction in which he thought the report disappointing.

Although the Prime Minister failed to get rid of Haig, he did succeed in getting the War Cabinet to remove Robertson. On 9 February, Haig was summoned to London and told that Wilson was to become CIGS and that Robertson had refused the offer that he should replace Wilson on the Supreme War Council. The matter was complicated by the fact that the military representatives on the Supreme Council had, on 4 February, been constituted as the Executive War Board, giving authority to the several members to transmit executive orders to the armies of their respective countries. The Board was also to have executive control of a general reserve. Lloyd George had apparently had many ideas, one of them that Plumer should become CIGS; but Plumer had refused. Another was that Haig should become Generalissimo, in London, of all the British forces, and that he should be replaced in France by Plumer.

Haig pointed out the disadvantage of changing command in France at a time when so grave an emergency threatened.[18] Haig's view prevailed and he agreed to allow Rawlinson to replace Wilson at Versailles. Plumer came back from Italy to take over from Rawlinson and the army reverted to his old number 'Second'. Haig was not happy with the change-over which had, in effect, removed his strong supporter in London and replaced him by Wilson, whom, as he told the Prime Minister, neither he, nor the army, generally trusted. Nevertheless, after the change was made, there was never any indication that Haig worked against Wilson or that his attitude to him as the Government's chief military adviser was anything but correct, though he was not slow to express criticism when he believed wrong policies were being advised.

The build-up of the German forces on the Western Front did not escape the notice of the Allied Intelligence Staffs. The total number of divisions had risen to 172 by the end of January and five more were added during the next fortnight. By mid-March, there were 187 divisions, including 80 in reserve, most of them opposite the British Third and Fifth Army front between the Scarpe and the Oise. The total number of Allied divisions was 165. There had been various moves to create a central Allied reserve and actual arrangements had been made for such a reserve to be at the disposal of the Executive War Board. It was Robertson's bitter opposition to the idea and to the Supreme War Council and the Executive Board generally which finally caused his dismissal. Incidentally, although Haig also opposed these concepts, he had told Robertson that he ought to agree to go to Versailles in the change-over with Wilson. He said that '. . . as the British member of the Versailles Committee he was in the position of "Generalissimo", and further, that this was no time for anyone to question where his services were to be given. It was his *duty* to go to Versailles or anywhere else if the Government wished it.' But Robertson was adamant and decided to go on half-pay.

Although there was all this fuss and all the arrangements for creating the Allied Reserve were made, there was in fact no reserve. Both Haig and Pétain were so short of divisions that they steadfastly refused to loose their hold on any of them. Both preferred to rely on reciprocal arrangements.[19] They both felt that the real reserve for the Western Front was the American Army. Both hoped that the American forces would first go into battle in British and French divisions so as to gain experience. Pershing made no secret

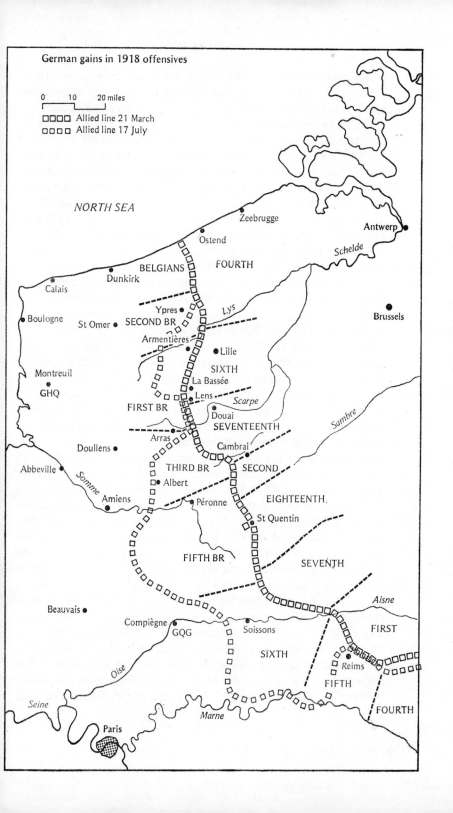

German gains in 1918 offensives

0   10   20 miles

▢▢▢▢ Allied line 21 March
▢▢▢▢ Allied line 17 July

NORTH SEA

Zeebrugge
Ostend
Antwerp
Schelde

BELGIANS    FOURTH

Dunkirk
Calais
Boulogne
St Omer
Ypres          Lys          Brussels
SECOND BR
Armentières
Lille
SIXTH
Montreuil
GHQ
La Bassée
Lens        Scarpe
FIRST BR
Douai
Arras        SEVENTEENTH
Doullens        Cambrai
Abbeville        THIRD BR      SECOND
Somme        Albert
Amiens        Péronne
EIGHTEENTH
St Quentin
Sambre
FIFTH BR
Beauvais
SEVENTH
Aisne
Compiègne        Soissons        FIRST
GQG
Oise        SIXTH
Reims
Seine        FIFTH
Marne        FOURTH
Paris

of his intention that the American Army would have its own front. He hoped to get his first four divisions in the line or in reserve soon and to have eighteen divisions in France or in transit by July.

On 16 February, Haig met his four army commanders for an intelligence briefing by Cox who emphasized the increased strength of the enemy and indicated that they must be prepared to withstand a very severe attack at any moment. The defensive arrangements and the use of reserves were discussed, and all the army commanders expressed to Haig their confidence of being able to hold their front. This is surprising in view of the qualms so often expressed by Gough about the extent of his front and state of his defences.

The Germans had not launched an important offensive since Verdun but, after Passchendaele, they determined that the winter would be spent in offensive preparations and that, freed from the Russian commitment, they would launch an offensive to win the war in the spring. Surprise and new tactical methods were essentials of their plan. Ludendorff entrusted the planning to Lieutenant-Colonel Wetzell, Head of the Operations Section, whose studies convinced him that a double attack was necessary. First, an attack at St Quentin to draw the British reserves and a fortnight later an attack at Hazebrouck to roll up the British front from the north.[20] Ludendorff did not fully accept this excellent plan because he decided he had only sufficient forces for one attack. He therefore decided to launch the attack at St Quentin about 20 March.

In the light of the knowledge that the placing of the German reserves indicated an attack south of the Scarpe, Haig's relative strength along his front is worthy of notice. In Flanders, Second Army had one division for every one and a half miles. Southward to the Scarpe, the First Army had one division for every two miles. From the Scarpe to the Cambrai battlefield, the Third Army was slightly stronger with a front of twenty-eight miles and sixteen divisions. The worst-off was the Fifth Army with only fourteen divisions to cover the forty-two miles from well north of St Quentin to south of the Oise. These figures must be looked at with the understanding that battles are not won by arithmetic and that the armies had differing scope for manœuvre without loss of vital areas. In Flanders, the enemy was already too close to the Channel ports while behind the Fifth Army the vital area was Amiens forty-five miles back from St Quentin. Moreover, the chances of taking advantage of Pétain's reciprocal deal over reserves diminished with every mile north from the inter-Allied boundary, and it was reasonable to assume that Pétain would do everything he could in the defence of Amiens. Apart from his wide front, Gough had the disadvantage that his army, after its grim fighting in Flanders, had only just taken over their positions from the French. Their forward positions had been reasonably kept up, but defences in depth had not even been marked out, let alone dug and wired.[21]

By a happy chance, Haig had to attend a meeting with the Prime Minister in London on 14 March and, on the 15th, his son, the present Earl Haig, was born. The next day Haig was summoned to Buckingham Palace where the King, the Queen and Princess Mary were warm in their congratulations and enquiries for Lady Haig. The meeting on 14 March was about the Allied Reserve, and there Haig met a staunch supporter in Clemenceau, who had succeeded Painlevé in November 1917, both as War Minister and Prime Minister. The solution of the vexed question was that the intention to form a Reserve should be adhered to and effect given to it as American troops arrived and set free British and French units. Foch, the chief exponent of the Allied Reserve, did not like the decision and Haig wrote in his diary: 'This led to a wordy altercation between Clemenceau and him, which finally ended by C. waving his hand and shouting "silence". Clemenceau then thoroughly sat on Foch!' Haig obviously enjoyed Foch's troubles with his Prime Minister more than his own.

A few days after Haig returned to France, in the early morning fog of 21 March, the German attack began. Just before five am, a terrific bombardment crashed down on the whole of Fifth Army front, and on most of the Third Army and part of the First. An hour later, at sunrise, visibility was only six yards. On the Fifth Army front, where the assault came at nine-forty am, the fog hung about until noon. The Germans made good use of the fog to further their new tactics of advancing in small groups, or storm troops, irrespective of what was happening on the flank, to overcome or find a way round and so disorganize the defence. The aim of the Germans was to destroy the southern flank of Fifth Army and so separate the British and French armies and roll up the British. They went far towards achieving their aim because Haig looked west towards Amiens and Pétain looked south-west to Paris. The reciprocal plan for use of the scant reserves soon dissolved. At first it seemed to be working. On 23 March, Pétain came to see Haig at his advanced headquarters and Haig received the impression that Pétain would do everything possible to keep the two armies together. He had put Fayolle in command of two armies on Haig's right to operate in the Somme valley. But by dawn the next morning, the Germans were across the Somme in some strength and when Pétain came to Haig at eleven pm that night, his attitude was very different. Haig asked him to concentrate as large a force as possible near Amiens, but Pétain replied that he was expecting to be attacked in Champagne at any moment and he had told Fayolle that if the enemy advanced further he was to retire south-west towards Beauvais to cover Paris. Haig wrote:

> It was at once made clear to me that the effect of this order must be to separate the French from the British right flank and to allow the enemy to penetrate between the two Armies. I at once asked Pétain if he meant to abandon my right flank. He nodded assent and added, 'It is the only thing possible, if the enemy compelled the Allies to fall back still further.' From my talk with Pétain I gathered that he had recently attended a Cabinet meeting in Paris and that his orders from his government were to *cover Paris at all costs*. On the other hand, to keep in touch with the British Army is no longer the basic principle of French strategy. In my opinion, our Army's existence in France depends on keeping the British and French Armies united.

Haig immediately telegraphed for Wilson and Milner to come to his headquarters. Haig admired Pétain for what he was, but he knew it would be a waste of time to try to dissuade him from his proposed action. Haig was slow to speak, but his mind worked quickly and he saw in a flash that the only hope in the immediate crisis was the appointment of a French commander of strategic insight and of resolution to have supreme direction of the operations in France. Foch seemed to him obviously the man.

Wilson lost no time. Summoned at three am on 25 March, he was with Haig at eleven am the same day. There was some difficulty in informing Milner, who was already in France, and Haig also failed to get Clemenceau for a meeting on that day. Only Weygand, Foch's staff officer, came and Haig gave him a note for Clemenceau telling him that, in order to avert disaster, it was essential for the French to concentrate as large a force as possible near Amiens. It was the next day before everyone, including Poincaré, the President, Foch and Pétain could be collected at Doullens. It soon became apparent that Pétain had somehow gained the wrong impression that the British Army meant to retire north because Clemenceau said he had been told that Haig intended to give up Amiens. Perhaps Haig's brief note sent by Weygand had strengthened that idea, but how such a misconception had arisen in the first place has never been explained. However, Pétain soon forfeited Clemenceau's confidence by saying, 'The Germans will beat the English in the open field, after which they will beat us too.'[22] Clemenceau, who could not tolerate talk of defeat, now saw that Foch, whom he had never liked but who would never say such a thing, was his man. Clemenceau proposed that Foch should be appointed to co-ordinate the operations of an Allied force to cover Amiens and ensure that the British and French armies were not separated. Haig's comment was:

> The proposal seemed to me quite worthless, as Foch would be in a subordinate position to Pétain and myself. In my opinion it was essential to success that Foch should control Pétain, so I at once recommended that Foch should *co-ordinate the action of all the Allied armies on the Western Front*. Both Governments agreed to this. . . . Foch seemed sound and sensible but Pétain had a terrible look. He had the appearance of a commander who has lost his nerve.

When Clemenceau congratulated him on his appointment as Generalissimo, Foch said 'A fine gift, you give me a lost battle and ask me to win it.'[23]

If it should be asked why Haig, who had so mistrusted the arrangement with Nivelle and who had refused to contribute a single division to the Allied reserve to be controlled by the Supreme War Council, was yet the promoter of Foch's appointment, the answer is not hard to find. On the first issue, the situation was far different. Nivelle remained Commander-in-Chief of the French Army when the British Army was subordinated to him. In this case Foch controlled Haig and Pétain as respective Commanders-in-Chief. On the question of the reserve, the answer is best given in Haig's own words, 'I can deal with a man, but not with a committee.'[24]

As may be imagined, Haig, in addition to his comings and goings on the command question, was in constant touch with his army commanders. At first he seemed most concerned about Byng's Third Army but, on 22 March, he visited Gough. Gough told him

that his casualty rate was exceeding by far the inflow of reinforcements, but that his army would go on fighting so long as there were
men to do so.[25] Haig's reply was non-committal, but the next day
he was surprised to find how far back Fifth Army had gone. Haig
then got in touch with Plumer and asked him to start thinning out
with a view to sending divisions down to the Somme. He remarked,
'It is most satisfactory to have a commander of Plumer's temperament at a time of crisis like this.' Haig brought all his army commanders, except Gough, to report to him at Doullens before the
Allied conference. He explained to them the areas in which he could
not afford to give ground if the French were to have time to concentrate near Amiens.

After the Allied conference, Milner and Wilson asked Haig about
Gough, who had been in bad odour with the politicians since
Passchendaele. In answer Haig said, '. . . whatever the opinion at
home might be and no matter what Foch might have said, I considered that he (Gough) had dealt with a most difficult situation very
well. He had never lost his head, was always cheery and fought hard.
Gough had told me at Doullens that Foch had spoken most im-
pertinently to him regarding the leadership of the Fifth British Army.'
Wilson's entry in his diary for the same day, 26 March, gives a
rather different account: 'Then I discussed removal of Gough, and
told Haig he could have Rawly, and Rawly's old Fourth Army
staff from Versailles, to replace Gough.' Wilson's record is supported
by the fact that on the next day, Haig's Military Secretary arrived at
Gough's headquarters to tell him that Rawlinson would supersede
him and would arrive on the following afternoon. Possibly Haig had
only a temporary relief in mind because he knew Gough and his
staff required rest. Certainly this was before the order for Gough's
dismissal came from the Government; when it did come, not until
4 April, Haig recommended to the War Cabinet that Cavan should
be brought back from Italy to replace Gough. In the meantime,
Haig had given Gough and his staff the task of making a defence
scheme for the Somme valley from Amiens to the sea, in case the
worst happened and the Germans separated the British from the
French.

On 3 April, Haig met Lloyd George at Beauvais where a conference
assembled to tie up details of the Doullens agreement and to apply
it to the American forces; Lloyd George told Haig that Gough must
go and the formal notification was sent by Derby next day. Haig

said, 'The PM looked as if he had been thoroughly frightened, and he seemed still in a funk. . . . Ll. G. is a fatiguing companion in a motor. He talks and argues so! And he appears to me to be a thorough imposter.' The Prime Minister and the CIGS returned to London the same night and Wilson's diary gives an illuminating account of the War Cabinet meeting on 4 April:

> Suddenly Smuts chimed in and said Haig has proved his complete unfitness for C-in-C. Then wild discussion about Plumer, Cavan, Robertson, Harington, Du Cane, Foch etc. There was no doubt the feeling of the Cabinet was, I think, unanimously against Haig, i.e. the whole of GHQ. No question that all *confidence* is lost. I said very little.

What little Wilson did say was against removing Haig. He said the Government would not find anyone to fight a defensive battle better than Haig, and the time to remove him was after the German attack was over.

In the first week of April, the German momentum against the Fifth (now renumbered Fourth) and Third Armies began to die down. The very merit of the German plan had been to exploit success wherever it was found, but the policy was carried too far and Ludendorff played into the hands of the Allies by pushing on southwestward rather than directing his efforts against Amiens. Despite the diminishing danger on the Somme, the Germans still had large forces there, and when intelligence reports showed them to be massing reserves opposite First Army, Haig was hard put to it to dribble back divisions, exhausted by battle, to form reserves further north. Ludendorff had, in fact, decided to switch to the attack on Hazebrouk, contemplated by Wetzell as part of the original onslaught. On 9 April, again in fog, the attack came. The blow fell on three weak Portuguese brigades, already earmarked for relief the next day. The Germans went right through to the River Lys and overran the British division to the north from flank and rear. Cyclists and cavalry and a division just arrived from the Somme were rushed up to close the gap. With the front not much more than fifty miles from Calais, the situation was grave and, on the 11th, Haig issued his famous 'Backs to the Wall' order of which the text, which was written in his own hand, is given in Appendix 2.

Haig had at first seemed very pleased with Foch's handling of his position as Generalissimo, but, as the battle moved northward, his attitude changed. Foch came to him on the day of the Lys breach and Haig records:

*Foch declined to take over any part of the British line*, but is determined to place a reserve of four French Divisions with their heads on the Somme immediately west of Amiens. In case of necessity he proposed to march them NE to take a share in what he calls the 'bataille d'Arras'. I pointed out the very great inconvenience caused by the insertion of these troops into the area of the Fourth Army. . . . It is also a sad fact that there are very few French Divisions with good enough morale to face the Germans in a stand-up fight.

I found Foch most selfish and obstinate.

This was most unjust. Although Haig's view of the disadvantage of sandwiching British and French troops was sound, so was Foch's refusal to relieve divisions in battle. Haig wanted Foch to relieve British troops on the left flank, next the Belgians, or on his right at the inter-Allied boundary. This would have been excellent, given time, but it was hardly an emergency measure for releasing British divisions.

Again on 14 April he records his talk with Foch: 'I explained the *urgent need* for the French to take a more active share in the battle, because, owing to very severe losses, the British Divisions are fast disappearing and our men are very tired. Foch spoke a lot of nonsense, that as we are in the battle, there must be no divisions withdrawn for rest. In support of his views he recalled to mind what the British did at Ypres in October and November 1914.'

The British Official History pays tribute to Foch's handling of his powers in the difficult days of April:

Professing the strongest belief, which was not unjustified, in the tenacity of the British troops against any odds . . . Foch in April declined to direct General Pétain to take over more of the line. He kept his main reserves near the junction of the Allied Armies and sent up reinforcements in driblets, divisions singly or in pairs, replacing those engaged by moving up others from the rear. His action in refusing to do more was justified by results, and this limitation of assistance to the absolute minimum may well be claimed as proof of the highest military judgment in relation to the Allied cause as a whole: he kept his head and declined to send his none too plentiful reserves in response to every call from General Pétain as well as from Sir Douglas Haig. But his decision cost the British Army heavy casualties, and was at the time the cause of overwhelming anxiety at GHQ.[26]

By the end of April, the Lys front was stabilized. Ludendorff was determined to make another effort in Flanders because, like Haig, he realized this was the vulnerable front; in order to facilitate the attack, he decided to draw off the reserves by an attack against the French in Champagne. He made two determined attacks. The first on 27 May made considerable progress across the Chemin des Dames, the second launched on 15 July gave Foch the opportunity for his counter-stroke on the Marne which marked the beginning of the end for Germany. The onslaught against the French gave Haig and Pétain the opportunity to change rôles; it was now Pétain's turn to call on Foch to order down British reserves. Haig protested to Foch, but he sent the reserves. A British corps of five divisions was involved in the Chemin des Dames disaster because Haig had agreed somewhat unwillingly to send tired divisions to replace fresh French divisions in quiet sectors; the fresh divisions going to Foch's reserve to help Haig. As soon as the British IX Corps arrived in its quiet sector, all hell was let loose. At one time Haig was down to his last division in reserve, but when the time came for Foch's counter-stroke on the Marne another British corps (XXII) of four divisions participated.

There was for a time a real battle of wills between Haig and Foch. Haig believed reserves were only being drawn away from Flanders to facilitate the next German stroke there. Foch was not persuaded. Yet, though there were such disagreements, the two men learned to know each other and the trust in the stubborn Haig which grew in Foch's mind was of inestimable value when the time came for the Allies to turn to the offensive.

Haig had not expected as much from the Second Battle of the Marne as Foch had achieved, but since mid-May he had been discussing with Rawlinson the return to the offensive. Many British and French soldiers and politicians believed the Allies should remain on the defensive for the remainder of 1918 and, with the participation of a large American army, deliver the final blow in 1919. Haig was not at all of this opinion. He believed the Germans would be unable to hold another major offensive. It must be confessed he had thought the same in 1916 and 1917, but this time he was right. Twenty-five United States divisions had landed in France by July 1918, but Haig was not relying on the United States. In May he had considered Pershing 'stupid and obstinate' and said: 'He hankers after a *"Great self-contained American Army"* but seeing that he has neither Commanders of Divisions, of Corps, nor of Armies, nor Staffs for same, it is ridiculous to think such an army could function unaided in less than two years' time.' Haig thought the Americans would do better to train their units integrated in British and French divisions – at that time, the Americans had only four divisions completely equipped – but seven days after the German offensive on 21 March Pershing had placed all his manpower resources in France at Foch's disposal and some divisions had fought well, interspersed in the French line in Pétain's defensive battle on the Aisne.

On 16 July, refreshed by a week's leave in London, Haig saw Rawlinson and told him that he had given orders to First and Third Armies for attacks which he hoped would draw away reserves. The main attack was to be made by Rawlinson with three corps, one Australian, one Canadian and one British. Foch had suggested attacks on Armentières, but had been persuaded by Haig's plan. He then agreed to give Haig command of Debeney's First Army to take part in the battle. The attack went in at Amiens on 8 August and was a brilliant success. It will be seen from the next chapter that the tactics and technique were far superior to anything Haig's armies had achieved so far. Ludendorff described 8 August as the black day of the German Army and the greatest defeat which the German Army had suffered since the beginning of the war.[27]

Despite the initial success, the Battle of Amiens did not lead to a strategic break-through and, after four days of fighting, the Germans had recovered. There was then some disagreement between Haig and Foch. Foch wanted the attack pressed but Haig had learned his lesson from Ypres. At Amiens, success had come through surprise and he did not want to attack the enemy where he expected it. On 14 August he wrote:

Foch had pressed me to attack the positions held by the enemy on the front Chaulnes–Roye. I declined to do so because they could only be taken after heavy casualties in men and tanks. I had ordered the French First and British Fourth Armies to postpone their attacks, but to keep up pressure on that front so as to make the enemy expect an attack on this front, while I transferred my reserves to my Third Army and also prepared to attack with the First Army. . . .

I spoke to Foch quite straightly and let him understand *that I was responsible to my government for the handling of the British Forces.*

Haig had his way and a surprise attack by the Third and First Armies extended the advance northwards so that, with the Fourth Army taking advantage, the enemy was cleared up to the Hindenburg Line. The French, too, had some success in the Soisson area and, in the north, the Second Army and the reconstituted Fifth had cleared the enemy back to the front from which he had started the Lys offensive.

Haig had already, on 22 August, sent to all army commanders a telegram drawing attention to the changed conditions of the battle and asking them to bring to the attention of all commanders 'the necessity for all ranks to act with the utmost boldness and resolution in order to get full advantage from the present favourable situation.' Three days later Foch sent a letter in similar terms to Haig, suggesting the progressive widening of the offensive. This drew from Haig a suggestion that things were going well on his front but more might be achieved by converging thrusts against Mézières from the south, St Quentin and Cambrai. He would look after the attack from Cambrai, but the French and the Americans might attack in the same direction.[28] Contrary thoughts came from London and Haig received a secret and personal message from the CIGS warning him not to incur heavy losses in an attack on the Hindenburg Line. Haig was disgusted, not only by the content of the message, but that it was not sent as an official one. He wrote:

It is impossible for a CIGS to send a telegram of this nature to a C-in-C in the field as a 'personal' one. The Cabinet are ready to meddle and interfere in my plans in an underhand way, but do not dare openly to say that they mean [not] to take responsibility for any failure though ready to take credit for every success! . . . How ignorant our present Statesmen are of the principles of war. In my opinion it is much less costly in lives to keep on pressing the enemy after several victorious battles than to give him time to recover and organize a fresh line of defence.

Haig's exchanges with Foch and his exasperation with the Cabinet stem from the same thoughts. He believed that the time had come for concentrated converging attacks on the Germans. The breaching of the Hindenburg Line towards Cambrai and on in the direction of Mézières was to be his share and the French and Americans should drive in the same direction from Champagne. The rôle of the American forces was crucial. They now had, ready for operations, two divisions with the British, five with the French and fourteen with their newly-constituted First Army prepared for an independent operation against the St Mihiel salient (east of Verdun) with exploitation towards Metz. All their divisions were about double the strength of the British and French. Haig had now persuaded Foch that the war could be ended in 1918 and Foch modified the St Mihiel operation although he did not, as Haig hoped he would, cancel it so that the preliminaries for a Franco–American attack could begin at once. The St Mihiel attack was successful and did much to inspire confidence in Pershing and the American Army. Foch was now thoroughly of the same mind as Haig and his cry was '*tout le monde à la bataille*'.

Haig's great attack against the Hindenburg Line and its extension north along the Canal du Nord and the Flanders position began on 29 September. The main attack was made by Fourth Army on the 29th and, in addition to three of his remaining armies, he again had the First French Army on his right. The Second Army, a Belgian and a French Army to the north operated under the King of the Belgians. Altogether, Haig had forty-four British and fourteen French divisions on his centre front from Lens to La Fere, and King Albert had ten British, six French and twelve Belgian divisions on his left from the sea to Lens. Further south, Pétain was attacking from Champagne with fifteen American and twenty-two French divisions.

The Germans fought bravely in heavily-defended positions but they were no longer in a condition to withstand the formidable attacks from Verdun to the sea. The Fourth Army and part of the Third, attacking the Hindenburg Line, took the advanced position and half the main position on the first day. This time there was no countering of early successes and, by 4 October, the whole of the Hindenberg Line was overrun. By 17 October, the First Army, in which two United States divisions played an active part, captured Le Cateau. In Flanders, the weather was almost as bad as in 1917, but Second Army avenged old scores by capturing the whole of the Ypres Ridge in their initial attack.

The last three months of the war saw the culmination of Haig's plans and the fulfilment of his hopes. By the end of September, Hindenburg knew that the war was lost and, on 11 November, the Armistice came. On 19 October Haig had, with the CIGS, attended a meeting of Lloyd George, Milner and Bonar Law to put forward their military views on the Armistice terms. Wilson wanted to demand that the Germans should lay down their arms and retire to the east bank of the Rhine. Haig said that he did not believe the Germans would accept unconditional surrender and asked: If the enemy 'refuses to agree to our terms, can the Allies continue to press the enemy sufficiently vigorously during the coming winter months to cause him to withdraw so quickly that he cannot destroy the railways, roads etc?' Haig thought the answer was No! He therefore believed that the essential terms were the immediate evacuation of occupied Belgian and French territory and of Alsace Lorraine, and Allied occupation of Metz and Strasbourg.

In his attitude Haig was less optimistic than Foch, who had already given him his paper on the terms he suggested, which were very similar to those actually imposed.[29] These allowed the German Army to withdraw with its personal arms to the east bank of the Rhine and the Allied occupation of the Rhineland was to include bridgeheads over the river. Haig told the Prime Minister: 'The British Army had done most of the fighting latterly, and everybody wants to have done with the war, provided we get what we want. I therefore advise that we only ask in the armistice for what we intend to hold, and that we set our face against the French entering Germany to pay off old scores.'

# 10

# A TACTICAL STUDY

The narrative of the course of the war will have shown that Haig had a sure sense of strategy: he knew where a blow would hurt and where the enemy must stand and resist; and in defence he knew where he must manœuvre and where he must stand to the end. He well understood the importance of surprising the enemy, although it cannot be claimed that, in a war where there was little scope, he had a flair for doing the unexpected. It may then be asked why victory came to him with such difficulty and at so great a cost, and why he never seemed to know when to break off his battles. In the first place it may be explained that war is a two-sided game. If two opposing commanders both handle their evenly-matched resources well, who will win the battle? In the second, but only as a part answer, it is certain that history is full of examples of battles lost because they were not pressed at the moment of imminent victory. And let it be remembered that the Germans have shown themselves in many wars to be the most professional and competent of soldiers.

Yet it must be confessed that Haig's lack of one characteristic must forfeit for him a place among the great Captains of History. He was not, as were Marlborough and Wellington, a master of the weapons and tactics of his day. As has been pointed out in the first chapter, the problem which faced commanders on the Western Front was more difficult than that faced by any commander before or since. Allenby's career illustrates this clearly. How brilliant was his performance when he had the wide open spaces of Palestine and Syria for his manœuvres. But he was not noticeably successful on his

Western Front. We must admit also that Haig did – at the end – solve the tactical problem. The Battle of Amiens is a model which has not been improved upon in a conflict on a restricted front between evenly-matched forces. It compares with El Alamein, with the Battle for Rome and with the Rhineland Battle of the Second World War. And so we must ask ourselves why it was that it took Haig so long and so many bloody battles before he arrived at the tactics which were used with such success in the Battle of Amiens on 8 August 1918.

In making comparison with Marlborough and Wellington and with Montgomery and Slim, the extent of the battlefield and the size of the forces must be remembered. Marlborough and Wellington could usually survey the whole battlefield; Montgomery and Slim had a more manageable front than a single one of Haig's armies. They had, in addition, the advantage of immediate radio speech with their subordinates. Haig could not be expected, therefore, to control closely the tactics with which his battles were fought. What he should have done, and in 1918 did do, was to ensure a continuous and objective study of the tactical problem. It was necessary to have a working section of GHQ seeking a technique which would take in all the weapons in the armoury, and every new device and invention and method of communication. Haig was himself a thoughtful soldier and his interest in tactics in his early days and in the wars in the Sudan and South Africa has already been shown. He had under him many thoughtful and ingenious soldiers. Among the higher commanders, Rawlinson, Plumer, Monash, Maxse and Jacob may be mentioned. There were many good gunners and sappers, without whom the very different techniques used at Messines and Amiens would not have been possible. And for the newer weapons there was Trenchard in the Royal Flying Corps whilst Elles and Fuller could speak for the tanks.

These men and others were constantly searching for a solution and trying new ideas. But their efforts were not sufficiently co-ordinated and were certainly not reflected in the spate of instructions which poured out from GHQ. The Germans had no better brains, yet, because of their objective staff studies, they were always tactically one step ahead. Owing to their war on two fronts, their studies were at first concerned with the defensive, but, by the time they were able to concentrate on the Western Front, they were ready with the tactics which they used with such success in March 1918.

It cannot be said that Haig was reluctant to adopt new tactical ideas or accept new weapons. He had always been interested in the military employment of aircraft and he made great use of Trenchard and his ideas. When the Germans used gas for the first time, Haig saw at once that they had failed to take advantage of the surprise they had gained. He was also quick to use this new weapon in his own plans. Some may say that Haig failed to avoid the same mistake with the tank as the Germans made with gas and it is true that tanks, when first used on the Somme, were not effective, but this was certainly not because Haig had belittled the idea.

On Christmas Day 1915, soon after he became C-in-C, Haig read a paper by Winston Churchill, who had just had his first experience of trench warfare with the Grenadier Guards. Churchill felt himself to be the bearer of one good gift, 'the conception of a battle and of a victory', and he had seen fit to write a paper for French suggesting the use of 'caterpillars' for wire cutting. He had already experimented with the idea in the Admiralty and knew that such a vehicle was being produced. Some of his ideas, for instance that these caterpillars should only be used at night, were impracticable, but Haig caught the idea. He had not previously heard of these caterpillar tractors, and he immediately sent one of his staff officers (Major Elles, later to become the commander of the Tank Corps) to Churchill to learn more. For reasons of secrecy, Churchill would say no more, so Elles went to the War Office and was told of the state of development.[1] On 14 April 1916, when he was making his plans for the Somme, Haig went to the War Office and saw Colonel Swinton. Even more than Churchill, Swinton has a claim to be the father of the tank and he was the moving spirit in its development and production. Haig was told that one hundred and fifty tanks would be ready by 31 July, but he said he must have fifty by 1 June. Swinton said he would do all he could to produce them. Haig's instructions to Swinton show that he understood the tactical problem involved in the use for the first time of this new weapon. Swinton was 'to practise and train tanks and crews over obstacles and wire similar to the ground over which the forthcoming attack was to be made'. Haig '. . . gave him a trench map as a guide and impressed upon him the necessity for thinking over the system of leadership and control of a group of tanks with a view to manœuvring into a position of readiness and during an action'.

There is no doubt that Haig underestimated the time necessary for mechanical training and the tactical training which he saw to be necessary. He could hardly be blamed for that on the mechanical side. A fortnight later Swinton wrote to GHQ, saying that no tanks could be sent until 1 August and that, by then, he hoped seventy-five crews would be trained. Haig had lost, through no fault of his own, the opportunity to launch fifty tanks in his opening offensive. It is possible they might have had an important effect. The question is whether it would then have been better, as Swinton and others advised, to leave the tanks to prepare for a specially-mounted action next spring. By New Year's Day, there would be not 150 but 350 tanks. However, Haig was not the man to leave until next year what what he thought he could accomplish this. On 28 July, he still thought there was hope that, by a renewal of his offensive, he might force the enemy out of his position before winter. The use of even a small number of tanks might just turn the scale.

Rawlinson was given the task of commanding the renewal of the attack. He wrote in his diary, 'The chief is anxious to have a gamble with all available troops about September 15, with the object of breaking down the German resistance and getting through to Bapaume. We shall have no reserves in hand, save tired troops, but success at this time . . . might bring the Bosche to terms.'[2] He was given fifty tanks, which he shared out among three corps, and behind him, he had Gough's army including the five cavalry divisions and six tanks for contingencies. As Liddell Hart wrote, 'The offensive that was to have broken through the German front resulted in a maximum penetration of little more than a mile. . . . The trickle of tanks made only a slight contribution to the day's success such as it was.'[3] It was certainly not a break-through.

Tanks were used again at Arras and Ypres in 1917 before their first brilliant success at Cambrai. Their early performance won them many detractors but Haig, although he had not the vision to see their full potentiality, never lost faith in their use in battle as an adjunct to infantry and artillery. Here it may be said that it is only when used properly in conjunction with artillery and infantry that tanks have ever been effective against a determined enemy. It is significant, too, that the Germans did not themselves develop an effective tank force in the Great War: their immediate reaction when the British used them was to study the use of guns to destroy them. This defence was successful up to, and including, Cambrai and it was only when suitable tactics using tanks, infantry and artillery in concert were evolved that tanks could play their full part. It is doubtful if the evolution of the successful attack, such as was seen at

Amiens, would have been possible without that experience in battle which paved the way to improvement in design and tactics. Rawlinson and Monash, commander of the Australian Corps, were both converts who, after doubts about their value, gave their keen minds to the problem of fitting the tanks into the pattern of battle. The only criticism that can be levelled at Haig over the use of tanks is that he did not guide thought into a more direct study of the tactical problem. Had he done so he might have achieved in August 1917 what he did in August 1918. But this is pure conjecture.

Haig's approach to the problem of battle seems to have been based on three pre-conceived ideas. The first two were part of the classic military tradition: that if infantry, in sufficient strength and sufficiently supported, press the attack with determination they will make a break and, through that gap or round an exposed flank, the cavalry will pass to complete the victory. The third was that, given enough artillery and ammunition, the infantry can be provided with the necessary support. This may be an undue simplification, but it does serve to illustrate Haig's outlook up to the end of 1917. The first two tenets were accepted too easily. With infantry, he did not appreciate that infantry advancing in extended line or waves, a formation learned in the South African War, put them at the mercy of machine guns in enfilade even in smoke and darkness. He *did* realize that cavalry could only be effective in open warfare, but he was never able, not even in 1918, to bridge the gap between the fight through areas defended in depth and the pursuit. Moreover, he did not appear to give weight to the lesson he ought to have learned from the South African War, that cavalry was only useful when employed as mounted infantry; that is to use the horse only for the purpose of movement and to fight on foot just as infantry.

Haig was an early believer in the machine gun and, as DSD, he had pressed for more of them for the expeditionary force. Both as Army Commander and as C-in-C, he sought to destroy the enemy machine guns and the entrenched defences with artillery fire. His belief that he could do so was reinforced by his near success at Neuve Chapelle and his comparative failure at Aubers Ridge and Festubert – it seemed to him, and to others, that if only he had had enough ammunition he would have got through. At Loos again he had insufficient artillery ammunition but, although he saw that this was not the chief reason for failure, be could justly blame French for withholding the reserves. But Haig did not realize the true reasons for failure. There were two. First, it was a matter of communications, the inability of the commander to gauge the moment to pass through his reserves and the difficulty of placing those reserves where they could be used when wanted. Secondly, it was the unsuitability of the infantry tactics and the failure to use such formations as would minimize the effect of enemy fire. There was also a subsidiary fault – the art of getting machine guns into action effectively to hold off the immediate counter-attack was never mastered. This was one of the main causes of the loss of so much ground gained at Cambrai. It is a sad fact that, although the British had as many machine guns as the Germans, they did not use them nearly so effectively.

When Haig became c-in-c, ammunition was more plentiful and he sought to send the infantry to victory chiefly by the effectiveness of his artillery. It is true that Haig asked for more time for training. It is often forgotten how, in war, training must be continuous and progressive, especially for British infantry which finds it difficult to take its training seriously. And in war there is little time left after duty in the line, working parties and essential rest. One of Haig's subordinates, Maxse, whom he knew well from Aldershot and I Corps days, was an excellent trainer of troops: the division he commanded and the corps in which he served scored almost the only success on the first day of the Somme. Plumer, far away up in Flanders, sent him a special message to ask about his training methods. There is no evidence that Haig remarked on them until June 1918 when he set him up in the new appointment of Inspector-General of Training with a team of officers to visit each division in turn. This showed Haig's foresight in envisaging the mobile operations that were to come, but it also emphasizes the fact that training in the difficult art of trench warfare had been neglected, except for the technicalities of bayonet fighting, bombing and raids.

So far as the artillery was concerned, there was no neglect of the study of new methods. Haig had a whole regiment of expert professionals working on the problem. The technique of preparatory bombardment, creeping barrage, counter-battery fire and counter-preparation (action against enemy artillery and reserves) was worked out and perfected down to the last detail. Two difficulties were not easily overcome: first, that surprise was easily forfeited by indications received from artillery fire, and, second, that prolonged artillery fire could create worse obstacles than those it destroyed – for instance, in wet weather, it churned up impossible quagmires. The second difficulty was never completely overcome and indeed reappeared in North West Europe in 1944 and 1945. But by progressive inventions and devices, such as sound ranging and flash spotting, it became possible to prepare a complete artillery programme for delivery at zero hour without previous indications. The necessary counterpart to this was the use of the tank as wire-crusher and obstacle-destroyer. Surprise was again possible, as was shown at Cambrai.

The picture was not complete at Cambrai because the infantry was not sufficiently trained to take advantage of tank action and because the German use of field guns against tanks had not been efficiently countered. But the lessons of Cambrai and of the German offensives in the spring of 1918 were learned, and enquiring minds were turned to the problem of training. Rawlinson and Monash were resourceful in ideas for infantry co-operation with tanks and, at divisional and regimental level, Australians and Canadians as well as other British initiators used their ingenuity in improving and perfecting the drills on which Elles and Fuller had long worked. Maxse's team was visiting divisions and teaching them that there was something better than the extended line in which they had advanced to their death. Monash devised new methods of forming up his troops before battle so that reserves were fresh and close at hand to take their opportunities, and he made improvements in the process known as the leapfrogging of divisions.[4]

All these changes showed their value on 8 August 1918 and in subsequent battles. But it must not be imagined that mobile warfare, even to the extent of that of 1914, or of Palestine in 1917 and 1918, was restored to the battlefield, for it was not easy to get a huge army used to fighting under almost static conditions out of the ingrained habits of three years of trench warfare. The Germans were again the masters of minor tactics. Their use of scattered machine guns and prepared artillery concentrations in their rearguard actions prevented the appearance of any romantic picture of war with cavalry flashing their swords and infantry at the double. Nevertheless, from August to November 1918, Haig's army advanced to victory in a series of well planned and competently-executed battles.[5]

Haig must be given the credit for seeing, even before Foch's counter-attack at the second Battle of the Marne, that his army would be the weapon for the achievement of victory in 1918 and that its methods must be adapted to the changed conditions. He saw to it that these new methods were devised and used. He can be praised also for his conduct of battles from Mons up to and including Neuve Chapelle. His tactical outlook then was probably ahead of that of his enemy and of his Allies. But after that the Germans learned more quickly and Haig stood on pre-conceived ideas. He had every excuse for doing so up to the Battle of the Somme, because shortage of ammunition had cloaked the real lessons and he was hurried, against his will, by Joffre into an offensive with a largely untrained army. Arras was nearly a success and here he had the excuse, as at Loos, that his reserve had been withheld from him, this time to take over part of the French line. What is not so easy to forgive is that, after the experiences of the Somme, he repeated almost the same methods at Ypres. The army was better trained at Ypres than on the Somme and this showed in the result on the first day; but it was trained in methods which had been shown to be fruitless except in breaking the forward defences.

The same methods with the same lack of success had been used by the French in several offensives and also by the Germans at Verdun. The state of the French Army demanded a British offensive in 1917. Even though Pétain had not directly asked for it and would have been satisfied with a series of limited offensives like Messines, Haig knew better and realized that the situation required the complete absorption of the German Army. This, the Third Battle of Ypres did. It is easy to rewrite history with hindsight, but it may not be out of place to suggest that the engagement of the Germans could have been achieved by Messines and possibly a second limited attack under Plumer with an extensive simulated concentration in Flanders. At the same time, training might have gone on for a large-scale operation further south on the lines of Cambrai, to be delivered, say, in mid-August. Such an attack might have had far-reaching results. On the contrary, it might have been only another Arras, but it must surely have achieved as much as Passchendaele and at lesser cost.

# 11

# MORALE, LEADERSHIP
# AND CHARACTER

In writing of Haig and morale, two quite separate aspects must be discussed. There is first his own spiritual outlook and his inner reaction to disaster, disappointment, criticism and success. The other is the extent to which he fostered the morale of his army, whether he inspired those who served under him and whether he cared, and they knew that he cared, for the burden that he necessarily laid upon them.

Of one thing there is no doubt: his will to win and his belief that, if everyone showed the same determination as himself, his army would succeed. He was always a man of faith. His mother had brought him up in the fear of the Lord in the true Presbyterian manner, mellowed in the gentle light of family love. As a young man, he had not shown himself to be outwardly religious except in so far as he had a strongly-developed sense of duty. It was as he advanced in rank that he seemed to feel the sense of destiny – this is apparent in his letters to his sister Henrietta and to his nephew Oliver. His commitment to service for the Empire in the struggle which he saw as imminent was even more pointed in his letters to Kiggell and to Philip Howell.

It is probable that his marriage deepened his spiritual outlook and his sense of destiny. What is certain is his complete commitment to his marriage, a fidelity which lasted his whole life yet offered no competition to his military vocation. After his marriage we learn a little more about his inner feelings, because his letters to his wife sometimes tell us what his reticent nature prevented him from revealing to anyone else. The Reverend George Duncan, a minister of the Church of Scotland, was his chaplain throughout his time as Commander-in-Chief and Haig made him also his friend. Every Sunday when he was at GHQ, Haig attended his services and almost invariably made a comment on the sermon in his diary. Duncan did not know this until he read the diaries after the war. Another thing that Duncan did not know at first was that Haig did not allow the staff officers who accompanied him to mention the war as they walked to church or talked to him afterwards. Yet Duncan says that he could count on the fingers of one hand the times when he talked to him of his own religion.[1]

It may be presumptuous to discuss the spiritual outlook of another, but the comparison between Haig and Montgomery seems apposite. There is no doubt, at any rate outwardly, that Montgomery's was the Old Testament God; the Lord God of Hosts Mighty in Battle called upon to give his army the victory. Haig was well versed in the Old Testament, from which he drew much spiritual strength, but in his public utterances, spoken or written, he never called upon God. Not even in his 'Backs to the Wall' message did he invoke his name as an ally in the cause in which he so devoutly believed. The faith was there and he would wish men to know it. It was expressed not by invocation but by his calm bearing, his clear instructions and his actions. Only occasionally did he put his faith into words. In a letter to his wife, in answer to her counsel that he should ask God's help in the imminent Somme offensive, he said:

> Now you must know that every step in my plan has been taken with the Divine help – and I ask daily for aid, not merely in making the plan, but in carrying it out, and this I hope I shall continue to do until the end of all things which concern me on earth. I think it is this Divine help which gives me the tranquillity of mind and enables me to carry on without feeling the strain of responsibility to be too excessive. I try to do no more than 'do my best and trust in God', because of the reasons I give above. Very many thanks for telling me your views of this side of my work, because it has given me the chance of putting my ideas on paper. For otherwise I would not have written them, as you know I don't talk much on religious subjects.

Another occasion was the Sunday three days after the Germans had struck in March 1918. It was the day on which Haig had seen

Pétain and realized the need to call in Foch. Before he had gone on to his advanced headquarters, he had gone to church. Duncan met him and, breaking the usual rule, he 'haltingly expressed the hope that things were not too bad'. Haig replied tersely that they would never be too bad. After a few more words from Duncan, accepting what he took to be almost a rebuke, Haig relaxed and said: 'This is what you once read to us from Second Chronicles: "Be not afraid nor dismayed by reason of this great multitude, for the battle is not yours, but God's".' He then went into the church without another word.[2] A few months later, when the Lys battle was at its height, Haig, who was away from GHQ at the scene of the fighting, wrote to Duncan: 'I know I am sustained in my efforts by the Great Unseen Power, otherwise I could not be standing the strain as I am doing.'[3]

Enough has been said of Haig's strength in adversity but what of his magnanimity in victory and success? His sense that he had a part to play prevented any false modesty. His was always a stand for the army and never for himself, as can be seen from what has been written about his relations with French and Nivelle. He did once or twice let himself go about French in intimate letters to his wife but, despite ample opportunity, there was no political intrigue. It was not until the publication of his diaries after his death that anything was known of the views he expressed, correctly and in answer to their initiative, to the King, the Secretary of State for War and the CIGS. And in the final victory in the war there can be no doubt of his humility. It was, to him, the victory of the British Army and not of himself. Foch, who as much as anyone knew the part he played in the victory, summed up the man when he said to Lady Haig after Haig's funeral: '*Il etait très droit, très sûr et très gentil.*'

Something will be said in the next chapter about Haig's critics. In the face of criticism, Haig was sometimes internally impatient, though he did not show it externally. His distrust of politicians was common to most soldiers of his generation, perhaps of all generations. The craft of the politician is so different from that of the soldier. Within reason, the soldier has only to give his order and all jump to obey him. The politician has to persuade his people that what he tells them to do is what they want to do. The soldier has to look only to his enemy. The politician has only to decide on a course of action for his friends secretly and his opponents openly to tell him he ought to decide differently. Haig did not quite understand how that could be in war-time, but he did understand perfectly that the soldier is the servant of the Government. In moments of bitter controversy, he never threatened resignation or public statement. The most he ever did was to say that, if the Government had lost confidence in him, he would give up his command and serve wherever they thought fit.

His attitude is best shown by his reaction to the Maurice controversy. Major-General Maurice, the Director of Military Operations in the War Office, had written to *The Times* to expose the juggling with figures by which Lloyd George and the Government had sought to cloak the shameful way in which they had starved Haig of men in early 1918. Because of his letter to the press, Maurice was made to resign and thus end a most valuable military career. Although Haig expressed regret for Maurice personally, he wrote in his diary: 'Reuter states Maurice has written to the papers. This is a grave mistake. No one can be both a soldier and a politician at the same time. We soldiers have to do our duty and keep silent, trusting to ministers to protect us.'[4]

There was nothing sectarian in Haig's approach to religion. He went to Duncan's church because it answered his spiritual needs. He frequently saw Bishop Gwynne, the Chaplain-General. His charge to him, and to the two Archbishops when they severally visited the army, was that the chaplains should work together so that Church and State could advance towards a great Church to which all decent citizens could belong, and next that the clergy should be enthusiasts and preach to the army on the great aims of the war, 'the freeing of mankind from German tyranny'.

Turning now to the second aspect, the heavy casualties and the awful conditions of the Somme and Ypres offensives certainly suggest a case against Haig which must be answered. Some see this evidence of a cold, heartless commander with no thought beyond bludgeoning his way through the enemy, a man incapable of counting the cost. This is far from the truth. Haig knew that the war could not be won without hard fighting, and he prepared his battles with all the resources he could muster. He believed in their success and he demanded from others the same determination that he himself possessed and the sacrifice he would willingly himself have given.

It is true that Haig's Chief of Staff, Kiggell, when he visited Passchendaele after the breaking-off of the offensive, wept and said, 'Good God! Did we really ask our men to fight in that?'[5] But Kiggell was a more tender plant than Haig. He was a courageous and highly-intelligent soldier, but it is not to be thought that the war could have been won under his command. Edmonds, who recounted the incident to Liddell Hart, added, 'Haig of course knew but did not flinch or care.' The word 'care' is ill-chosen, but Haig certainly did not flinch from what he believed to be the essential cost of victory.

There is no doubt that some of the conditions of the Ypres battlefield were terrible but, as Edmonds himself testifies,[6] they did not apply to the whole battlefield. It was on the routes up and back from the line that they were at their worst and this is obviously the part Kiggell visited. On the whole, contrary to public belief, the conditions on the Somme in 1916 were worse than those at Ypres, although it is not pretended that that affords any defence of Haig. What is a defence is a comparison between the conditions on the two battle-fields and the hardships which the Fourteenth Army had to bear in Burma in 1944 and 1945. Certainly the casualties were not so large, but the armies were smaller and Slim's army was certainly fighting against a more cruel enemy. Also, his men were further away without periodical short leave at home to look forward to and without the improvement in conditions when they were out of the line. Yet Slim, rightly, has the reputation that, although he made his men fight, he understood them and cared for them. But the difference between Haig and Slim was not in how much they cared, but in their outward demeanour and in Slim's ability to unbend without any consequent loss of dignity. Both men demanded all that they considered necessary for victory. Slim could, and Haig could not, be the bluff 'Uncle' of his army.

This comparison of two such different men in their relationship with those under their command must not be taken to infer that Haig's men believed he did not care. In the first place, the social changes that had taken place between 1918 and 1939 must be remembered. It is important to avoid judging the past by the habits and standards of today. In 1918, there was a bond but there was also a gulf between officers and men. It was the same in civilian life; it had its hierarchy and most men knew their place in it. So it was natural for Haig to be a distant and unapproachable figure. Even men like Plumer and Raw-linson, so much easier in their external manner, were yet equally distant from the private soldier. Then there is the question of up-bringing; most men had been taught to 'fear God and honour the King' and, broadly speaking, they did so. It is not too much to say, therefore, that for the most part the officer and man had, in the depths of his heart, a concept of duty not very different from Haig's own. If it had not been so, it would not have been possible for the army that had gone through the Somme, Ypres, and the retreat of 1918, to emerge as a victorious army. One thing too is certain: Haig retained to the end the full confidence of his army. That is one of the reasons why Lloyd George could not get rid of him.

Haig did not have any facility in talking to his soldiers in his frequent visits to units, but he could listen and he did not forget. One little incident recorded in his diary for 12 January 1916 may serve as an example:

> We lunched in a cottage at Flesselle. On my way there, I passed the 6th Battn. of the Cameronians – a Territorial Battalion which fought so well in May and June at Festubert. (The Regular Battalion did splendidly at Neuve Chapelle.) It was proposed to put the 6th Battn. (Territorials) into a Highland Brigade. The Battalion demurred and many said their grandfathers had fought against the Highlanders. So the Battn. is now under Divisional Hd. Qrs.

It would be quite wrong to judge Haig, as many do, from the disenchantment expressed in so many of the novels, plays and personal memoirs written between the wars. The War Poets are dealt with separately below, but the others were, for the most part, inspired not so much by what had been felt or suffered during the war as by disgust at what came afterwards. So much had been endured to secure the bright flower of victory, but the flower had quickly faded and was soon followed by disillusionment. Today a large number of personal diaries written in the war are being published. Many give a poignant account of hardship and distress, but the theme that runs through most of them is one of courage and a willingness to endure for victory. It was not what was written during the war but the comments of the modern editor that pose the question, at least by inference, whether it was all necessary and worthwhile.[7]

Major-General Essame, a regular soldier and military historian who saw both wars at the sharp end, including the Somme and Passchendaele, is a stern critic of Haig. He agrees wholeheartedly with Liddell Hart about the casualties and will have none of Edmonds's figures (see p. 116). But he does accept that the army gave Haig its confidence to the end. Of its attitude to the war he writes: 'I would say that the regimental officers and NCOs were, in the slang of the period, "bitter enders" to a man. The majority, I think, went to their graves with a feeling of contempt for their contemporaries who missed their experience.'[8]

The War Poets must be considered on their own because their poems were written at the time, and often in the trenches. But there is also another reason for dealing with them separately from the diarists who wrote under the same conditions. Poets are a race apart, men with a deep sensitivity and a feeling for the sound as well as the meaning of words. What they say is often an expression of what is best or what is worst in us, but it can hardly be used to measure the morale of an army. The poet is not usually a man to seek out the profession of arms, despite such famous exceptions as Raleigh, Philip Sidney and Montrose, yet the Great War inspired much of the best poetry of its generation.[9]

Men of every rank and type wrote their lovely or their soul-tearing lines. Isaac Rosenberg wrote beautiful poetry but there can never have been a man so unfitted, physically and temperamentally, for the life of a soldier in war or peace, although because of his cockney humour he made not a bad job of it. His poem *Louse Hunting* was an epic of trench warfare of another kind. He was killed in action in April 1918. Quite different are poets like Julian Grenfell and T.P.Cameron Wilson, who lifted up the idea of conflict and the inevitable death in action to which they went. Edward Thomas' poems might have been written in a country vicarage; in only two of his poems does he mention the war at all. He was killed in action at Arras in 1917. Wilfred Owen was one of three friends who served in the same Regiment. He was awarded the Military Cross in October 1918 and killed in action a week before the Armistice. The other two, Siegfried Sassoon, who, like Owen, gained the MC, and Robert Graves both survived.

Wide as is the range of these and other poets, there is one common thread that has significance in the study of morale. That is, as Edmund Blunden remarks,[10] the inevitable change in tone as the war goes on. Yet something of the idealism of 1914 remains right up to the height of the Ypres battle in 1917. But he thought Passchendaele brought murder 'to their singing faiths and hopes'. After that their visions were 'generally a cry'. Yet the spirit of the army remained intact up to the moment of victory.

There remains for discussion Haig's relationship with the more senior officers with whom he worked and with his own staff. It can be said at once that, with a few exceptions, those who dealt with him most closely were able to see the staunchness of his character and to feel his support and his outstanding leadership. They could also realize the warmth that might have been hidden from others. Enough has been said already about Robertson, and it has been shown how Haig was able to work with Wilson, whom he distrusted. He had some distrust for Rawlinson too, but he realized his outstanding qualities and was able to bring him on and made of him the spearhead commander who gave him the tactical victory. He was doubtful about Plumer when he first became c-in-c, and, on 17 February 1916, wrote to Robertson saying that air photographs showed that the defences on Second Army front were not being properly maintained. He went on: 'I am going to see Gen Plumer tomorrow to hear what explanation he has to offer. I fear he cannot have any worth having. In fact he has always assured me, in reply to my personal questioning, that everything was "all right" and that he was quite "satisfied". It is therefore possible I may have to recommend his removal from the command, because this is no time for having *doubts* about anyone's fitness. If I have to come to this decision . . . please try to give him some other job so as to let him down lightly.'

Happily, when he saw him, Haig did not remove the man who was to become his most steadfast and reliable army commander. As he informed Robertson the next day, he told Plumer he must get things right. He told him 'to take hold of his corps commanders and to make them in their turn grip their generals of divns. and so on down the scale'.

Haig's handling of Gough was less happy. It has been shown how Gough became misplaced because there was no break-through on the Somme. But it was certainly a mistake to give him the Ypres battle in 1917. Haig's first thought of using Plumer and Rawlinson was much sounder. Gough had not proved himself to be a master of the infantry battle. Essame says of the decision: 'What on earth possessed [Haig] to bring Gough into the Ypres battle: he must have realized that his slapdash approach as compared to Plumer's disqualified him for serious study of a problem which the Germans in fact solved without tanks in March 1918.'[11] Gough was a thruster, but neither he nor his chief staff officer knew how to get the best out of their corps and divisional commanders. Haig knew this. In October 1917 he became aware that the Canadian Corps (they were thrusters too) did not want to move into Fifth Army. Haig remarked: ' . . . the idea seems to be prevalent that he drove them too hard on the Somme last year'. In December, after the Ypres fighting had died down, he went to Gough and mentioned to him how many divisions had said they hoped that they would not be sent to Fifth Army to fight. He wrote: 'This feeling I put down to his staff. I had not mentioned it to him before because I thought it might have an effect on his self-confidence during the battle. It was, of course, a surprise to Gough to learn this, but from the facts which I gave him, he realized that there were cases bearing out what I told him.'

As has been seen, Haig did not dismiss Gough nor send him home until he was directed to do so by the Secretary of State for War. It may be asked whether Haig was justified in complying with this order when he himself believed that Gough was not responsible for the disasters of March 1918. He did not think Gough was without blame, but he did not want to dismiss him. After Gough had gone home, Haig wrote to his wife on 16 June: 'As regards Gough I am sorry he is talking stupidly, but I don't think it would be any use writing to him. Some of his friends are advising him to keep quiet. I am doing all I can to help him, but as a matter of fact, some orders he issued and things he did were stupid.' One of Gough's admirers and defenders was Beddington, who was his Chief of Staff during the retreat. In February 1919, Haig confessed to him the real reason why he did not do more to defend Gough, saying: 'After considerable thought I decided that public opinion at home, whether right or wrong, demanded a scapegoat, and that the only possible ones were Hubert or me. I was conceited enough to think that the army could not spare me.' Beddington was still very sore, and remained so, but he was forced to admit that Haig was right, as indeed he was.[12]

There were inevitably removals of other commanders. Of these, Maxse told Liddell Hart in 1926: 'When Haig gave anyone their congé he did so in a way that they never felt injured. He was alway so impersonal. That was a contrast to Rawlie and Gough.' When, because of his health, Haig had to replace Kiggell, he did so with great regret. Kiggell always worked too hard and he was not well off. Haig took pains to ensure that Kiggell got an appointment where he could recover his health and would be properly remunerated. On 14 May 1918 he wrote to Kiggell:

I am delighted to hear that you have accepted the Guernsey command, but there is to be no idea of 'resigning yourself to the shelf' or any nonsense of that sort. You go to Guernsey to pick up after your *many years of overwork*. And when you have had a rest, there will be lots of active work for you in connection with this great Army. Even if I am moved out of the way, there are *many* in high places who know your worth and will not fail, I know, to make use of you – so make up your mind to get strong and don't talk rubbish about shelves!!

We have had anxious times here.

Haig had a deep sense of loyalty to those who served him, and his several chiefs of staff and his staff generally reciprocated this and almost all had a strong affection for him. This mutual regard perhaps went too far in the case of Charteris, for Haig allowed himself to be misled as to the state of the German Army, despite plenty of contrary evidence from the War Office. Strangely enough, Lady Haig did not like Charteris whom she had known from the time of her marriage. But in this respect Haig allowed no petticoat influence. Lady Haig retained her prejudice after the war and would not co-operate with Charteris in his writing of the life of her husband, and was unjustly critical of it when it appeared.[13]

There was one exception to the near-worship of the junior staff who worked personally with Haig. Major Sir Desmond Morton, who had been ADC to Haig for six months to April 1918, wrote to Liddell Hart:

I have rarely met so self centred a man. Curly Birch [Haig's Major-General, Royal Artillery] confessed that though he had known him for many years in the army and socially he still did not know him. He was intensely courageous physically and morally. He could talk – he never chatted – freely on certain subjects which had nothing to do with war and about his past experience as a soldier ... but what he was thinking about the war as it stood on any particular day, no one, not even his Chief of Staff, could fully make out. He gave his orders quick enough but never explained them. He was certainly tongue tied in anything like public speaking. He was anyway a silent man but such silence was babbling compared with what he said when he gave an oral instruction instead of a written order. You had to learn a kind of verbal shorthand, made up of a series of grunts and gestures. His bedside books were *The Bible, Scottish Metric Psalms, Pilgrim's Progress* and a life of Cromwell. His sense of mission was to do his duty as he saw it in the sphere of life in which God had been pleased to call him.

Morton expanded on this for Liddell Hart, saying:

He was very fair, just and kind to his junior subordinates, and loyal as well; though a holy terror to his equals, superiors and possible competitors. He had a strict sense of what was apt and fitting for a gentleman to do and how a gentleman should behave towards his superiors – intrigue and so on. He never shouted nor swore, nor raised his voice in anger, which last he never showed outwardly. Self-discipline was his guide.

He was a quick-thinking man within himself and therefore rarely taken aback by the unexpected. But his intellectual powers were distinctly average. He had no sort of genius in him.

He utterly disliked new ideas especially in respect of soldiering and making war. He hated being told any information, however irrefutable, which militated against his pre-conceived ideas or beliefs. Hence his support of John Charteris, unbelievably bad as a DMI, who always concealed bad news or put it in an agreeable light. Hence his utter disbelief in tanks, the machine gun etc.'[14]

The last sentence is palpably untrue, as has been shown in the last chapter. What persuaded Morton to say it is not known. It may help readers to understand this sketch, part of which is so perceptive and part so controversial, to know that staff officers in the War Office found Sir Desmond Morton not easy to deal with when he was personal assistant to Churchill in 1940.

A different picture is given by Sir Frank Fox, an Australian journalist who was wounded on the Somme and later served on the staff of GHQ. In 1920 he wrote:

I cannot help intruding a reply to some criticism of Lord Haig that he was too inclined to stand by his officers, that he was reluctant to 'butcher' a man, and that in consequence he did not get the highest standard of efficiency. Faithfulness to his friends and servants was certainly a marked characteristic of Lord Haig as Commander-in-Chief. He chose his men cautiously and, I believe, with brilliant insight. Having chosen them he stood by them faithfully in spite of press or political or service thunderings, unless he was convinced they were not equal to their work.

It is a characteristic which, even allowing that there was an odd case of over-indulgence, of giving a man a little too much benefit of the doubt, worked on the whole for good. Men do not do their best with ropes round their necks; and I believe that a great newspaper magnate whose motto at first was 'sack, sack, sack' very soon found that it was a mistake.

Charteris also must be allowed his say, because whatever his faults as an Intelligence Chief, he was a remarkable man who knew Haig as well as anybody. Liddell Hart followed up the strictures of Morton and received from Charteris a letter of 11 October 1931, in which Charteris denied that Haig was prejudiced. He said:

He never closed his mind to an addition to the facts and was always ready to amend his former judgments in the light of further facts. He did not resent the expression of a judgment contrary to his own from others he trusted, but while he did not resent it it rarely altered his own confidence in his own judgment. But his confidence was only in his own *judgment*. He made no claim to knowledge above other people's and tended to draw the lines of his own limitation of knowledge far lower than was necessary or justified. One saw, therefore, the queer blend of confidence in *judgment*, diffidence in *claim to knowledge*. This made him very (unusually so) open to new ideas. His confidence in his judgment was I think justified. He rarely erred but like all human beings he erred at times. . . . I sometimes think it was recognition of these errors, still unaccountable to him, that led him into his deep religious tendency which came late in life and afforded to him the explanation of the unexplainable.

He had a very real generosity in mind and in dealing with others, a generosity that was limitless until it impinged on the 'cause' as he saw it. Then it was cut off as by a guillotine.[15]

The doubts of those who wondered if Haig really cared must surely be set at rest by his activities after the war. His life was devoted to the cause of those who had served. His one wish was that the comradeship that had bound all ranks in the war should continue afterwards, that those who had suffered should be helped and that the others should be able to live a full life. He fought hard for improvement in pensions, not without some success. His labours also bore fruit when the British Legion was born in June 1921. He had fathered an organization in which all ranks could participate, and one which was free from all political affiliation and bias. He himself kept free from all controversy; he wrote no memoirs and he did not allow his diaries to be used until after his death and they were not published until 1952.

Haig's despatches hurt Pétain, but Pétain himself, when Haig went to see him to say good-bye, had admitted to him the fears he had had for the French Army. Haig wrote in his diary on 3 April 1919: 'After dinner Pétain, in a private talk referred to the terribly insubordinate state of the French Army in 1917, and said there were two occasions when he had deserved well of his country, the first was at Verdun, and the next "after Nivelle's failure in 1917 when he kept the French Army from mutinying". Referring to his visit to me that summer, he said that the state of the French Army was much worse then he had dared to tell me at the time.' Edmonds consulted Haig and countless others on what he wrote in the official histories. Haig's attitude to his criticisms can best be illustrated by what he said to Davidson, his Chief of Operations, who wished to object: 'I have no doubt that the Official History will do full justice to us all, so let us leave it at that.'[16]

One well-known act of magnanimity must be recorded here. Haig was ill during the victory march on 19 July 1919, but he forced himself to ride. After the march he went to Haldane's flat to see the man who had done so much but had been politically rejected. Haig left with him a bound copy of his despatches and, after he had gone, Haldane opened it and found that it was inscribed: 'To the greatest Secretary of State for War England has ever had.'

The personal reward for Haig after the war was an earldom and £100,000. This may be compared with what the country had given its Commander-in-Chief in the preceding great war. Wellington was granted £2,000 a year for life before the end of the Peninsular War, and before he fought Waterloo he was made a Duke and his bounty made up to £500,000.[17]

But a gift which was of priceless value to Haig was Bemersyde, the ancestral home of the Haigs, which, as a result of public subscription, was bought from another branch of the family and presented to him. He spent happy years there with his family but, sadly, they were few. He died of a heart attack in London on 29 January 1928. By his own wish he was buried near Bemersyde and his grave lies beside that of Sir Walter Scott at Dryburgh Abbey.

# 12

# HAIG AND HIS CRITICS

In the course of the narrative, particularly in the last two chapters, certain of the criticisms levelled at Haig have been discussed. There remain the more general criticisms of him. These come not only from politicians and from distinguished military critics, but also from less experienced military writers; some of these come into the category which John Terraine has aptly labelled 'Instant Historians'. No man did more to take away from Haig all credit for victory in the war than Lloyd George. He does not even acknowledge the masterly conduct of the last hundred days. Such credit as he does allow he attributes to the fact that Haig was under the direction of Foch. No reading of the facts can possibly sustain this interpretation. Little need be added to what has already been said except to say that the 'War Memories' illustrate the truth of Blake's couplet:

> A truth that's told with bad intent
> Beats all the lies you can invent.[1]

But one thing must be said and one of Lloyd George's criticisms further examined.

Haig's great weight of responsibility must have been vastly increased by the knowledge that Lloyd George thoroughly mistrusted his military opinion and ability. Haig made it clear that if the Government had lost confidence in him they should replace him, and he would be willing to serve where they directed. A lesser man, left in command and knowing the doubts and fears of the Government, might have been tempted to resign. But Haig was not deflected from his purpose.

Only a man of outstanding integrity and great strength of character would have remained and done what he did. He continued to follow the strategy which he considered to be right. The events of 1918 proved that it was right. It is doubtful whether anyone else could have done it so well.

The criticism by Lloyd George which deserves further examination is that Haig lacked imagination. John Terraine quotes one of the Prime Minister's sons as having reported that his father said Haig was 'brilliant to the top of his army boots'[2] and Lloyd George himself wrote: 'He was a painstaking professional soldier with a sound intelligence of secondary quality. He had the courage and stubbornness of his race and also a large measure of their business capacity. . . . But he did not possess the necessary breadth of vision or imagination to plan a great campaign against some of the ablest Generals of the War. I never met any man in a high position who seemed to me so utterly devoid of imagination.'[3] The question of whether Haig lacked imagination will come up when we discuss the military critics, but here we must consider the context of Lloyd George's remarks. Lloyd George disliked Haig's strategy because Haig believed a decision must be sought on the Western Front, whereas Lloyd George thought it could be found where victory in battle was less costly. In short, Lloyd George judged Haig as if he were the chief military adviser to the Government. But he was not, his sole responsibility was the conduct of the war on the Western Front. It would have taken more than a little imagination on his part to suggest that his troops should be taken away to fight elsewhere. Haig thought the war could be lost or won on the Western Front. Not only did Lloyd George not believe that the Germans could break through the front, but he did not believe that the Allies could succeed there. In 1918 he was proved wrong on both counts. It might have been better if Haig had been CIGS from the beginning of the war, as Haldane wanted, but he was not and it was quite wrong to judge him as if he had been.

It was a tragedy that Haig and Lloyd George did not get on better with each other. It must not be forgotten that Lloyd George's drive and decision were potent factors for victory. He played much the same role as Churchill in the Second War. He did so, moreover, without the experience and the machinery which came from the first war. The disparaging remark about Haig's lack of imagination quoted above was written in Lloyd George's memoirs with hindsight after Haig's death. It is worth considering their first meeting after Haig became Commander-in-Chief. The meeting was a great success, and Lloyd George, who was then the Minister of Munitions, wrote to Haig on 8 February 1916: 'I want to thank you for the great courtesy which you showed me during the interesting visit which I paid to your Headquarters. I was specially touched by the kindness shown to my two boys. The visit, if you will permit me to say so, left in my mind a great impression of things being *gripped* in that sphere of operations; and whether we win through or whether we fail, I have the feeling that everything that the assiduity, and the care, and the trained thought of a great soldier can accomplish, is being done.'

Working together, the two men had much to give to each other and to the country. Esher knew this and wrote to Haig: 'There are upon the side of the Allies only two fighters; you and Lloyd George. I apologize for the bracket but it is a hard fact.' Courage in adversity was the only quality they had in common. Otherwise each was the complete antithesis of the other in all he did and was. Lloyd George was the brilliant communicator with the mercurial temperament, whose individual contribution towards winning the war was at least as great as any other. Haig was steadfast, deliberate, true and loyal, always limiting himself strictly to his own personal duty and responsibility.

It was the Somme which altered Lloyd George's opinion of Haig, and it was the Nivelle affair which caused Haig to feel he could never again trust Lloyd George. Haig's attitude to other politicians tells us something about his character. Haldane and Clemenceau were two politicians he really admired. The first for his breadth of thought and his shrewd judgment, the second for that pugnacity which to his own generals matched that of Lloyd George. He had a poor opinion of Churchill as a strategist, but he took him seriously as a soldier. He was hard on Derby, who was a good friend to him and a strong supporter. On 14 January 1918, he wrote Lady Haig: 'D is a very weak-minded fellow I am afraid, and, like the feather pillow, bears the marks of the last person who has sat on him!' It may surprise some that he had a high opinion of Asquith and Carson. They came to see him in September 1917. Carson told Haig that he realized the dangers of Lloyd George, but that he must be supported as Prime Minister because of his driving power. Carson also told Haig that Asquith in opposition had great influence. Of Asquith, Haig wrote: 'I felt that the old gentleman was head and shoulders above any other politician who had visited my Hd Qtrs in brains and all-round knowledge. It was quite a pleasure to have the old man in the house. So amusing and kindly in his ways.' He also said: 'I took quite a liking to Carson and think that it is fortunate for the Empire that he is in the War Cabinet.'

Something of schoolboy delight, not often suspected in Haig, came out over the discomfiture of F.E.Smith during Lloyd George's first visit. Haig's account differs slightly from that published in Gilbert's *Life of Churchill*.[4] On 2 February 1916 he wrote to Philip Howell:

> Recently I had Lloyd George and Bonar Law here. The latter seems too honest for the crowd he is with. ... There was an amusing incident when the two Cabinet ministers were here. It seems F.E.Smith jumped into the back of their car when they were leaving Boulogne and came here without a pass. I have recently stiffened up the rule about passes and Lt Col F. Smith was duly reported to the A-G's branch as having passed in without a pass. Meanwhile he had gone on to dine with Winston and about 11 at night he was arrested by the Provost Marshal and brought to St Omer . . . fairly spitting blood I hear. 'The Attorney-General and a Cabinet Minister under arrest etc.' I soon settled the matter and he went home a wiser man I hope. But he is desperately afraid of the story getting into the press and of the ridicule of his friends.

Turning now to the lesser critics, there are probably few works that have so misled uninformed opinion as the book *The Donkeys* and the play *Oh What a Lovely War*.[5] Probably the play gets its information from the book, because the personal twists are similar. In *The Donkeys*, many of the facts are well stated and are not dissimilar from those discussed in Chapters 6 and 7 above. There are a few unpardonable mistakes such as the suggestion that, in the advance to the Aisne, Haig had the cavalry under his command and moved them behind his infantry. As has been shown, Haig was strongly critical of the way the cavalry was used. To go into all the fallacies of Alan Clark's exposition would mean going over all the ground again. The greatest misrepresentations are those directed at Haig's personal life and character. Let it suffice to point out that to anyone reading the book it must appear that Haig lent money to French in order to put him in his power; that Haig caused the King to sack French, and that only Haig's bad choice of a mount for His Majesty endangered the intrigue. The play, which takes a similar line, may be good entertainment, that is a matter of taste, but it cannot be regarded as even a good caricature of Haig.

Liddell Hart and Fuller, two strategists and military historians with an international reputation, were both critical of Haig. Liddell Hart started as a great admirer. He wrote in the *Daily Express* of 21 December 1916:

> A modern general has not only to be a master of strategy and tactics, but he has also to be a good organizer. It is the possession of such organizing ability added to a genius for pure generalship which has made Sir Douglas Haig fit to rank with any general of past or modern times. One great change Douglas Haig has made is in the selection of young leaders. In fact, our leaders, under Sir Douglas Haig's regime, average quite twenty years' younger than those of any other army. The result is seen in increased initiative and energy.

In his notes on the British generals Liddell Hart remarked that Haig 'had a ready mind, ever able to seize and improve on new ideas, and a wonderful organizer. He was tongue-tied ... but his ability instilled everyone with confidence in him.'⁶ Liddell Hart also approved Haig's wide study of military history, especially that of the American Civil War, which the Germans had not studied.

It was not until after the war that Liddell Hart became critical of Haig through his study of infantry tactics and his development of the theory of what he called 'the expanding torrent'. His ideas were similar to those used by the Germans in March 1918 and advocated in the British Army by Maxse before that. Liddell Hart was a great admirer of Maxse and thought Haig should have developed these tactics earlier. Then Liddell Hart's study of military history taught him to advocate the strategy of the indirect approach and persuaded him that 'the longest way round is often the shortest way there'. The suggestion that Haig failed in that respect is unjust because, on the Western Front, which was Haig's only domain, there was no longer way round. Wherever Haig attacked, he had first to break through and then to exploit before the gap could be closed. Liddell Hart extolled the value of surprise. But Haig achieved surprise in the opening phase of every one of his attacks except Third Ypres, both when he was Army Commander and c-in-c. It was in the repetition of the attacks after the Germans had recovered that Haig's battles became unimaginative.

When in 1928 Liddell Hart published a scintillating and provocative collection of essays on the principal Allied and German commanders,[7] his view of Haig was well balanced and not so critical as it was to become later. He did however castigate Haig for the misuse of tanks, thus:

> The premature use of a handful of tanks gave away the jealously guarded secret of the newly-forged key to the trench deadlock, sacrificing the birthright of decisive strategic surprise for the mess of potage of a local success. The metaphor has a satirical aptness, for military ignorance has never made a worse mess of any new weapon. The progenitors of the tank had long before sounded the warning, in a memorandum, that the secret must be preserved until masses of machines could be launched in a great surprise stroke, and that on no account should they be used in driblets as manufactured. As Haig had expressed his agreement with the memorandum in the spring of 1916, the military historian is driven to the conclusion that the tanks were literally 'pawned for a song'. . . . If so, the greater price (sic) thus lost beyond recall was a heavy forfeit to pay for an attempt to redeem some fragment of the failure of the Somme.[8]

Liddell Hart's summing up of Haig is severe but not altogether unjust:

> As an executive commander there has hardly been a finer defensive general; in contrast, among those who have gained fame as offensive generals none perhaps have made worse errors. In the last phase he did much to rebuild his reputation, but the scope for more than method and determination was not wide. His mind was dominated by the instinct of method, a valuable asset; where he failed was in the instinct of surprise, in its widest sense – originality of conception, fertility of resource, receptivity in ideas. And without the instinct of surprise – the key to economic and decisive success in war – no man can take rank among the Great Captains. But as a great gentleman, also in the widest sense, and as a pattern of noble character, Haig will stand out in the Roll of History, *chevalier sans peur et sans reproche*, more spotless by far than most of Britain's national heroes. Most of all, perhaps, because in his

190

qualities and defects he was the very embodiment of the national character and the army tradition.[9]

It was in the great controversy of the 1930s repeated in the 1950s about the relative casualties on the Somme and at Ypres that Liddell Hart became much more critical of Haig. It was an argument about figures that will never be resolved. But it was more, because Liddell Hart's view took away the one merit of Haig's offensive strategy, that these battles destroyed the German Army and made possible the victories of 1918. On the side of Haig stand, not only the testimony of many German commanders and historians, but the fact of victory.

In the course of the controversy about the cost of Ypres and Passchendaele, Liddell Hart had one more complaint. He contended that Haig invented, after the war, the excuse that Pétain had asked him to press the offensive to save the French Army. Liddell Hart's argument[10] was that neither Foch, nor Pétain, approved of an offensive towards Ostend and that Pétain would have been satisfied with a series of limited attacks. Both facts are true, but they do not alter the fact that Haig's appreciation of the state of the French Army, made from what Pétain told him, was right. Anything less than the full engagement of the German Army would have left them free to engage the French at least sufficiently to find out their weakness and then to turn against them.

It is not surprising that Fuller had criticisms to make of Haig. He had a highly-developed critical sense and, in his study of war, a brilliant perception of what it would have been better to do, only Marlborough has his unstinted praise. He has harsh things to say about Napoleon and few commanders of any nationality escape the cutting lash of his pen. It is surely a sign of some perversity that one of the commanders in whom he finds most to commend is Grant, whose warlike achievements more resemble those of Haig than anyone else. But Fuller finds cause for some praise as well as blame:

> It is indeed strange that the man whose stubbornness in the offensive had all but ruined us on the Somme, should from August 1918 onwards have become the driving force of the Allied armies. Yet this was so and it must stand to his credit, for no man can deny that, during the last hundred days of the war, he fitted events as a hand fitted a glove.[11]

Let the last word go to Trenchard, father of the Royal Air Force. It was under Haig's command that he did much of his pioneering work on a new weapon in a new element. He knew Haig well and was not likely easily to forgive that lack of sensitivity to a new idea of which Liddell Hart complains or that lack of ability to see the obvious which was Fuller's chief criticism. In December 1952 he wrote:

It has been the fashion since 1918, to decry Haig's reputation as a man and as a soldier. . . . The power of this criticism, some of which came from people in high positions, in my opinion has tended to dim the work of a great man and a great soldier. . . .

Haig knew, as few did, that it was touch and go whether France went out of the war. When morale begins to weaken, it may at any moment go with a rush, the smallest crack in the dam may produce an overwhelming flood.

He knew if France went out of the war the British Army on the continent was doomed – four or five million men would have been lost. He knew if he fought on he would save not only Britain but the world.

In spite of the British Army having suffered during the battles of 1915, 1916 and 1917, the high standard of leadership of the young officers and non-commissioned officers showed no signs of deterioration.

In spite of all the differences of opinion about tactics, and the grumbling which inevitably goes on in any long war, the morale of the armies was excellent, due in a very large measure to the Commander-in-Chief. It never weakened. In fact at the Hindenburg Line in 1918 it was greater than ever – there was no denying it. I feel if anyone but Haig had been in command then, and the break in the Hindenburg Line had not been accomplished, the war could have gone on quite easily for another year, if not two years.

Haig was inarticulate and this handicapped him greatly when talking to his officers and men, in numbers or individually. He had no glib tongue, or the gift of words, but his spirit and morale were of the highest. The British Army's spirit of determination not to be beaten – to win in the end – was inspired by its Commander-in-Chief.

I am one of those who believed then, and still believe, that after the terrific battles of the Somme and Passchendaele, and the great offensive of April 1918, all ranks trusted Haig. Their faith in him was unshaken. This was shown particularly by the wonderful morale and spirit of the whole British Army on 8 August 1918, when, under Haig's leadership, the Army attacked with an enthusiasm that few at home realized, and the long drawn out struggle was ended. That was Haig's triumph. . . .

I feel one day in years to come – it may be fifty or even a hundred years – history will relate what the world owes to Haig.[12]

# APPENDIX 1

## Officers who were students
## at the Staff College with Haig 1896–7

(Taken from the Edmonds Papers)

### Haig's Year

| | | |
|---|---|---|
| Major | Heath H.N.C. | 1/. Yorks L.I. |
| Major | Douglas W. | 1/. Royal Scots |
| Major | Buchanan-Riddell H.E. | K.R. Rifle Corps |
| Capt | Findlay N.D. | Royal Artillery |
| Capt | Johnston J.T. | Royal Artillery |
| Capt | Allenby E.H.H. | 6th Innis. Dragoons |
| Capt | Sandbach A.E. | Royal Engineers |
| Capt | Haking R.C.B. | 2/. Hampshire Regt |
| Capt | Anderson W.J. | 1/. W. Riding Regt |
| Capt | Stopford L.A.M. | 1/. Derby Regt |
| Capt | Edmonds J.E. | Royal Engineers |
| Capt | Brikbeck W.H. | 1/. Dragoon Gds |
| Capt | O'Donnell H. | 1/. W. Yorks Regt |
| Capt | Phillips H.G.C. | 1/. Welsh Regt |
| Capt | Phipps P.R. | Dorset Regt |
| Capt | Haig D. | 7th Hussars |
| Capt | Capper T. | 1/. E. Lanc Regt |
| Capt | Colomb F.C. | 42nd Gurkhas |
| Capt | Vallentin J.M. | 2/. Somerset L. |
| Capt | Macdonogh G.M.W. | Royal Engineers |
| Capt | Holloway B. | 2nd Madras Cav. |
| Capt | Furse W.T. | Royal Artillery |
| Capt | Climo V.C. | 2/. W. Indian Regt |
| Capt | Forestier-Walker G.T. | Royal Artillery |
| Capt | Willoughby M.E. | 2nd Bengal Cav. |

194

| Lieut | Dyer R.E.H. | 29th Punjab Inf. |
| Lieut | Burbury F.W. | 2/. R.W. Kent Regt |
| Lieut | Buckley E.J. | 1/. R. Innis Fus. |
| Lieut | Gogarty H.E. | 2/. R. Scots Fus. |
| Lieut | Biddulph H.M. | 1/. Rifle Brigade |
| Lieut | Blair A. | 1/. K.O. Scot Bord. |

## Senior Division in Haig's First Year

| Major | Barter B.St.J | 2/. Lincoln Regt |
| Capt | Du Cane H.J. | Royal Artillery |
| Capt | Perceval E.M. | Royal Artillery |
| Capt | Haden J.R.F. | 2/. E. Yorks Regt |
| Capt | Sloman H.S. | 2/. E. Surrey Regt |
| Capt | Bridge W.C. | 2/. S. Staff Regt |
| Capt | Barthorp A.H. | 1/. Northn Regt |
| Capt | Wise H.E. | 2/. Derby Regt |
| Capt | Hamilton L.A.H. | 1/. Yorks L.I. |
| Capt | Strachey R.J. | 2/. Rifle Brig. |
| Capt | Skinner F.St.D | 2/. R. Sussex Regt |
| Capt | Lawrence Hon H.A. | 17th Lancers |
| Capt | Graham H.W.G. DSO | 5th Lancers |
| Capt | Knox J.S. | 1/. E. Yorks Regt |
| Capt | Jennings-Bramly | 1/. R. Highlanders |
| Capt | Vertue N.H. | 2/. E. Kent Regt |
| Capt | Ewbank W. | Royal Engineers |
| Capt | Spearman C.E. | 2/. R. Munster Fus. |
| Capt | Walker H.S. | 2/. Scottish Rifles |
| Capt | De Gruyther C.M. | 1/. Suffolk Regt |
| Capt | Carter E.E. | Army Service Corps |
| Capt | Kirkpatrick G.M. | Royal Engineers |
| Capt | Clay C.H. | 43rd Gurkhas |
| Capt | Tod J.K. | 7th Bengal Cav. |
| Capt | Thompson W.A.M. | Royal Artillery |
| Capt | Tennant H.L. | Royal Artillery |
| Capt | Maude F.S. | 2/. Coldstream Gds |
| Capt | Young F. de B. | 6th Bengal Cav. |
| Capt | Earle S. | 2/. Coldstream Gds |
| Capt | MacBean J.A.E. | 2/. R. Dublin Fus. |
| Capt | Friedericks D.A. | Royal Engineers |

## Junior Division in Haig's Senior Year

| | | |
|---|---|---|
| Bd Maj | Mackenzie E.J. | Seaforth High |
| Capt | Urquhart B.C. | 1/. Cameron High |
| Capt | Anstruther C.J. | 17th Lancers |
| Capt | Thompson C.W. | 7th Dragoon Gds |
| Capt | Murray A.J. | 2/. R. Innis Fus. |
| Capt | Fowle T.E. | 1/. Bedford Regt |
| Capt | Banon F.L. | 2/. Shrops L. |
| Capt | King Salter H.P. | 3/. Rifle Brig. |
| Capt | Wyndham G.P. | 16th Lancers |
| Capt | Nugent O.S.W. DSO | 1/. K.R.R. Corps |
| Capt | Molony F.A. | Royal Engineers |
| Capt | O'Meara W.A.J. | Royal Engineers |
| Capt | Everett H.J. | 1/. Somerset L.I. |
| Capt | England T.P. | 1/. Royal Fus. |
| Capt | Cumming-Bruce Hon J.F.T. | 2/. Royal High |
| Capt | Fox-Strangways T.S. | 1/. R. Irish Rifles |
| Capt | Oxley R.S. | 4/. K.R.R. Corps |
| Capt | May W.S.K. | 2/. E. Yorks Regt |
| Capt | Henstock F.T. | 2/. West Ind. Regt |
| Capt | Blackburn L.D. | 2/. Scottish Rifles |
| Capt | Climo V.C. | 2/. West Ind. Regt |
| Capt | Robertson W.R. DSO | 3rd Dragoon Gds |
| Capt | Tuson H.D. | 1/. Border Regt |
| Capt | Barrow G de S. | 4th Bengal Cav. |
| Capt | Stewart R.S. | 1/. Liverpool Regt |
| Capt | Bannatyne W.S. | 1/. Liverpool Regt |
| Capt | Perrott W.H.W. | Royal Artillery |
| Capt | Symonds G.D. | Royal Artillery |
| Lieut | Ruggles-Brise H.G. | Grenadier Gds |
| Lieut | Seagrim D.G. | Royal Artillery |
| Lieut | Burrows A.R. | 1/. R. Irish Fus. |
| Lieut | Owen F.C. | Royal Artillery |
| Lieut | Holman H.C. | 16th Bengal Cav. |

# APPENDIX 2

SPECIAL ORDER OF THE DAY

BY FIELD-MARSHAL SIR DOUGLAS HAIG, KT,
GCB, GCVO, KCIE, COMMANDER-IN-
CHIEF, BRITISH ARMIES IN FRANCE

TO ALL RANKS OF THE BRITISH ARMY
IN FRANCE AND FLANDERS

Three weeks ago today the enemy began his terrific attacks against us on a fifty-mile front. His objects are to separate us from the French, to take the Channel Ports and destroy the British Army.

In spite of throwing already 106 Divisions into the battle and enduring the most reckless sacrifice of human life, he has as yet made little progress towards his goals.

We owe this to the determined fighting and self-sacrifice of our troops. Words fail me to express the admiration which I feel for the splendid resistance offered by all ranks of our Army under the most trying circumstances.

Many amongst us now are tired. To those I would say that Victory will belong to the side which holds out the longest. The French Army is moving rapidly and in great force to our support.

There is no other course open to us but to fight it out. Every position must be held to the last man: there must be no retirement. With our backs to the wall and believing in the justice of our cause each one of us must fight on to the end. The safety of our homes and the Freedom of mankind alike depend upon the conduct of each one of us at this critical moment.

D. HAIG, FM
Commander-in-Chief, British Armies in France
General Headquarters, Thursday, April 11th, 1918

# NOTES

*Chapter 1*
1 Duff Cooper, *Haig*, I, Ch. 1.
2 Duff Cooper, I, p. 20.
3 Edmonds Papers.
4 *Douglas Haig, the Educated Soldier*, p. 7.
5 Letter to the author, 13 September 1974.
6 Duff Cooper, I, pp. 37–9.
7 Letter to the author, August 1974.
8 Letter to the author, 4 February 1975.
9 Conversation with the author, September 1974.
10 Kiggell Papers.
11 Howell Papers. Also Rosalind Howell, *Philip Howell, a Memoir*.

*Chapter 2*
1 A nominal roll for each year, taken from the Edmonds Papers, is at Appendix 1.
2 Barrow, *The Fire of Life*, pp. 43–4.
3 Ibid., p. 44.
4 Goldsmith, *The Deserted Village*.
5 Wavell, *Allenby*, pp. 62–3.
6 Edmonds Papers.
7 *The Fire of Life*, p. 46.

*Chapter 3*
1 Winston Churchill, *The River War*.
2 Sir Evelyn Wood had been Midshipman and served in the Naval Brigade in the Crimean War; he was commissioned in the 13th Light

Dragoons (afterwards 13/18 Hussars) and had been awarded the Victoria Cross in the Indian Mutiny while serving with the Central India Horse. He then transferred to the infantry and had commanded 90th LI, afterwards 2nd Battalion The Cameronians (Scottish Rifles), in the Zulu War of 1879.

3 Maurice, *Life of General Lord Rawlinson of Trent*, p. 38.
4 Duff Cooper, I, p. 63.


*Chapter 4*

1 Elgin Commission *Evidence*, I, p. 465.
2 Maurice, *The War in South Africa*, IV, p. 174.
3 Quoted by Liddell Hart, *Through the Fog of War*, p. 47.
4 Elgin Commission *Evidence*, II, p. 403.
5 Ibid., p. 110.
6 Ibid., p. 404.
7 Ibid., p. 413.


*Chapter 5*

1 Duff Cooper, I, pp. 95–6.
2 Letters to Howell are taken from the Howell Papers.
3 Duff Cooper, I, pp. 103–4.
4 Viscount Esher, *Journals & Letters*, I, p. 391.
5 Ibid., II, p. 69.
6 John Terraine, *Douglas Haig, the Educated Soldier*.
7 Duff Cooper, I, pp. 109 and 113.
8 Command Paper 4948.
9 This, and subsequent quotations from letters in this chapter, are from the Kiggell Papers.
10 Charteris, *Field Marshal Earl Haig*, p. 60.
11 Ibid., Ch. 7.
12 Among others . . . Duff Cooper, I, pp. 122–5 and Charteris, *Field Marshal Earl Haig*, pp. 70–4.


*Chapter 6*

1 Charteris, *At G.H.Q.*, p. 17.
2 Spears, *Liaison, 1914*, pp. 263–4.
3 *Douglas Haig, the Educated Soldier*, p. 98.
4 *At G.H.Q.*, pp. 118–20.


*Chapter 7*

1 Edmonds, *France and Belgium 1915*, I, p. 307.
2 Edmonds, *France and Belgium 1915*, II, p. 114.

3 Bonham-Carter, *Soldier True: the Life and Times of Field Marshal Sir William Robertson 1860–1933*, p. 133.
4 Spender and Asquith, *Life of Lord Oxford and Asquith*, II, p. 191.
5 Robertson Papers.
6 Wilson Diaries, 16 and 17 December 1915.

*Chapter 8*
1 This and subsequent quotations from the correspondence between Haig and Robertson is taken from the Robertson Papers. Many of Haig's letters to Robertson are in his own handwriting and there are no copies in the Haig Papers.
2 Falkenhayn, *General Headquarters*, pp. 209–20.
3 Ludendorff, *My War Memoirs 1914–18*, I, pp. 276–8 and 304.
4 Quoted in Edmonds, *France and Belgium 1916*, I, p. 494.
5 Quoted ibid., II, p. 555.
6 Ibid., II, pp. xiii–xv and 553.
7 See Oman, 'A Correction to the World Crisis' in *Nineteenth Century and After* (May 1927); Churchill, *The World Crisis* (revised edition), p. 548; Lloyd George, *War Memoirs*, VI, p. 3414.
8 *Douglas Haig, the Educated Soldier*, p. 353.
9 Letter to the author dated 18 February 1968.
10 Spears, *Prelude to Victory*, p. 40.
11 Hankey, *The Supreme Command 1914–1918*, II, p. 616.
12 Ibid. and Spears, pp. 144–54.
13 Blake, *The Private Papers of Douglas Haig, 1914–1919*, p. 199; Spears, p. 149.
14 Blake, pp. 203–6: these two letters are published in full here.
15 Spears, pp. 570–2: Haig's letter of 9 March and Nivelle's comments are published in full.
16 Edmonds, *France and Belgium 1917*, I, p. 493.

*Chapter 9*
1 Hankey, II, p. 654.
2 Wilson Diaries, 26 May and 2 and 4 June.
3 Lloyd George, IV, pp. 2141–3.
4 Lloyd George, IV, p. 2129.
5 Robertson, *Soldiers and Statesmen*, II, p. 241.
6 Bonham-Carter, p. 248.
7 Farrar-Hockley, *Goughie*, p. 213; Edmonds, *France and Belgium 1917*, II, pp. 126–7.
8 Ibid., pp. 100–1.
9 Ibid., p. 105.
10 Ludendorff, II, pp. 488–90.

11 *At G.H.Q.*, p. 259.
12 *War Memoirs*, IV, p. 2265.
13 Wilson Diaries, 23 August 1917.
14 *Haig as Military Commander*, p. 237.
15 Hankey, *The Supreme Command 1914–1918*, pp. 755–6.
16 Edmonds, *France and Belgium 1918*, I, pp. 40–1.
17 *War Memoirs*, IV, p. 2267.
18 Edmonds, *France and Belgium 1918*, I, pp. 80 and 87–9.
19 Ibid., p. 69.
20 Ibid., Appx 20: a translation of Wetzell's paper is given in full.
21 Ibid., p. 122.
22 Duff Cooper, II, p. 255.
23 Ibid., p. 260.
24 Ibid., p. 258.
25 Farrar-Hockley, *Goughie*, p. 292.
26 Edmonds, *France and Belgium 1918*, II, p. 487.
27 *My War Memories 1914–18*, p. 690.
28 Edmonds, *France and Belgium 1918*, IV, pp. 315–16.
29 Barclay, *Armistice 1918*, pp. 146–52; a summary of the terms of the Armistice is given here.

*Chapter 10*
1 Liddell Hart, *The Tanks*, I, pp. 47–8.
2 Ibid., p. 69.
3 Ibid., p. 71.
4 Monash, *The Australian Victories in France 1918*, ch. v.
5 *British Generalship in the Twentieth Century*, chs. 5–8: the author has published here a more detailed study of the subjects raised above.

*Chapter 11*
1 Duncan, *Douglas Haig as I knew Him*, p. 120.
2 Ibid., p. 120.
3 Ibid., p. 122.
4 Beaverbrook, *Men and Power 1917–1918*, ch. 8: a full account of the Maurice episode is given here.
5 Liddell Hart Archives – 'vouched for by Swinton and Gen. Aspinall'. Letter 7 October 1927.
6 Edmonds, *France and Belgium 1917*, II, p. v.
7 For example, *A Place Called Armageddon*. Also, Fussell, *The Great War and Modern Memory*.
8 Letter to the author, 7 October 1975.
9 *Up the Line to Death* includes poems by all mentioned below.
10 Ibid., Foreword, p. vii.

11 Letter to the author, 7 October 1975.
12 Farrar-Hockley, *Goughie*, p. 324.
13 Edmonds Papers.
14 Liddell Hart Archives, 9 July 1931.
15 Liddell Hart Archives.
16 Davidson, *Haig, Master of the Field*, p. xiv.
17 Duff Cooper, II, p. 411.

*Chapter 12*
1 William Blake, *Auguries of Innocence.*
2 *Douglas Haig, the Educated Soldier*, p. xiii.
3 *War Memoirs*, IV, pp. 2266–7.
4 Gilbert, *Life of Churchill*, III, pp. 694–7.
5 By Alan Clark and Theatre Workshop, respectively.
6 Liddell Hart Archives.
7 Liddell Hart, *Reputations.*
8 Ibid., pp. 102–3.
9 Ibid., p. 123.
10 Liddell Hart, *Through the Fog of War*, pp. 178–9.
11 Fuller, *Memoirs of an Unconventional Soldier*, p. 341.
12 Davidson, *Haig, Master of the Field*, vii–xi.

# BIBLIOGRAPHY

OFFICIAL HISTORIES AND REPORTS

Edmonds, J.E., *Military Operations. France & Belgium 1914–1918*, 14 vols plus maps and appendices (Macmillan, 1927–39)

Maurice, J.F., *History of the War in South Africa*, 5 vols (Hurst & Blackett, 1906–10)

Royal Commission on the war in South Africa (Elgin Commission) *Report, Minutes of Evidence & Appces*, 4 vols, Comd. 1789–92 (HMSO, 1903)

*Report on the Colonial Conference of 1909*, Comd. 4948 (HMSO, 1909)


BIOGRAPHIES, MEMOIRS, HISTORY AND MILITARY STUDIES

Amery, L.S., *The Times History of the war in South Africa* (1902)

Barclay, C.N., *Armistice 1918* (Dent, 1968).

Barnett, Correlli, *The Swordbearers* (Eyre & Spottiswoode, 1963)

Barnett, Correlli, *Britain and Her Army 1509–1970* (Allen Lane, 1970)

Barrow, George, *The Fire of Life* (Hutchinson, 1941)

Baynes, John, *Morale* (Cassell, 1967)

Beaverbrook, Lord, *Men and Power, 1917–1918* (Hutchinson, 1956)

Blake, Robert, *The Private Papers of Douglas Haig, 1914–1919* (Eyre & Spottiswoode, 1952)

Bond, Brian, *The Victorian Army and the Staff College 1854–1914* (Eyre Methuen, 1972)

Bonham-Carter, Victor, *Soldier True: the Life and Times of Field Marshal Sir William Robertson 1860–1933* (Muller, 1963)

Buchan, John, *Memory Holds the Door* (Hodder & Stoughton, 1940)

203

Callwell, C.E., *Field Marshal Sir Henry Wilson: his Life and Diaries*, 2 vols (Cassell, 1927)

Callwell, C.E., *Stray Recollections* (Arnold, 1929)

Charteris, John, *Field Marshal Earl Haig* (Cassell, 1929)

Charteris, John, *At G.H.Q.* (Cassell, 1931)

Churchill, Winston S., *The River War: The Reconquest of the Sudan* (Eyre & Spottiswoode, 1899)

Churchill, Winston S., *The World Crisis 1911–1918*, abridged & revised edition (Thornton Butterworth, 1931)

Clark, Alan, *The Donkeys* (Hutchinson, 1961)

Cooper, Duff, *Haig*, 2 vols (Faber, 1935)

Davidson, John, *Haig, Master of the Field* (Peter Nevill, 1953)

Duncan, J.S., *Douglas Haig as I Knew Him* (Allen & Unwin, 1966)

Dunlop, John K., *The Development of the British Army 1899–1914* (Methuen, 1938)

Esher, Viscount (ed.), *Journals & Letters of Reginald, Viscount Esher*, vols i–iv (Ivor Nicholson & Watson, 1934–8)

Essame, H., *The Battle for Europe, 1918* (Batsford, 1972)

Falkenhayn, E., *General Headquarters 1914–1916* (Hutchinson, 1919)

Falls, Cyril, *The First World War* (Longmans, 1960)

Farrar-Hockley, Anthony, *The Somme* (Batsford, 1964)

Farrar-Hockley, Anthony, *Goughie* (Hart-Davis MacGibbon, 1975)

Fuller, J.F.C., *Memoirs of an Unconventional Soldier* (Ivor Nicholson & Watson, 1931)

Fox, Frank, *G.H.Q.* (Allan, 1920)

Gardner, Brian, *Allenby* (Cassell, 1965)

Gilbert, Martin, *Winston S. Churchill*, vol. iii (Heinemann, 1971)

Godwin-Austen, A.R., *The Staff and the Staff College* (Constable, 1927)

Gooch, John, *The Plans of War* (Routledge & Kegan Paul, 1974)

Haldane, Viscount, *An Autobiography* (Hodder & Stoughton, 1929)

Hankey, Lord, *The Supreme Command 1914–1918*, 2 vols (Allen & Unwin, 1961)

Henderson, G.F.R., *The Science of War* (Longmans Green, 1905)

Howell, Rosalind, *Philip Howell, a Memoir* (Allen & Unwin, 1942)

Kruger, Rayne, *Good Bye Dolly Gray, The Story of the War in South Africa* (Cassell, 1939)

Liddell Hart, B.H., *Reputations* (Murray, 1928)

Liddell Hart, B.H., *Foch, Man of Orleans* (Eyre & Spottiswoode, 1931)

Liddell Hart, B.H., *Through the Fog of War* (Faber, 1938)

Liddell Hart, B.H., *The Tanks* vol i (Cassell, 1959)

Liddell Hart, B.H., *Memoirs* vol i (Cassell, 1965)

Lloyd George, David, *War Memoirs*, 6 vols (Ivor Nicholson & Watson, 1933–6)

Ludendorff, E., *My War Memories 1914–18* (Hutchinson, 1920)

Magnus, Philip, *Kitchener, Portrait of an Imperialist* (Murray, 1958)

Marshall-Cornwall, James, *Haig as Military Commander* (Batsford, 1973)

Maurice, Frederick, *Life of General Lord Rawlinson of Trent* (Cassell, 1928)

Maurice, Frederick, *Life of Viscount Haldane of Clone* (Faber, 1937)

Monash, John, *The Australian Victories in France in 1918* (Angus & Robertson, 1936)

Montgomery, Viscount, *A History of Warfare* (Collins, 1970)

Robertson, William, *Soldiers and Statesmen* (Cassell, 1926)

Roskill, Stephen, *Hankey, Man of Secrets* vol I (Collins, 1970)

Sixsmith, E.K.G., *British Generalship in the Twentieth Century* (Arms & Armour Press, 1970)

Smithers, A.J., *Sir John Monash* (Leo Cooper, 1973)

Spears, Edward, *Liaison 1914* (Eyre & Spottiswoode, 1930)

Spears, Edward, *Prelude to Victory* (Cape, 1939)

Spender, J.A., and Asquith, Cyril, *Life of Lord Oxford and Asquith* vol II (Hutchinson, 1932)

Swinton, Ernest, *Eyewitness* (Hodder & Stoughton, 1932)

Taylor, A.J.P., *English History 1914–1945* (Oxford, 1965)

Terraine, John, *Douglas Haig, the Educated Soldier* (Hutchinson, 1963)

Terraine, John (ed.), *General Jack's Diary* (Eyre & Spottiswoode, 1964)

Wavell, A.P., *Allenby, Soldier and Statesman* (Harrap, 1946)


POETRY, PLAYS AND EDITED WAR LETTERS

*Oh What a Lovely War!* Theatre Workshop (Methuen, 1965)

*The Ordeal of Alfred Hale*, ed. Paul Fussell (Leo Cooper, 1975)

*A Place Called Armageddon*, ed. Michael Moynihan (David & Charles, 1975)

*Up the Line to Death: the War Poets 1914–18*, an anthology ed. Brian Gardner (Methuen, 1964)

*The Great War and Modern Memory*, Paul Fussell (Oxford, 1975)


PAPERS AND PRIVATE RECORDS

*An Artillery Officer in the First World War*, Roderick Macleod (Imperial War Museum)

The Edmonds Papers (Military Archives, King's College, London)

The Haig Papers (National Library of Scotland)

The Howell Papers (Military Archives, King's College, London)

The Kiggell Papers (Military Archives, King's College, London)

The Liddell Hart Archives (States House, Medmenham)

The Maxse Papers (Imperial War Museum)
The Rawlins Papers (Royal Artillery Institution)
The Robertson Papers (Military Archives, King's College, London)
The Wilson Diaries (Imperial War Museum)

# INDEX

Aisne, Battle of, 77, 188
Albert, King of Belgians, 162
Alexandra, Queen, 19, 53, 59
Allenby, F-M. Visc., 12–15, 47, 77, 105, 129, 144, 164, 194
Amiens (8 Aug 1918), 108, 153, 165, 168, 170, 191–2
Anthoine, Gen., 142
Anzac Corps, 142–3, 168, 170
Armistice, 163
Army Council, creation of, 53
Arras, Battle of, 108, 129, 131, 133, 137, 171
Askwith, Lord, 3
Aspinall-Oglander, Brig-Gen. C. F., 206
Asquith, H. H. (Earl of Oxford and Asquith), 67, 86, 91–2, 103, 105, 108, 113, 187–8
Atbara, Battle of the, 24–6
Aubers Ridge, 86, 90–1, 95, 168
Australian Army, see Anzac Corps
Austrian Army, 139

Bacon, Adm. Sir Reginald, 109
Baird, Maj-Gen. H. B. D., 64
Balfour, Earl, 53
Baring, Maj-Gen. Sir Everard, 22
Barrow, Gen. Sir G. de S., 12, 23, 196
Beddington, Brig. Sir Edward, 180
Belgian Army, 69, 79, 80, 107, 162
Bemersyde, 2, 140, 184
Bergendal, Battle of, 42

Birch, Gen. Sir Noel, 181
Blair, Brig-Gen. A., 13, 19, 20, 195
Blunden, Edmund, 178
Bonar Law, Andrew, 139, 162, 188
Botha, Gen. Louis, 44, 46
Braithwaite, Gen. Sir Walter, 61
Briand, Aristotle, 123, 126, 128
British Army, regts., cav: 5 D.G., 33; 5 L., 33; 7 H., 4, 5, 7, 30, 51; 13/18 H., 74, 203; 17 L., 45–6, 49, 51, 84; 21 L., 21; regts., inf: Gr. Gds., 166; Coldm. Gds., 74; Devons, 34; R.S.F., 106; Cameronians (Sco. Rif.), 88; Manch., 34; Mx., 88; K.R.R.C., 106; Gordons, 34; bdes: 1st Cav, 30–1; Gds., 39; divs: Cav, 36–42; Gds., 96, 100, 106; 2nd, 97; 6th, 39; 7th, 80, 92; 8th, 87, 89; 9th, 96; 15th, 96–8; 24th, 96–8; 36th, 1; corps: I, 70, 72–5, 77–81, 84, 89, 96; II, 72–4; IV, 79, 80, 84, 89, 96–7, 105; IX, 159; XI, 96–100; XXII, 159; armies: First, 86–92, 105, 110, 112, 129, 152, 157, 161–2; Second, 141, 143, 150, 152, 162; Third, 102, 110, 129, 150, 152, 161–2; Fourth, 112, 140, 156–7, 160, 162; Fifth, 115, 137, 140, 143, 150, 153, 156–7, 167, 179, 180
British Legion, 184
Broadwood, Lt-Gen. R. G., 20–3, 26–7

Brooke (F-M. Visc. Alanbrooke), 104
Buller, Gen. Sir Redvers, 11, 30, 36–8, 42
Bulow, Gen. von, 76, 79
Butler, Lt-Gen. Sir Richard, 105
Byng. F-M. Visc., 44, 47, 144

Calais Conference, 124–8, 131
Cambrai, 108, 119, 144–5, 167, 170
Cambridge, Duke of, 8–9, 52
Cameron-Wilson, T.P., 178
Canadian Corps, 129, 142–3, 170, 172
Caporetto, Battle of, 108, 143, 145
Capper, Maj-Gen. Sir Thomas, 12–13, 19, 20, 61, 194
Carleton, Col., 35
Carson, Sir Edward, 187
Castelnau, Gen. de, 109, 111
Casualties, 77, 91, 100, 116–17, 130, 134, 142, 144, 191
Cavan, F-M. Earl, 156–7
Chamberlain, Sir Austen, 113
Chamberlain, Joseph, 45
Chantilly Conference, 110–11
Charteris, Brig-Gen. John, 64, 73, 76, 80–1, 139, 146, 181–3
Chemin des Dames, 77, 130, 159
Churchill, Sir Winston, 21, 23, 27, 69, 89, 105, 116, 166, 187
Clark, Alan, 188
Clausewitz, Karl von, 60
Clemenceau, Georges, 113, 154–5, 187
Clifton College, 2
Congreve, Lt-Gen. Sir Walter, 4
Cooper, A. Duff (Visc. Norwich), 2–3, 51, 53, 55
Cox, Brig-Gen. E.W., 147, 152
Craddock, Dr S., 3
Creagh, Gen. Sir O'Moore, 58–9, 63
Cronje, Gen. Piet, 39–40
Crosigk, Col., 8
Curragh Incident, 65–6, 86
Curzon, Marquess of, 52, 139

Dardanelles (incl. Gallipoli and Suvla), 87, 89, 93–5, 101–2, 105, 112
Davidson, Maj-Gen. Sir John, 184
Davies, Gen. Sir Francis, 87–8

Debeney, Gen. E., 160
De La Rey, Gen. K., 42–3, 46
Derby, Earl of, 55, 140, 147, 156, 187
De Wet, Gen. C., 39–43, 46
Diamond Hill, Battle of, 42
Douglas, Gen. Sir Charles, 69
Doullens Conference, 154–6
Dubois, Gen., 82
Du Cane, Gen. Sir John, 157
Duncan, Revd. George, 173–5
d'Urbal, Gen., 90

Edmonds, Brig-Gen. Sir James, 4, 12–15, 116, 176, 184, 194
Edward vii, King, 7, 19, 47, 53, 59, 60
Egyptian Army, 16–29
Elandslaagte, Battle of, 33–5
Elgin Commission, 35, 40–1, 49, 53
Elles, Gen. Sir Hugh, 144, 165–6, 170
Ellison, Lt-Gen. Sir Gerald, 55
El Obeid, Battle of, 16
Erroll, Col. the Earl of, 38–9
Esher, Visc., 53–4, 103, 187
Essame, Maj-Gen. H., 177, 179
Eugénie, Empress, 83
Ewart, Lt-Gen. Sir Spencer, 66

Falkenhayn, Gen. von, 79, 80, 111, 116–17
Falls, Capt. Cyril, 116
Fayolle, Gen., 154
Festubert, Battle of, 90–1, 168
Fisher, Lt-Gen. Sir Bertie, 51
Fitton, Brig-Gen. H.G., 24
Fletcher, Lt-Col. Alan, 51, 84, 97
Foch, Marshal, 79, 81, 95–6, 120, 134, 142, 146, 154–63, 170, 173–4
Fox, Sir Frank, 182
Franchet d'Esperey, Gen., 76, 120, 128–9
Fraser, Gen. Sir Keith, 7, 8
French, F-M. Sir John (Earl of Ypres), 8, 9, 30–7, 50–1, 62, 66, 69–83, 85–8, 90–105, 166, 174, 188, 191
French Army, 7 & *passim*; morale of, 130–1, 135, 144, 171, 191–2
Fuller, Maj-Gen. J.F.C., 144, 165, 170, 184, 189, 191
Furse, Lt-Gen. Sir William, 12, 194

Gallioni, Gen., 79
Gallipoli, *see* Dardanelles
Gatacre, Lt-Gen. Sir William, 37
Geddes, Sir Eric, 124–5
General Staff, creation of, 53, 56–57
George v, King, 19, 62, 65, 70, 78, 83, 93, 101, 104, 113, 120, 126, 133, 174, 188–9
German Army, 7–9 & *passim*; offensive 1918, 150–9, 170, 173–4, 177, 179, 192
Gheluvelt, 81, 141
Givenchy, Battle of, 90–1
Gladstone, William Ewart, 16
Gordon, Maj-Gen. Charles, 17, 19
Gough, Gen. Sir Hubert, 66, 92, 96, 101, 115, 137, 141, 152, 155–6, 167, 179, 180
Gough, Brig-Gen. John, 66, 72, 87–8, 105
Grant, Capt. R.N., 44
Graves, Robert, 178
Grenfell, F-M. Lord, 44
Grenfell, Julian, 178
Grierson, Lt-Gen. Sir James, 55, 71
Gwynne, Bishop, 175

Haig, Dorothy (Countess), 53, 76, 78, 83–4, 86, 102, 106, 113, 133, 172–4, 180–1, 187
Haig, Douglas (F-M. Earl), principal personal events: birth, 1; religious faith, 2, 9, 172–5; B.N.C. Oxford, 3; Sandhurst, 4; commissioned, 5; Staff College, 9, 10–15; Subst. Lt-Col., 45; Bt. Col. and C.B., 49; appt. I-G. Cav. India, 52; betrothal and marriage, 53; DMT, 54; DSD, 55; org. of BEF and creation GS, 55–7; writes *F.S.R.*, 57; CGS India, 60; GOC Aldershot Commd. and I Corps, 64; embarks with BEF, 71; promoted Gen. & commd. First Army, 83; receives GCB, 93; decision on gas at Loos, 98; conflict of loyalties with French, 99–102; replaces French, 104; directive to Haig as C-in-C, 107; pr. F-M., 120; review of war, 1 Aug 1916, 118–19; appreciation before Ypres, 137–8; refuses peerage, 140; birth of son, 153; calls for Foch as Supreme Comd., 154–5; issues Special Order, 157; belief in victory 1918, 162; bedside reading, 181; post-war work, 183; at Victory Pde., 184; personal rewards, 184; death and burial, 184
Haig, 2nd Earl, 153
Haig, Hugo, 48
Haig, John, 2
Haig, Oliver, 48, 172
Haig, Rachael, 2, 172
Haig, Victoria (Lady Victoria Scott), 9–10, 59, 83
Haking, Gen. Sir Richard, 12, 101, 194
Haldane, Visc., 54–6, 62, 66–7, 69, 70, 100, 102, 104, 120, 184, 186–7
Hamilton, Gen. Sir Ian, 34, 42, 47, 50, 54
Hankey, Lord, 123, 125–6, 148–9
Hardinge, Visc., 60
Harington, Gen. Sir Charles, 157
Helbronner, Col., 75
Henderson, Col. G.F.R., 11–15, 38
Hertzog, Gen. J.B.M., 43
Hicks, Col., 16, 20
Hildyard, Maj-Gen. Sir H., 11
Hindenburg, F-M. von, 163
Hindenburg Line, 125, 128, 161–2, 192
Holford, Sir George, 47
Horne, Gen. Lord, 72, 91
Howell, Brig-Gen. Philip, 10, 53, 55, 57, 63, 66, 109, 172, 188
Hunter, Gen. Sir Archibald, 21, 27
Hutchinson, Lt-Gen. H., 54

Imperial Light Horse, 33
Indian Army, 58–61, 63; commissions for Indians, 63–4; Indian Corps, 84, 89
Italy and Italian Army, 113, 117, 123, 135, 142–3, 145, 148

Jacob, F-M. Sir Claude, 141, 165
Jameson, Mrs Henrietta, 7, 19, 20–21, 23, 27, 37, 41, 46–8, 51, 56, 172
Jameson, William, 7
Jellicoe, Adm. of the Fleet Earl, 132, 139

Joffre, Marshal, 73, 75–7, 79, 86, 90, 92, 94–5, 104, 107–10, 113, 118, 120, 124, 132, 171
Joubert, Gen. Piet, 33

Khalifa, 17, 21, 26–7
Kiggell, Lt-Gen. Sir Lancelot, 10, 57–9, 61–4, 88–9, 105, 125, 128, 139, 146–7, 172, 175, 180–1
Kimberley, Relief of, 37–9
Kitchener, F-M. Earl, 17–29, 38–40, 42, 44–7, 51–4, 61, 67–70, 75, 85, 87, 91–3, 95–6, 99, 101–3, 105, 107, 110, 112
Kluck, Gen. von, 74, 76, 79
Kock, Gen., 33–4
Kritzinger, Gen., 43
Kruger, President, 31, 40–2

Ladysmith, 31–6, 40, 42
Landon, Maj-Gen. H.J.S., 81
Lanrezac, Gen., 72, 75–6
Lawrence, Gen. Sir Herbert, 12, 38, 45, 146–7, 195
Laycock, Brig-Gen. Sir Joseph, 38
Le Cateau, Battle of, 72–4
Le Gallais, Col. P.W.J., 22
Liddell Hart, Capt. Sir Basil, 116, 176, 180, 189–92
Lloyd George, David (Earl), 92, 108, 114, 116, 119, 121, 123–6, 132–5, 139, 140, 142, 145–9, 156–157, 163, 177, 185–8
Loe, Gen. von, 7–8
Lomax, Maj-Gen. H., 76, 78, 80–1
Lombards Kop, Battle of, 35–6
Loos, Battle of, 96–9, 168
Louis of Battenberg, Prince, 69
Ludendorff, Gen., 116, 141, 152, 157, 159, 161
Lyautey, Marshal, 120
Lys, R., Battle of, 108, 174

Macdonagh, Lt-Gen. Sir George, 12, 72, 139, 194
Machine guns, 20–3, 25, 77, 168–70, 182
Mackenzie, Maj-Gen. Colin, 58, 196
Magersfontein, Battle of, 37–8
Mahdi, 16
Mahmud, 21, 24
Mahon, Gen. Sir Brian, 22

Malan, Dr, 45
Marlborough, Duke of, 1, 164–5
Marne, Battle of, (1st) 78; (2nd) 108, 159, 170
Marshall-Cornwall, Gen. Sir James, 9, 147
Mary, Princess, 153
Mary, Queen, 153
Maude, Lt-Gen. Sir Frederick, 5, 12, 195
Maud'huy, Gen., 75, 86
Maurice, Maj-Gen. Sir Frederick, 175
Maxse, Gen. Sir Ivor, 141, 165, 169, 180, 184
Mercer, Maj-Gen. H.F., 87
Messines Ridge, 109, 134, 137, 165, 171
Methuen, F-M. Lord, 37
Micheler, Gen., 129
Miles, Maj-Gen. S.H.G., 62
Milner, Visc., 45, 139, 154–6, 163
Moltke, Gen. von, 71, 79
Monash, Lt-Gen. Sir John, 165, 168, 170
Monro, Gen. Sir Charles, 76, 81, 102, 105, 112
Mons, Battle of (and retreat from), 72–5, 78, 171
Montgomery, F-M. Visc., 1, 165
Morley, Lord, 60
Morton, Maj. Sir Desmond, 181
Murray, Gen. Sir Archibald, 12, 70–1, 73, 75, 86, 100, 105, 196

Navy, Royal, 44, 57, 69
Neuve Chapelle, Battle of, 86–9, 90–3, 168, 171
Nicholson, Gen. Sir William, 58, 62
Nivelle, Gen., 108, 119–30, 132–3, 155, 174, 184, 187
Northcliffe, Visc., 146

Oman, Sir Charles, 116
Omdurman, Battle of, 26–9
Owen, Wilfred, 178
Oxford University, 2–3

Paardeburg, Battle of, 39
Painlevé, Paul, 128
Passchendaele, 79, 142–3, 152, 171, 175, 177, 191–2
Pater, Walter, 2

Pershing, John, Gen. of the Army, 160, 162

Pétain, Marshal, 91, 128–30, 132–9, 148, 150, 152–4, 158–9, 161, 171, 173, 184

Plumer, F-M. Visc., 15, 44, 90, 134–137, 141–3, 149, 156, 165, 169, 177, 179

Poincaré, Pres., 126, 154

Polo, 3, 5, 52, 64

Poplar Grove, Battle of, 39–41

Portman, 3rd Visc., 3

Portuguese Bde., 157

Rawlinson, Gen. Lord, 26, 59, 62, 79, 87–9, 105, 109, 112, 115, 135, 140, 150, 156, 159, 165, 167–8, 170, 177, 179, 180

Reading, Marquess of, 148

Reid, Col. Hamish, 5

Repington, Col. a'Court, 61, 85, 91

Reserve, Allied, 150, 155

Rhodes, Cecil, 37

Rice, Maj-Gen. Sir S.R., 82

Ripon, Bishop of, 19

Roberts, F-M. Earl, 11, 38–42, 50, 54

Robertson, F-M. Sir William, 12, 86, 89, 93, 99, 100–5, 108–12, 118–119, 123–31, 135, 137, 139, 140, 145–7, 149, 150, 157, 179, 196

Rosenberg, Isaac, 178

Rothschild, Leopold de, 113

Royal Flying Corps, 87, 141

Russia and Russian Army, 95, 108–109, 113, 117, 145

Ryan, Col. E., 73

St Albans, Duke of, 51

Salisbury, Marquess of, 31

Salonica, 101, 112, 123

Sandhurst, R.M.C., 4

Sassoon, Siegfried, 178

Scheepers, Comdt. G.J., 44–6

Secrett (Haig's soldier-servant), 84

Seely, Brig-Gen. Sir John (Lord Mottistone), 65

Slim, F-M. Visc., 165, 175

Smith, Sir F.E. (Lord Birkenhead), 188

Smith-Dorrien, Gen. Sir Horace, 62, 71–4, 84–5, 90

Smuts, F-M. Jan, 46, 139, 148–9, 157

Somme, Battle of the, 108–10, 115–118, 140, 166, 171, 173, 175–9, 187, 190–2

Staff Colleges, Camberley and Quetta, 5, 6, 8, 11–15, 59, 60–2

Stamfordham, Lord, 78, 101, 126

Steyn, Pres., 31, 40–2

Stokes, Brig. R.S.G., 10

Stormberg, Battle of, 37–8

Straker, Maj., 84

Submarine warfare, 62, 132, 139

Supreme War Council, 145, 147, 150

Swaine, Col., 7–8

Swinton, Maj-Gen. Sir Ernest, 166–167

Symons, Maj-Gen. Penn, 33

Tactics (and Haig's tactical thought), 9, 20, 24–6, 28–9, 49–50, 61, 165–71, 192

Talana Hill, Battle of, 31

Tanks, 117, 130, 141, 144, 166–8, 170, 182, 190

Terraine, John, 5, 55, 80, 116, 186

Thiepval, 118

Thomas, Edward, 178

Tillett, Ben, 92

Trenchard, Marshal of the Royal Air Force Visc., 87, 141, 165–6, 192–3

Ulster Controversy, *see* Curragh

US Army, 137, 145, 150–1, 159, 160, 162

Verdun, 108, 111, 113, 117–18, 120–121, 152, 171, 184

Vimy Ridge, 91, 96, 99, 108, 129, 133

War Cabinet, Council and Committee, 103, 118, 123–4, 139, 140, 146, 149, 166, 188

Warren, Gen. Sir Charles, 11

Wavell, F-M. Earl, 2, 13

Wellington, Duke of, 164–5, 184

Wetzell, Col., 152, 157

Weygand, Gen., 154

White, Gen. Sir George, 31–7
Wigram, Col. Lord, 93–4
Wilhelm II, Kaiser, 7–8, 81
Willcocks, Gen. Sir James, 89
Wilson, F-M. Sir Henry, 54, 59, 71–72, 77, 80, 86, 105, 108–9, 127–8, 133–4, 145–50, 154, 156–7, 179
Wolseley, F-M. Visc., 6, 9, 11, 16–17, 20, 31, 37

Wood, F-M. Sir Evelyn, 6, 8, 11, 16–17, 20, 24–9, 37, 202–3
Woods-Sampson, Col., 47

Younger, Maj-Gen. Ralph, 5
Ypres (1st), 79–81, 158; (2nd), 90; (3rd), 108–9, 135–44, 167, 171, 175–80, 189, 191
Yule, Brig-Gen., 35